L   d
Cha   ent

Leadership and Change Management

Annabel Beerel

Los Angeles | London | New Delhi
Singapore | Washington DC

First published 2009
Reprinted 2010

SAGE Publications Ltd
1 Oliver's Yard
55 City Road
London EC1Y 1SP

SAGE Publications Inc.
2455 Teller Road
Thousand Oaks, California 91320

SAGE Publications India Pvt Ltd
B 1/I 1 Mohan Cooperative Industrial Area
Mathura Road, Post Bag 7
New Delhi 110 044

SAGE Publications Asia-Pacific Pte Ltd
33 Pekin Street #02-01
Far East Square
Singapore 048763

Library of Congress Control Number: 2008939498

British Library Cataloguing in Publication data

A catalogue record for this book is available from the British Library

ISBN 978-1-84787-340-8
ISBN 978-1-84787-341-5 (pbk)

Typeset by C&M Digitals (P) Ltd, Chennai, India
Printed in Great Britain by the MPG Books Group
Printed on paper from sustainable resources

CONTENTS

PREFACE

As this book goes to press the world economy appears to be falling apart. Every corner of the globe is experiencing some version of the global economic meltdown. The United States benchmark stock index, the Dow Jones, has fallen well below 7000, a level it has not held since 1997, twelve years ago. Unemployment in many countries is ratcheting up at a rapid pace. Banks are failing, companies are going bankrupt and individuals are losing not only their life savings but also the roof over their heads. The TARP (troubled asset relief program) set up in the US with the goal of saving banks by taking over their toxic assets and pumping in taxpayers' money, has so far not achieved many of its intended goals. The Bank of England is desperately trying to resist nationalizing one of its largest banking entities while also shoring up a bleak economic situation. Everywhere it seems mortgage defaults are on the rise as is the collapse of many businesses previously considered sound. What is going on? How is one to understand this emerging new reality?

This book, *Leadership and Change Management*, emphasizes that the fundamental task of leadership is the management of change and all that entails. Change always arrives by way of new realities. Effective leaders recognize new realities when they are new! This is not easy to do for many reasons. First, new realities often emerge in covert and intricate ways. They do not make themselves immediately obvious and can only be detected by an eye attentive to what is really going on in the present moment. Second, new realities always have a systemic impact. This means that in order to correctly identify and read new realities requires adeptness at systems thinking. Third (and by no means last), communicating new realities to others meets with their resistance. In general people resist new realities because they know new realities always signal some kind of change. In particular they resist unpalatable new realities, preferring to deny or ignore that these exist. If they have to deal with new realities, people prefer to deal with ones that are hopeful or favourable. Unpalatable realities are readily deferred.

The current crisis we find ourselves in is a result of many deferred realities we have collectively chosen to ignore or to repackage into fantasies we would rather deal with. For example, the financial system has demonstrated over and over again it is not able to self-regulate without devolving into excess and corruption. Remember the 1980s and Michael Milkin; the 1990s and the crazy support of the dotcoms soon to be dotbombs, and the beginning of this century marked by Enron, Worldcom, Parmalat and so on?

The banking sector, as with most of our other more mature industries, such as automobiles and major consumables, has excess capacity. Excess capacity, a problem Karl Marx foresaw as part of capitalism's downside, creates huge problems of finding new demand or creating it. The relentless pursuit of new markets, and the pressure to create consumerist behaviour wherever we go, is our attempt to deny the reality of excess capacity and the need to address the capacity issue. We prefer instead to create unrealistic and unsustainable markets. Our new free market hope is that we can convert the billions at the bottom of the pyramid, as we refer to them, into avid consumers so that we do not need to address the huge number of unpalatable capacity problems. If we were to face our industry capacity problems head on we would realize that many, many organizations need to be allowed to fail. This reality is particularly prevalent in the financial services sector. The shadow financial market, which ingenious financial innovators have created with their collateralized instruments, derivatives and hedge funds, have provided some sophisticated techniques in creating market activity without really adding productivity utility. At the end of the day, as we now see, much of it is smoke and mirrors. Rather than address the reality of overcapacity head on, we are going to prop up many failing organizations citing the argument they are too large to fail. In the short term, this seems easier to deal with than the reality that we have created a world of excess (capacity), dependent on excess (consumerism). Somehow we hope this will all 'come out in the wash.' Unfortunately this wash is going to cost taxpayers around the world not only billions of dollars but also faith and trust in a system that used to pride itself in faith and trust.

The text *Leadership and Change Management* points out that reality, by definition, never goes away. It is here to stay. We have a choice: do we embrace new realities as soon as we can or do we try to manipulate them and respond to them according to our own comfort or timing? Effective leadership, this book argues, is about helping people and organizations embrace reality head on, regardless of how challenging the reality might be. The better able we are to deal with new realities, the more adaptive we become. Given that change is relentless and is arriving faster, with more systemic implications than ever before, there is no greater asset, personal or organizational, than having an adaptive outlook that encourages the following.

- Integrity by facing reality, as reality is the truth.

- Wisdom by working with the systemic nature of what is truly happening here and now.

- And resilience by willingly and openly embracing change no matter how uncomfortable it might be.

This book explores all of these issues. It provides insights, examples and opportunities for reflection. This book is essentially a call to everyone's own ability to exercise leadership and to manage change, thereby living life well.

Annabel Beerel
Sudbury, Massachusetts
March 2009

ACKNOWLEDGMENTS

This book has been ten years in the making. While in some ways it is a sequel to my previous book on leadership, *Leadership Through Strategic Planning*, the ideas in this book are far more adventurous and challenging than those in my previous text.

There are many, many people to whom I owe a huge thank you for guiding me as I formulated the ideas included in these pages. Most specifically I would like to thank Ronald Heifetz of the J.F.Kennedy School of Government who, fourteen years ago, presented me with a new perspective on leadership, and who inspired me to wrestle with my own adaptive work in new and challenging ways. My thanks also go to the many individuals, colleagues and friends who engaged tirelessly with me on leadership issues and who supported me when I put my ideas on leadership into practice.

Over the past three years, Chris and Mary Papoutsy, the endowers of the Christos and Mary Papoutsy Distinguished Chair in Ethics, which I have the privilege to hold at this time, provided an unending source of energy, creativity and support. Enormous thanks go to Dawn Simes, PhD, who generously gave many hours to carrying out all kinds of research that would inform and test my ideas. My appreciation goes to Kiren Shoman and her team at SAGE Publications, who have been an absolute pleasure to work with.

I also extend my thanks to my many clients and students who have been some of my best teachers. And last but by no means least I thank my family for their loving support and tireless patience during the many months I was preoccupied with this project.

Annabel Beerel, PhD
Sudbury, Massachusetts
March 2009

INTRODUCTION

Leadership and Change Management takes a very specific approach to the topic of leadership. This approach is called the **Systemic Leadership** approach. The Systemic Leadership approach views leadership as fundamentally concerned with the process of change. The change process begins with why and what needs to change and continues right through to the execution and implementation of change.

In *Leadership and Change Management* we do not dwell on the execution and implementation aspects. A great deal has been written on those topics to the point where execution and implementation have in many instances become the ends rather than the means to important ends or goals. In this book, we focus instead on what we believe is the main purpose of change. The main purpose of change is to attune and align the organization to new realities that are continuously emerging and presenting themselves. New realities, by definition, are both new and real. The sooner the organization recognizes new realities, the more time and opportunity it has to initiate appropriate strategic responses. Failing to recognize new realities or instigating change initiatives based on a false reading or understanding of new realities, is a sign of poor organizational leadership and inevitably has a detrimental effect on the organization's future survival.

Because new realities always signal change, effective leaders are attentive to environmental changes and trends. Environmental changes and trends are detected by mindfulness and an insatiable curiosity regarding what is currently taking place in the environment and its impact on different systems. A systems thinking mindset helps identify new realities and their systemic ramifications.

Staying attuned to new realities is difficult for a host of reasons. In this book we investigate these reasons in detail. One critical reason is that change always creates some form of loss. Both people and organizational systems resist accepting unpalatable changes for as long as they can so they can defer dealing with those losses. Since reality does not go away, nor can it be deferred, the longer the organization resists – or if it elects to change to a more palatable reality – the greater the negative impact on the organization's ability to adapt to change. Leadership is about holding the organization's feet to the fire to recognize, face, embrace and adapt to change. The measure of effective leadership is the extent to which leaders have helped the organization and its members enhance their adaptive capacities. Enhancing adaptive capacities takes time.

There are many reasons why change efforts fail or are minimally effective. Two important reasons are that the organization does not respond appropriately to new realities, and/or organizational leaders do not provide a sufficient containing function for the anxiety and distresses that change creates. *Leadership and Change Management* stresses these two aspects of the change process and delves in detail into how mistakes in the reading of new realities and insensitivity to the emotional life of the organization can be avoided. The ideas with regard to dealing with organizational distress have been inspired by Ronald Heifetz of the J.F. Kennedy School of Government, who developed the concepts of adaptive challenge, and adaptive and technical work. The ideas of the Tavistock Institute and its Group Relations approach have also shaped many of the ideas presented in the discussions of human behavior and their defenses against anxiety.

Because the critical task of Systemic Leadership is wrestling with new realities, leadership adopting this approach is an inherently ethical endeavor. New realities represent new truths. What is real is what is true. Wrestling with the truth and trying to be aligned to the truth represents this ethical quest. Effective leadership is thus ethical leadership; they represent two sides of the same coin.

In *Leadership and Change Management* I explain these ideas and many more in detail. Each chapter includes practical exercises and case studies. This is an excellent text for anyone interested in leadership, management, organizational behavior and ethics. It also provides interesting insights to the discerning general business reader.

Some of the key points of each chapter are summarized below.

Chapter 1 introduces the concept of new realities and how the organization needs to stay attuned to new realities in order to remain relevant and survive. New realities are always arriving. They always signal change, hence change is continuous and the call to change never ends. Change always challenges people's values. This explains their tendency to resist change. In order to be more flexible and accepting around change, organizations need to become more adaptive. Organizations must develop their adaptive capacities so that they may become better at anticipating and responding to change. Effective leaders identify new realities and help the organization enhance its adaptive capacity.

Chapter 2 focuses on the importance of systems thinking and having a systems mindset if one wishes to be adept at recognizing new realities and grasping their implications. A systems thinking mindset sees the world as interrelated systems that are in perpetual motion and change. Patterns and relationships are more important than individual units or events. A systems thinking mindset provides opportunities for understanding the environment from multiple perspectives and from more than one dimension. Since new realities are always systemic in nature, effective leaders use systems thinking and approach problems systemically.

Chapter 3 explores a range of normative leadership theories and introduces the Systemic Leadership approach. Systemic Leadership is a transformational approach that differs from other leadership approaches in that it emphasizes the tasks of leadership rather than the qualities or traits of leaders. While certain dispositions and talents will contribute to effective Systemic Leadership, anyone can essentially exercise leadership. There is no one blueprint model for leaders or leadership.

Chapter 4 develops the Systemic Leadership approach in detail. It explains important concepts such as adaptive and technical work and sets out the twelve steps of effective Systemic Leadership. It also explains the conflicting roles of leadership and authority and the implications of leading with or without authority.

Chapter 5 is devoted to the topic of authority. The notion of authority plays a huge role in our lives beginning in our earliest infancy. Our early experiences of authority shape our understanding and responses to people in authority in a variety of ways. Two important responses include our fear of authority and our tendency to cede our own moral authority to those who have authority over us. It is important that leaders understand the powerful influence the role of authority has over people and how easy it is to abuse one's authority. Leaders also need to understand that naming and defining reality is not the preserve of those in authority but requires the collaboration of others.

Chapter 6 focuses on the organizational behavioral aspects of change. At this time new realities are arriving faster than ever before and are challenging once sacred ground. New realities increase the stresses and anxieties already inherent in organizational life. Systemic leaders understand this dynamic and are attentive to the group dynamics that result. In this chapter we adopt the Group Relations approach to human behavior to provide a framework for understanding the emotional undertow of organizations, the anxieties that exist and the individual and group defenses against those anxieties. We also explain how the key task of the leader is containment of anxiety so that the creative energy of organizational members is not inhibited.

Chapter 7 addresses the shadow side of leadership. Here we explain how unethical, corrupt and ineffective leadership begins with leaders who are out of touch with reality, especially their own. Leaders who are focused on reality, especially the arrival of new realities, are far less likely to fall into the many moral traps that a leadership role invites and attracts. Narcissistic leaders and people in positions of power and authority who are distracted by fear are the most dangerous types of leader. They abuse their power, encourage dependency in their followers and surround themselves with sycophants. Only self-aware and self-reflective leaders can survive and remain effective.

Chapter 8 introduces the two important concepts of ethics and morality and explains their difference. It discusses how Systemic Leadership is primarily concerned with new realities so is concerned with the truth. What is real is true. New realities refer to new truths. Wrestling with the truth is essentially an ethical endeavor. Systemic Leadership thus equates with ethical leadership. Leadership and ethics are directly related. Therefore, according to Systemic

Leadership, effective leaders are ethical. Systemic leaders also understand the moral power of groups and how group pressure lowers the ethical standards of most groups.

Chapter 9 discusses the role of leadership in the strategy development process. Strategy addresses new realities and sets out the plans for the organization's response. Adaptation to change always requires a certain amount of transformation and learning. Effective leaders ensure the organization engages in continuous learning and uses that learning to strategic effect. Strategy development is in essence a continuous learning process. Scenario planning is a powerful tool for reality testing new realities and for developing key assumptions around change that require a strategic response.

Chapter 10 brings together the challenges and opportunities leaders face, especially those who adopt a Systemic Leadership approach. It highlights self-awareness, mindfulness, the ability to see the big picture and courage as four particularly important ingredients of Systemic Leadership. Systemic leaders realize that organizational leadership and management is as much a rational as an emotional process. In order to survive the pressures and projections of the group while holding up new realities they need to form strategic alliances. Above all, effective leaders understand that leadership begins with oneself. In reality, one cannot change others, only oneself!

1 NEW REALITIES AS THE FORCE OF CHANGE

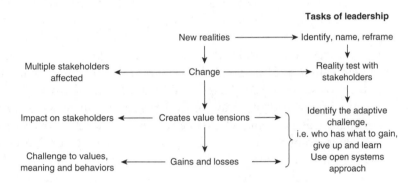

Figure 1.1

INTRODUCTION

This chapter introduces important themes and concepts that underpin the rest of the book. It begins with a discussion of the need for organizations to remain **relevant** to their stakeholders if they wish to survive. To remain relevant requires the ability to read and respond to **new realities**. New realities are the forces that herald change. New realities are pervasive and are continuously arriving at our doorstep, whether we invite them or not. 'New realities' is the most important concept of this book. As we shall discover, leadership and new realities go hand in hand.

Our virtual world, where time and space are collapsed into a virtual here and now, has speeded up the arrival of new realities and compounded their number. We are easily overwhelmed by the amount of new realities we are expected to embrace. We also need to create new mindsets that recognize perpetual change is the only true reality. The notion that change is a series of one-off events that can be anticipated, planned and tidily managed is fallacious. This mindset is outdated. New realities are continuously arriving and change arrives swiftly on their heels.

To remain relevant and alive in today's world requires a **shift in consciousness**, new ways of perceiving the world, and new ways of wrestling with the challenges of change. We also need to understand that there are good and bad responses to change. Simply changing is insufficient. If we do not change in response to new realities but rather in favor of some fantasy of our imagination, this will not serve us in the long run. Good change aligns us with new realities; bad change does not. Good change keeps us relevant, bad change does not.

By and large we do not like change. We resist it if we can. Change frightens and inconveniences us. One reason for our often deep resistance to change is that it always implies loss of some sort. Adapting to change requires **transformation**. Transformative change results from learning, and learning is not always easy. Change creates value tensions that require us to reprioritize or compromise our deeply held values or cherished beliefs. Harder still, change usually tests our own self-esteem or sense of self. Adapting to change is hard work.

Since we live in a world of continuous change the only way to survive and even thrive under this perpetual challenge to who we are and how we see ourselves is to strengthen our **adaptive capacity**. This is not easy. It requires adaptive work, which is different from **technical work**. This book argues that the most important tasks of leadership are to identify the new realities facing the organization and to help build the organization's adaptive capacity. This chapter explores these ideas in greater detail.

PRIMARY GOAL OF ORGANIZATIONS

The Criticality of Relevance

All organizations, regardless of their purpose or mission, have one common, primary goal. That primary goal is to remain **relevant**. Organizations must remain relevant to their societies and relevant to the stakeholders interested in and affected by their actions. As a key organizational purpose this seems obvious and even trite, yet this essential requirement for continued organizational existence is often forgotten or overshadowed by fancy discussions about strategy, competitiveness and profits.

Relevance must be the major driving force behind all the actions of the organization. If relevance does not remain at the forefront of organizational thinking, the organization will soon lose its attraction to its markets and customers, slip into dysfunctional behaviors, decay, and ultimately disappear. Many, many organizations fade into the zone of non-relevance (for example Singer Sewing Machines or the well-known Digital Equipment Corporation) and, despite all efforts, they cannot regain their previous position. The world has moved on!

Relevance is Relational Power

Being relevant is about 'engaged power.' When something or someone is 'relevant' this describes their relational significance. If someone is considered significant, it means he or she has a 'power' that has traction when engaging with others. With power one can do and achieve things. Powerless people or organizations are insignificant and readily become irrelevant. Power is a relational concept. Power as a force does not exist unless it can be exerted, expressed or used in relation to something else. Power and relevance go hand in hand. Being relevant generates power. Without power the individual or the organization 'dies' (May, 1972). (authority, obedience and power are discussed in Chapter 5)

The key challenge leaders of organizations face is how to ensure their organizations remain relevant so that they have the power and the resources to do meaningful things. Leaders need to consider what 'relevance' means from the perspective of the organization's mission or purpose, and to whom; which markets to target and where geographically they should position themselves. It is unlikely that any organization can be relevant in the eyes of everyone. Even the mighty Wal-Mart cannot make that claim. According to *Business Week*, July 2007, Wal-Mart retreated from the German market by selling eighty-five of its stores to the local competition. Wal-Mart could not adapt to German culture and was thus unable to become relevant to sufficient German consumers. The consequence: exit the market or die. It exited.

Relevance Requires Responding to New Realities

To remain relevant requires organizations to be adaptive, creative and innovative.

This means that the mission or underlying purpose of the organization must be made relevant through vision statements that lay out goals and strategies that cohere with the organization's competencies and above all address changing realities. Being in tune with new realities is what makes organizations adaptive and creative. This task is by no means easy. New realities are always arriving. Some realities are obvious and explicit, e.g. the looming retirement of baby boomers; some are not that readily obvious and are more implicit, e.g. a change in the structure of households away from the traditional nuclear family model; and some changes slowly creep up on one and suddenly appear to be a big new reality although they have been emerging for some time, e.g. global warming and climate change. Often, identifying the current reality is not easy. Identifying new realities when they are still new is even more difficult for the many reasons we discuss throughout this book. Easy or difficult, there is nothing more important for any system that wishes to remain alive and relevant than to orient its activities to responding to new realities.

NEW MEDIA REALITIES

Google has radically overturned the newspaper industry. Google's search results track how many people click to view an ad thus providing advertisers with a measure of how many people actually read their ad. Advertising on the web linked to Google's search engine provides advertisers with a benefit they cannot get from traditional print media.

Newspapers and magazines have had to reposition. Large advertising budgets have been redirected to online advertising. Without repositioning, print media will become increasingly irrelevant. (Charan, 2007: 31)

THE FORCES OF CHANGE

The Pervasiveness of Change

Whether it is news on TV, the newspaper, discussion at the boardroom table or in the corridors of offices or manufacturing plants, everyone is talking about change. Change, they say, is the only constant. (Heraclitus, the Greek philosopher, told us this over 2,000 years ago – no new reality!) Everyone claims to be in so-called change mode. Products and processes are being revised, revamped, and re-engineered to respond to change. New industries are emerging, new types of companies are being created; new partnerships forged; new territories 'invaded'; new departments established; and newly skilled employees hired. Evidence of rapid and radical change is everywhere.

Change is pervasive. Many assert that never has there been so much change, such radical change, or such swift change as now. They insist we are facing change of new dimensions and proportions that exceed anything ever experienced. Is that true? Consider the time of the industrial revolution when, seemingly overnight, factories appeared; people left their traditional work at home to be employed by others; steam engines and automobiles replaced donkey carts and bicycles; and new types of medicines cured century-old diseases. Songs and discussions on the local commons were supplanted by the gramophone and the wireless, and flying machines soon ushered in the jet age. People living in those times must have been overwhelmed by the impact of change and are likely to have said much of what we are saying today about the radicalism and rapidity of change.

If we go further back in history we are likely to find many similar turning points where massive changes were the order of the day. If we look carefully we will note that not just every century, but every country heralded a series of spectacular changes.

EXAMPLES OF RADICAL CHANGES

- Horses to chariots
- Sailing ship to hydrofoil
- Morse code to the telephone
- Printing press to the computer
- Bicycle to the automobile
- Radio to television
- Kites to aeroplanes
- Library to the world wide web

Change: A Shift in Space and Time

The twentieth century brought with it a major change in our experience of space. One example is that thanks to advances in aerodynamic technology we can now travel faster than the speed of sound. This reality can hardly be grasped conceptually!

If we look back over the centuries we can mark our progress in the realm of travel. We evolved from walking, to riding the horse, to the donkey cart, to the bicycle, to the automobile, to the propeller plane, to the jet plane, and now to supersonic flight. Along with our new technical abilities, our consciousness has shifted in order to keep up with our changing understanding of distance. Distance, we know, relates to space.

Several hundred years ago, a once in a lifetime physical journey from, say, Casablanca to Mecca would take months. Now this trip is possible within several hours. We can also repeat this journey weekly or even daily without undue hardship. Our twenty-first-century understanding of journey is thus quite different to that of say four hundred years ago. There is no place on earth we cannot physically reach within twenty-four to forty-eight hours.

If for a moment we set aside the physical element of traversing distance and transport ourselves instead to the intellectual or mental plane, we recognize that here too we have made dramatic strides. In earlier centuries we could only communicate face to face via oral messages or handwritten briefs. Communication took time and space (distance had to be covered). Now, with the computer, the internet, and satellite communication, we can communicate almost instantaneously. There is no perceived space between us. Distance is collapsed into the immediate here and now. Space and time no longer exist. Everything is *virtually* here and now. The communication revolution has eradicated the 'space between.' Thus new happenings or new news is not new for long. We are relentlessly assailed with new realities. New realities are made known to us by seemingly instantaneous data feeds. No matter how much you and I might glue ourselves to the news or the internet, there is no way we can absorb, never mind grasp or embrace, all the new realities being communicated.

The communication revolution is likely to continue. The speed of communication has stimulated the development in new technologies, which in turn has improved the technology of communication. The so-called information revolution has resulted from these new technologies that have spawned and fed the ubiquitous world wide web. One important reminder is that the bombardment of information we experience does not guarantee its relevance or quality. Our new challenge is not paucity of information but how to sift out the grains of relevant truths from the mounds of data, facts and fanciful narratives. This too is one of the key challenges of organizational leadership. How does one lead in a **virtual world**? How does one identify the most salient information required for good decision making?

Change as the Only Reality

Judging by the enormous hype regarding the change we are experiencing one might be led to believe we are living in a new era. Well, are we? What makes this time so spectacular, so different? Is 'change' really a special phenomenon? Contemporary physics tells us that everything, everywhere, is always (and always has been) in perpetual motion and change. Nothing is static; everyone and everything consists of continuously vibrating molecules of energy. The cosmos comprises one pulsating mass of particles in continual movement toward new potentials, new possibilities and new outcomes (Capra, 1991; Laszlo, 2007). Waves of change perpetually wash through the cosmos. If this is true, and the new science is the governing scientific paradigm at this time, then it is clear that change is inherent in all that we are and do. Change *is* a constant; has always been with us, and will continue to dictate reality. In fact change *is* reality. Nothing can remain the same for any length of time. Change is as inevitable as night follows day.

So what is so different about our present time? Maynard and Mehrtens in their book *The Fourth Wave* (1993), argue that we are moving from an era of interconnectedness (third wave) to an era of integration (fourth wave). (The first wave was the agricultural revolution and the second wave industrialization.) In the fourth wave, as we come to realize how integrated the world is, we experience a shift of consciousness. As we learn and experience that China, for example, is only a few jet hours away and that China's culture and industrial activity can be brought into our living rooms via TV, we apprehend China differently. The charming notion that the flap of a butterfly's wings in Brazil can impact wind currents over Asia is now understood as an existential reality. Our perception of what is and can be has altered. The combined forces of technology and communications have not only removed or destroyed old fences and archaic stereotypes but have ushered in a profusion of new possibilities and choices. Entrenched ideas have always been challenged, but never at the same rate as now. Old technologies have always faded away, but never at the current pace. The more we realize how interrelated we are with one another and with the environment, the more interrelated we become. The collapse of space and time brings to our consciousness something the sages have always insisted on: the only thing we need to pay attention to is the present moment. As Peter Drucker claimed in one of the books he wrote at the turn of the twentieth century, the future is now!

Given this reality the phenomenon of change is not what requires our attention as much as the impact and meaning of the change. Robert E. Quinn, author of *Deep Change: Discovering the Leader Within* (1996), writes 'If we want to make the world a better place, we need to understand change.' He claims that every person and every organization continually faces a core dilemma: deep change or slow death. Unless work is done to the contrary, all living systems move toward **entropy** or loss of productive energy. He claims that if we do not make deep change we are doomed.

I say more about change in Chapter 2. At this juncture we recognize that change is reality and not keeping apace with change soon renders a person or an organization irrelevant. If one ignores the reality not only of change, but also the need for continuous change, one dies!

A STORY OF RELEVANCE

Recently I moderated a panel discussion on leadership. One of the panelists, the CEO of a small high-tech engineering company in New Hampshire, mentioned during her presentation that 80 percent of the tools and gadgets that are in common use today did not exist over ten years ago. She was making an important point about the rapidity of change. The audience nodded agreement. Further on in the discussions, when it was my turn to say a few words, intent on building on her comment, I asked the audience if they recognized my pen, which I held up for them to see. The pen at the time was a blue fountain pen. Over half the audience indicated they had never seen a fountain pen, never mind used one! When I carried out the same exercise in my class of juniors and seniors a week later, only five out of sixty students had ever seen a fountain pen before. How times change! Certain fountain pen makers have remained relevant to people like me who love all forms of special writing materials. Their market is surely a dwindling one and they are challenged to continuously recreate themselves to ensure their relevance. Not only are most people not that intrigued with fountain pens

(Continued)

(Continued)

any more, most people depend on computers to do their writing for them. Writing by hand is a 'dying' art. There is no longer much *need* for fountain pens or any pens at all for that matter. How will organizations that make any kind of writing instrument or writing materials remain relevant in this kind of a world? Well, notice the growing market in specialized journals! If we do not write for work any more maybe we can be encouraged to handwrite in a beautiful journal with special pens, possibly fountain pens, as part of our reflection or leisure pursuits. This is one attempt at keeping writing materials relevant in changing times.

Change Theories

Many theories of organizational change exist. Christiane Demers provides a synthesis of some of the predominant change theories in *Organizational Change Theories* (2007). In this book she illustrates how change theories have evolved over time and how our understanding of what initiates or motivates organizational change has altered from the 1970s to our present-day understanding. I do not wish to provide a synthesis of her synthesis but simply to highlight some of the different approaches to organizational change that she mentions.

Change theories address the issue of change from a number of different perspectives. One perspective considers whether change is internally determined or environmentally determined. I argue in this book that all change is and should be driven by environmental change. In other words, the stimulus for change is external to the system changing.

Another discussion about change rests on whether change is a radical or incremental phenomenon. Here the focus is on whether change is a transformational or evolutionary phenomenon. This theory looks into the implications of radical turnarounds as opposed to creeping strategic, structural and behavioral change. I argue that both types of change occur simultaneously in a far less definable and/or controlled fashion than we like to imagine.

Yet a further perspective on change focuses on the actions of management either selecting certain specific change strategies in a strategic and controlled manner or responding to crises and driving change through urgency and haste. In both cases change initiatives are considered to be highly rational and top-down-driven activities where leadership is exercised from the top. I resist this view of the management of change, as we will explore in Chapter 4.

The late 1990s and the twenty-first-century vision of change is different in that, instead of being deemed a one-off event, it is seen as pervasive, continuous and indeterminate. Here managers have less control as the organization grapples with change at all levels all the time. All members of the organization are caught up in change initiatives and everyone in the organization needs to see him or herself as an agent of change. The life cycle approach to change is less relevant at this time as industries and organizations break up or recreate new paradigms that do not follow the classic life cycle path. Change is less of a specific initiative in the strategic plan and more a phenomenon of daily organizational life. Just like the atoms and molecules that are in continuous motion, creating new possibilities, organizations are in perpetual motion too. This latter approach is the most consonant with our discussions in this text.

CHANGE AND LOSS

We Dislike Change

If change is inherent in all things and is the order of each and every day, why are we so bad at it? Few would disagree that in general we dislike change and resist it if and when we can. We tend to favor the status quo. We provide all manner of reasons for justifying our preference for what currently exists, especially in the organizational context. At the personal level we may be somewhat open to trying out that new electric car and reluctantly acknowledging that our gas-guzzling SUV has to go. Times have changed. The cost of gas, not the cost of the automobile, is what now determines our buying decisions. If we are part of the organization that is losing market share with its gas-guzzlers and is now retooling and recreating itself to become an electric car maker, we are likely to be even more resistant to the change from making SUVs to electric cars. Why are we so resistant to change? What ups the stakes? What makes organizational change so complex? To answer these questions let us begin by considering the nature of change.

New Realities

As discussed earlier, change arrives by way of new realities. Realities by definition do not go away. They are real and must be heeded. We also know that new realities are always arriving. Some new realities have direct relevance and immediacy to us and our organization, some less so. Because so many new realities are continuously arriving on so many fronts, we cannot apprehend or deal with them all. We have therefore developed coping strategies. Our coping strategies include screening out those realities we consider irrelevant or too insignificant to be concerned with. Often we identify new realities that will affect others, but thankfully not us! 'Look what they have to deal with!' or 'Thankfully that is not my problem!' are well-known sighs of relief.

There are times when our coping strategies incorrectly screen out new realities that have direct relevance to us. This can occur due to inattention, negligence, distraction, denial or fear, or because we feel overwhelmed. Whatever the cause of the oversight, the ramifications of overlooking important new realities can range from inconvenient (I did not realize I had to fill out those new forms) to dire (I should have taken the opportunity to be retrained when it was offered to me).

Organizations screen new realities both formally and informally. They do this through formal processes, such as environmental scanning or strategic planning, as well as informally via the collective consciousness of employees encouraged to be attentive to the changing environment. The result of these processes drives plans for change. Changes are usually initiated through the use of planning documents that lay out goals, set benchmarks, calculate discounted cash flows and use other managerial techniques aimed at ensuring the change will generate a net positive contribution to the bottom line. The predicted addition to profits, however, does not guarantee success, nor does it mean that the change initiative(s) will ensure enduring or even continued organizational relevance. Organizations too can fail to respond to poignant new realities, can respond to the wrong ones, or even to the right ones but in the wrong way. New realities are a tricky business! As we discussed briefly, new realities can be obscure; can be deceptive; can arrive in a fragmented fashion; can readily mislead; and most importantly can be difficult or downright brutal to absorb. The bombardment of new realities contributes to making change so overwhelming. We continuously have to ask ourselves: which new reality is the most critical one? How and why?

At the time of writing one existing reality is that North Korea, much to the alarm of many nations, is flexing its nuclear muscles. In response, the United Nations sponsored moves to tighten financial sanctions and to ban imports of luxury goods into North Korea. According to *The Economist*'s World report, the Kim regime has been the biggest customer for Hennessy's top cognac.[1] Cognac fell under the import ban. The brutal reality of losing this large market due to the embargoes must have been a challenging 'new reality' for Hennessy to absorb and adapt to. Did Hennessy's new realities screening mechanism anticipate this challenge? How did Hennessy adapt, one wonders.

NEW REALITY WARNING SIGNALS

- Nascent industries emerging.
- Non-traditional competitors start to appear.
- New technology challenges existing price–performance relationships.
- Existing business model no longer effective.
- Competitor market positionings alter.
- New customers emerge.
- Customer needs and satisfaction level change.
- New (seeming distant) legislation appears.
- Foreign markets develop imitations.
- Suitably skilled people are in abundance.

(Adapted from Charan, 2007: 51)

Value Tensions

New realities create **value tensions**. Let us see what this means. Pause for a moment and think of the most recent change you have experienced: a new job, a new house, a new baby, a broken tooth, or possibly flooding in the basement. That change, or new reality, challenged your sense of self; your value systems; your priorities. The new house means less money for golf: what will your golfing friends say? You are no longer part of their in-crowd. That new baby means less overtime in the office: what will your boss think of you? You can no longer be relied upon for those special urgent projects. Your new priorities mean you can no longer be the 'up and comer.' That broken tooth means yet another imperfection in your looks you have to deal with. Someone is going to have to artificially fix that smile. That flooding in the basement challenges you: why me? What will the neighbors think about the quality of my house? Am I the only one with lousy foundations? Am I the cheapskate in the neighborhood?

New realities require us to give up, change or mediate our values and often change our priorities and behaviors. This cuts deep! Our values are hard come by. Our values have developed over time, shaped by our life stories and experiences. They are part of who we are. We are invested in them. They reflect what is important to us, who and what we believe in, what we stand for and how we make meaning in the world. Our values give us identity and community. Changing, mediating or reprioritizing our values is no trivial project! Change that challenges our values, therefore, most immediately results in a sense of loss since we are required in some way to relinquish or compromise on one value or another. All change, even good change, signifies loss of some kind. Even 'loss' as a consequence of a welcome new reality invariably has an impact on one's sense of self, or self-esteem (Beerel, 1998; Heifetz, 1994).

Value tensions cut to the chase. They challenge who we are and the world of self-perceptions we have created around us. Often they pierce our most vulnerable spots and tear at the pillars on which we have built our world views, our sense of pride and our self-esteem. Identifying the value tensions that arise as a result of change is known as defining the **adaptive challenge** (Heifetz, 1994). Acknowledging the adaptive challenge is the beginning of the road of adaptive work – something we discuss in great detail in Chapter 4.

New realities may require us to change our ideas; our belief systems; our loyalties; our concepts; our habits; and our skill sets. As one example we have only to look at the role of technology in our lives to grasp the value tensions that new realities can create. Many a specialized craft, managerial function or professional skill has been replaced by technology of all sorts. For example software tools for graphics and design have replaced the work of draughtsmen. Decision support systems can now perform certain planning functions that used to be the preserve of management. Medical systems can now diagnose diseases that used to be the responsibility of specialists in the medical profession. The most dramatic outsourcing we have witnessed and will continue to witness is not to India or China, but to the advance of wireless technology, advanced microchips and intelligent machines. How does it feel to know that a large portion of humankind's basic skill set can be replicated faster, more accurately, more reliably and more consistently by a machine? That truth is an old reality. The new tasks that machines will take over from us are destined to provide a stream of new realities in the foreseeable future.

On that rather somber note this does not mean that change only brings loss, it also brings gains, and important ones. Sometimes those gains are not that easy to recognize, as in the flooding of the basement, losing one's job, or having to be retrained because a machine now performs our former tasks. As Jack Welch, the well-known, former CEO of the huge multinational, General Electric says, change provides a huge opportunity to shuffle the deck, to replay the game. Opportunity is the gateway to tomorrow. If we do not find the gains in change, we will have to change our minds, because change is here to stay.

CHANGE REQUIRES ADDRESSING PEOPLE'S FEELINGS

Harvard Professor Peter Kotter claims the central issue around change is never strategy, structure, culture or systems. The core of the matter is always about changing the behavior of people. He says CEOs are often as resistant to change as anyone and just as prone to backsliding. Behavior change happens mostly by speaking to people's feelings.

In a world where change is constant and often radical we are constantly dealing with 'loss' around our sense of self and who we are. This throws us into a continuous state of renegotiation with ourselves about ourselves. This is hard work – very hard work! It is not always pleasant work, as we are continuously asked to give up some things in favor of others. If we can develop our adaptive capacities by consciously engaging in adaptive work, new realities can bring us new freedoms and new opportunities for developing our infinite human potential. For example having to find a new job may mean we find new competencies and new strengths we never knew we had. In those cases where our sense of self or self-esteem is challenged we are provided with opportunities to consider whether they were grounded in healthy or sustaining values. If nothing else, having to respond to change in creative ways enhances our adaptive capacities, even when it hurts. Mature adaptive capacities provide us with **resilience,** and resilience is a capacity worth working for! Resilience improves the chances of healthy survival in a world of change.

Adaptive Capacity

Identifying and responding to change requires alertness, agility and energy. As we saw, change is hard work. To be good at it, like all things, takes practice. We need to do it repeatedly. Jokingly we often say: 'No rest for the wicked!' This well-worn phrase refers to the need to continuously create, shift, change, rearrange, do whatever it takes, to keep up. The work of 'keeping up' is never done. However, being adaptive is much more than keeping up.

To be good at responding to change refers to our capacity to adapt. As humans we have innate adaptive capacities. These are part of our built-in survival mechanisms as a species. As Darwin has explained to us, to ensure our legacy we need to adapt. To be sure, some of the species (individuals or groups), will elect not to adapt or will not have the wherewithal to adapt, and will, therefore, die and disappear. Losing some is inevitable. The question for our consideration is: do we want to be that individual who disappears? Does our organization want to be that group that falls behind and ends in the dustbin of history?

Adaptation is about learning: not superficial, rote learning, but a deep learning that is transformative. Deep learning is difficult because it challenges our relationship to reality and our mental paradigms. Transformative learning is not easy as it means transforming ourselves. We resist because we exist in the comfort zone of where we are now. Transformation takes us to new territory. That is scary. Adaptation requires strength and courage. It requires a shift in consciousness; a recognition that a new paradigm has come into being. Adaptation requires participating in this paradigm in a meaningful way and including it as part of one's reality.

Adaptation is not the same as coping. Adaptive strategies are different from coping strategies. Adaptation refers to the ability to integrate new realities into one's world view and to work consciously with the changes and value tensions these present. Adaptation means developing a new mindset and new skill sets that can integrate and competently handle new circumstances. Adaptation means being creative and active, not passive and submissive, in the face of change. Adaptation calls for working with the energy of change: guiding, shaping and harnessing that energy in innovative ways.

Coping strategies are less assertive, energetic and creative than adaptive strategies. Coping strategies imply a certain resignation to the inevitability of change whereas adaptive strategies are active, outgoing strategies that do the best they can to meet change on their own terms. Consciously developing our adaptive capacity is what makes us more competent at responding to change. It builds our resilience and our self-confidence. Developing our adaptive capacity also takes us out of the realm of simple survival to greater autonomy and personal moral agency.

Developing one's adaptive capacity is not something that is explicitly taught. Growing into adulthood is an adaptive process. Some do it well and some take a little longer. Even so, not all adults end up with the same adaptive capacities. In fact, our continued resistance to change, even though it is the essence of life, signals the need for us to become more adaptive.

From a leadership development perspective, MBA programs do not teach students how to read new realities and how to create adaptive responses. Regrettably, most MBA curricula place emphasis on technical and procedural, rather than **adaptive work**. (See Chapter 4 for a discussion on the difference between adaptive and technical work.) Adaptive work is left to life in the organization, and organizations have the responsibility of developing the adaptive capacity of their employees. Those organizations that specialize in developing the adaptive capacities of their employees are likely to remain more relevant and to achieve superior results. Through adaptation, creativity and innovation organizations maintain relevance in the eyes of their markets and customers. As they hone their adaptive strategies, they become more adept at adapting to new realities, as well as becoming the creators of new realities themselves. Organizations that do not place emphasis on developing their adaptive capacities will most certainly, in the medium to longer term, struggle to survive.

Adaptive people and adaptive organizations can embrace the future with greater confidence and an enhanced sense of autonomy. If you think about it, there is no greater gift than to help enhance others' adaptive capacity. Isn't that one of the major responsibilities of good parenthood, good education, and good governance? The idea of adaptive capacity and its role in leadership and change management will be discussed in more detail in Chapter 4.

PERSONAL EXERCISE

1 Consider your most recent significant new reality. List the various aspects that made it significant.
2 Who else was affected by this new reality?
3 Did you experience any personal resistance to this new reality? Any resistance from others?
4 Identify the value tensions you experienced. Do the same for the others who were affected.
5 What have you learned as a result of this new reality? What have you had to give up as a result of this new reality?
6 Have you discussed these steps with others? (If not, give it a try.)

The Complexity of Organizational Change

By now we understand well why people resist change. Within the organizational context resistance to change escalates. Let us look at some explanations for this phenomenon.

- People feel less in control when operating within the organization as they are part of a power hierarchy that has control over their future. The system is larger than they are.
- Usually there is someone else ultimately in charge of the change process, so there are usually power dynamics going on (see Chapter 5). Other people's issues have to be taken into consideration and these might take precedence over one's own.
- The losses people experience as part of a change process may be more visible to others than if they are within the realm of their personal lives. Exposure makes them feel more vulnerable.
- There is fear that change may result in people losing their jobs and hence their livelihoods.
- The group dynamic of the organization. Groups always fear for the survival of the group; employees are thus caught in the 'groupthink' around resistance to change. (See Chapter 6 on the anxieties existent in organizational life.)
- Overall, change in the organization appears to raise the stakes.

The group dynamic around resistance to change will be explored in detail in Chapter 6. At this point let us simply note that organizational change is more complex than personal change. Even where organizational leadership has clearly and accurately interpreted the new realities and devised appropriate strategies to move forward, organizational resistance to change can torpedo even the very best efforts. Identifying new realities is only the first part of the challenge of remaining relevant. These efforts must be followed by adaptive work or change initiatives will be sabotaged. Let us also for the moment note that 'execution,' a now popular concept, is not the same as adaptive work! We discuss this further in Chapter 9, on **Systemic Leadership** and strategy.

MANAGEMENT AND THEIR APPROACHES TO CHANGE

Ackoff identifies three primary forms of management based on their attitude toward time and change.

1 *Reactive* managers prefer the way things were in the past. They attempt to remove or suppress the effects of change in the hope of returning to the status quo ante.
2 *Inactive* managers also resist change; they like the way things are. Their objective is to prevent change. Their attitude tends to be 'if it

(Continued)

(Continued)

ain't broke why fix it?' These managers do not react until there is a crisis. They try to suppress the symptoms of a problem that signal the need for change. These are the characteristic behaviors of bureaucracy.

3   By contrast to the other two, *preactive* managers look to the future. For them change is an opportunity to be exploited. They predict and prepare. The most change-oriented leaders are preactive managers. They try to create the future as much as possible. Their possibilities of survival and remaining relevant are the most promising.

(Ackoff, 1999)

GOOD CHANGE AND BAD CHANGE

An important thing for organizational leaders and for executive management to grasp is that there is good change and there is bad change. Good change responds directly to new realities. Good change acknowledges the adaptive challenge and includes engaging in adaptive work along with the required technical work. Good change reinforces the organization's potency and relevance to its customers, markets, employees and shareholders. Good change sets the organization on a forward-looking and healthy trajectory. Good change advances the adaptive capacity of the organization as a whole as well as that of its executives and employees. Good change is recognized as an ongoing process.

Bad change detracts from the organization's potency and relevance. Bad change corrupts an organization's healthy trajectory and impairs its adaptive capacity. Bad change affects morale and people's willingness to be adaptive in the future.

Bad change can be worse than no change, especially where it deludes the company into thinking it is a good change. Bad change is particularly 'bad' if the organization has not truly dealt with the new realities that it needs to respond to in order to remain strategically relevant. Leaders that initiate badly aligned change initiatives do the organization serious damage. Alas, although examples of bad change efforts proliferate, many errant CEOs or executives are oblivious of the damage they have done and have moved on to their next big job, while the organization is stuck with reorienting and revitalizing itself.

It is possible that some change initiatives keep the organization on some course but not the most critical or salient one. That too is bad news. Not only has the organization used enormous energy and resources to achieve mediocre results but also the organization will remain convinced that it has changed and an important goal has been accomplished. Change is the means to an end, and not the end in itself. Change is an ongoing process. The end of one change effort is the beginning of another. In the strenuous efforts around change initiatives, these truths are easily forgotten.

Why Change Fails

Here are several reasons for the low success rate of change projects in organizations:

- The change did not really respond to new realities, but was a response to the reality the CEO and strategic management wanted to perceive was occurring rather than that which was really occurring.

- The change required in order to truly respond to the new realities was not fully understood, as the new realities were not adequately '**reality tested**'.

- The change engaged in was a technical fix to an adaptive problem (see Chapter 4).

- People involved in implementing changes did not truly believe that the change project was responding to new realities, so they were coerced into action rather than feeling self-mobilized.

- The anxieties inherent in the organization impeded its ability to adapt and learn.

- People's resistance to change was not properly dealt with.

- People affected by the change were not included in the decision-making processes.

- Leadership did not or could not convey the urgency of the requirement to change, resulting in poor timing of change.

- The extent of the change initiative was not fully thought through, hence shortly after launch trouble spots creating further stress occurred.

- The full impact of value tensions on stakeholders to the change initiative had been only superficially explored.

- The focus on the change was strategic, tactical and technical but not ethical.

As we discuss throughout this text, identifying new realities and managing the change process is the critical task of leadership. When leadership is exercised effectively the organization's change initiatives will be effective and there will be 'good change.' When leadership is exercised ineffectively, change initiatives will be mediocre, ineffective or will fail miserably. Leadership challenges that arise due to new realities and change will be explored from many angles in the following chapters.

ADAPTIVE, CREATIVE AND INNOVATIVE RESPONSES TO CHANGE

Organizations need to be adaptive, creative and innovative to survive and prosper. Being adaptive, creative and innovative requires enormous attention and energy. To sustain these efforts demands a culture of openness to change. The adaptive and creative work cannot be the sole responsibility of the CEO and strategic management or that of a single division or department. The adaptive and creative mindset must pervade every corner of the organization to make it effective and sustainable.

A change mindset must permeate the entire organization:

- Due to the amount of energy and focus needed to be adaptive and creative, organizations need to optimize group synergy around creative efforts.

- Departmentalizing creativity creates artificial barriers that foster a 'them versus us' attitude.

- Organizations are only as progressive as their weakest link; therefore their weakest link had better be adaptive and creative.

- Organizations need to encourage the creative potential of all their employees, not just those in special functions or departments.

- A culture of openness to change heightens the organization's awareness of new realities and reduces resistance to change.

- In order to foster a **learning organization** – see below – all the individuals in the organization need to bring their adaptive capacities to bear. (See Chapter 4.)

Adaptive Learning Organizations

We have discussed the concept 'adaptive' and the notion of adaptive capacity. What we can add at this point, and something we explore in more detail in Chapter 4, is that adaptive organizations are fundamentally continuous learning organizations (Argyris 1999).

Many organizations claim they have the characteristics of a learning organization. They insist they are creative and innovative and engage in healthy risk taking. Creating a learning organization requires more than this! True learning is to 'know differently.' It is the process of exploring, enquiring, searching, reflecting and in the end knowing something for the first time. The learning process alters the way a person constructs meaning and re-charts her mental maps. True learning results in transformation, not the addition of more information. True learning does not mean acquiring new skills or new technical solutions. True learning creates new understandings, new paradigms and new adaptive strategies and new behaviors.

Let us take a simple example: learning to drive a motor vehicle. Think back on the adaptive work and learning that took. There was certainly all the technical work: learning how to use the pedals, what the information on the instrument panel meant; using the rear-view and side mirrors; what lay under the hood; how to change a tire and so on. Well and good. Prior to learning to drive you had no doubt been driven around by your parents, teachers and friends. Now you are to take over and drive for yourself. This is big! There is a lot of adaptive work here too. You are going to be responsible for your actions behind the wheel. You have new autonomy and thus a new sense of self. You are a real grown-up now as you can take yourself places on your own terms. On the other hand, now you will be asked to fetch and take other people. You may even lose some of your freedom. Driving has opened up a whole new world of opportunities and responsibilitie as new realities always bring both 'losses' and gains.

Recall the first days of driving. You get in behind the wheel and now you are driving. Yes, you know all the technical stuff, but putting it all together is another matter. You run out of hands to activate the turn signals, you brake too late and nearly miss the stop sign, you forget to look in the rear-view mirror when you make a turn and nearly hit an overtaking car ... and so it continues for quite some time. You also learn about your understanding of speed. What it means to accelerate; you feel exhilarated and scared. What it means to stop and how long that can take if you are driving too fast. You learn that reading the map while you are driving is not a good idea as you will most likely miss the turn-off. Driving in a thunder or snow storm presents a whole other number of challenges.

Learning to drive changes your world. It changes the way you feel about yourself and it changes your relationship with others. You have a new understanding of go, speed and stop. You have a new awareness of yourself and your ability to multi-task in this environment. You know why you cannot drink and drive or should not drive when you are drowsy. You know this through the deep personal understanding of being in control, or not, of this metallic capsule that hurtles you and others through space. No one can really grasp the mindset of driving unless they drive. Driving requires an 'altered state of consciousness.'

If we remain with our driving metaphor, a true learning organization provides its employees with opportunities to develop and experience 'new vehicles,' 'new speeds,' and 'new mental maps.' It encourages 'altered states of consciousness' in that it acknowledges that these states provide opportunities for new problems to be identified and new paradigms of understanding to be found.

In this vein the characteristics of a learning organization include the following:

- The organization is open to changes in the environment.

- It allows those changes to flow through the organization and does not block them, check them, or unduly try to control them.

- Employees are encouraged to look at change from multiple perspectives and to reality test the new realities inherent in the winds of change.

- New realities often require new learning. Learning is experiential and so risk taking is encouraged.

- Learning is recognized as affective as well as cognitive, so people are encouraged to share their feelings, not just ideas about change.

- Interdisciplinary dialogue is encouraged to explore and heighten the learning that is taking place.

- Active and constructive feedback is considered part of the learning process.

Learning Can Be Unlearning

A key part of learning is unlearning. This too is part of the adaptive process. Organizations, like individuals, become accustomed to approaching familiar problems in familiar ways. Often unfamiliar problems are categorized as familiar ones as it is more convenient to deal with them using tried and tested solutions than to find new ones. In these cases differences are ignored and similarities are accentuated. The tendency to look at problems in this manner can easily lead to an ever-wider range of problems being solved the old way. In truth, they are not really solved.

The successful solution of problems also reinforces the fallacy that the same strategies are infallible and can be used time and again. Discarding or revisiting well-ingrained, old behaviors or problem-solving strategies becomes increasingly difficult over time. Unless organizational leadership persists in finding new ways to handle both old and new challenges, past success readily breeds complacency and apathy. Getting members of the organization to unlearn accustomed ways of interpreting the world and to relinquish old behaviors is often the greatest barrier to the next level of learning. New realities challenge us to new levels of learning and new behaviors. If we wish to adapt we have to be prepared to unlearn, give up, reorient and change.

THE SHAPE OF NEW REALITIES – THE FUTURE IS NOW

When thinking about new realities it is easy to fall into the trap of trying to predict the future as if it is a one-off event. The future is not a one-off event. It is *always arriving*! It is as ceaseless as the waves that wash up on the seashore. And the future is the past before we know it. No sooner has it arrived than it is past. There is no way and no point in trying to stargaze and anticipate future out-of-the blue events. Everything we wish to know about the future is being revealed to us in the present. Remember, every minute now was in the future a moment ago!

The future lies in the present; the future is now. Our understanding of the future and new realities depends upon our ability to pay attention and understand what is going on now. If we read today's tea leaves correctly we will see the new realities emerging and unfolding.

Organizations that excel, work intensively with current realities. Their mindfulness and attention to developments both in their markets and in others provides them with insights into new solutions and new creative opportunities. These organizations are observant and curious. They tend to investigate corners where others are not paying attention. They are essentially idea-driven, rather than market share- or profit-driven. They continuously change the rules for themselves to avoid complacency and arrogance. They see change as an opportunity. The entire enterprise is committed to change and action. Above all they employ adaptive, creative, self-motivated people.

ONLY THE CHANGE LEADERS SURVIVE

Peter Drucker in *Managing for the Future* (1992) claimed one cannot manage change. One can only be ahead of it. The only ones who survive are the change leaders; they see change as an opportunity; they actively look for and anticipate change. Their attitude is to abandon yesterday; to feed opportunities, and inculcate a policy of systematic innovation.

Gary Hamel in his chapter 'Be Your Own Seer' (in *Leading the Revolution*, 2002) provides some profound advice on how to be alert to new realities and how to respond effectively. He advocates the importance of freeing oneself from the stranglehold of the familiar by leaping over our mental constraints. We are prisoners to tradition and our eyes are dimmed by precedent, he claims. Familiarity is the enemy. He stresses the importance of the imagination, curiosity and creativity that come with learning to see and be different. He suggests that we become novelty addicts and heretics, willing to challenge the status quo and to proactively shape the environment.

Hamel insists it is essential to become 'addicted to change' and to perpetually seek new possibilities. Predicting the future is for fools; what is important is to develop strategies to deal with unpredictability. He argues that the future is different rather than unknowable. Opportunities are found by looking where others are not looking, and that requires us to really pay attention. He advocates that we challenge our mental models and deconstruct existing beliefs.

John Kotter of the Harvard Business School insists that the central issue is never strategy, structure, culture or systems. The core of change lies in changing the behavior of people, and behavior change happens mostly by speaking to people's feelings. The task of leadership is primarily about dealing with people's capacity for adapting to new realities, i.e. their ability to transform and change.

THE PRIME TASK OF LEADERSHIP – IDENTIFYING NEW REALITIES

Leadership is about facilitating, guiding and managing change. Where there is no change, we do not need leaders. Exercising leadership concerns mobilizing oneself and others (the group or the organization) to adapt to the new realities of change (Beerel, 1998).

The first responsibility of the leader is to define reality in collaboration with others in the organization. This requires sizing up the current situation as it really is; not as it used to be, or as people would like it to be. It is essential that the current realities are viewed from every angle; that bad news is confronted, and that creative attention is given to new realities that are continuously arriving.

Max De Pree, ex-chairman of Herman Miller, the highly specialized furniture manufacturers, describes in his two well-known books, *Leadership is an Art* (1989) and *Leadership Jazz* (1992), an approach to leadership that resonates with this attention to new realities. In *Leadership is an Art*, his advice for leadership is deeply consonant with the systemic and interrelatedness concepts of the new science discussed earlier. He claims that the first step of the leader is to define reality (De Pree, 1989: 11). According to him leaders should also liberate people to do what is required of them: to change, grow and strive to achieve their potential. They can only do this if they are aligned to the changing realities of the world and are in touch with the consequences.

Defining reality is difficult as we tend to mute or downplay those parts of reality we do not want to deal with. Entire organizations and even entire societies (see p. 23 below) collude in this fashion. In order to define reality effectively, therefore, leaders need to reality test their perception of what is changing. Reality testing means involving others in dialogue and investigation so as to arrive at a co-created understanding of the current new reality. Leaders must include views and opinions of people across all sectors of the organization, across all disciplines, and preferably across all points of view. Frequently the organization's outliers have insights into 'reality' that others may not see or grasp. Leaders must also persist in exploring current new realities that are being ignored, no matter how trivial they may initially seem.

DENIAL OF NEW REALITIES

Climate change is bottom of the priority list for Britain's largest companies.
    More than half the companies surveyed by YouGov for KMPG, the professional services firm, said there were more urgent issues, such as brand awareness, marketing strategies, and corporate social responsibility. Just 14 percent of them had a clear strategy for tackling climate change. Only half of the 73 companies surveyed claimed to understand fully the implications of climate change. In a separate report by HeadLand Consultancy, the feeling among 19 fund managers surveyed is that climate change is outside their limit. Long term for them is about three years out; they are not looking at 2012, let alone 2050. Industry efforts are aimed at getting the green fraternity off our backs).

Jared Diamond gives us some interesting insights into the devastating results of ignoring new realities and how and why this occurs. His book *Collapse: How Societies Choose to Fail or Succeed* (2005: 6), chronicles the collapse of past civilizations. He reveals how humankind's use and abuse of the environment throughout the centuries reveals the truth behind the world's greatest collapses. History, he claims, is filled with patterns of environmental catastrophes. The processes by which past societies have undermined themselves include deforestation and habitat destruction, soil problems, water management problems, overhunting, overfishing, the effects of introduced species on native species, uncontained human population growth, and increased per capita impact of people on the local environment, and we are calling these phenomena new realities!

His examples include the history of Easter Island, Norse Greenland, and the Native American Mayan society. In recounting the events that led to their demise he highlights the warning signals that were present and visible but ignored by the populations and their leaders. In fact some of the leaders' strategies exacerbated the situation rather than raising it to public attention or confronting the signs of impending doom.

Diamond asks the question: why do some societies make disastrous decisions? He refers to the collapse of the Easter Island people who cut down all the trees on which they radically depended. Easter Island was discovered by Jacob Roggeveen on Easter Sunday April 5, 1722. It is famous for its gigantic stone statues of human faces. Over several centuries the islanders systematically destroyed their forests. Without constraint they used wood for building houses and canoes, for platforms to haul the enormous statues across the island, and used bark for ropes. Clans competed to build bigger and bigger statues, destroying forests as they sought to outdo one another. The result of the native tribes' overexploitation of resources and destruction of a fragile ecosystem led to the society's eventual demise.

In order to answer his own question, Diamond refers to the work by archaeologist Joseph Tainter in *The Collapse of Complex Societies* (1988). Tainter describes how societies sit by and watch their encroaching weakness without taking corrective action. Many of their stories appear to reflect idleness in the face of looming disaster. Tainter (1988: 421) goes on to analyze this baffling phenomenon. He claims that there are four main reasons why groups fail to make decisions when realities reflect danger signals:

- failure of anticipation of problem before it arrives;
- failure in perception that there is a problem;
- even once they perceive it, failure to solve the problem;
- despite attempts, lack of success in solving the problem.

Tainter explains his analysis as follows:

1   Failure of anticipation – the society is facing a new problem; it has no prior experience; it has not been sensitized to the possibility; its reasoning processes fail as it uses old analogies to try to grasp the problem.

2   Failure to perceive – the origins of the problem appear imperceptible; people distant from one another, as in large corporations, are not able to piece the issues together. The new reality arrives in the form of a slow trend concealed by up and down fluctuations; it becomes creeping normality; this leads to landscape amnesia where people forget what the terrain looked like in the past due to the gradual changes.

3   Failure to attempt to solve a problem, once it is perceived – people over-rationalize the problem; there is a clash of interests between stakeholders; the blinding force of the lust for power distracts competing leaders from actually solving the problem; maintenance of the problem is good for some people. There is also irrational behavior, where people are torn by a clash of values and resist doing something new. An interesting question is: at what point do people prefer to die rather than compromise their values and live? Then there is the sunk-cost effect where people feel reluctant to abandon a policy in which they have invested heavily.

4   Failure to solve the problem – the problem is beyond the group's present capacities to solve.

What we observe from Tainter's analysis is that the failure to respond to new or unpleasant realities applies equally well to organizations. There too leaders and senior management readily fall into one or more of Tainter's four categories of decision-making inertia or failure. The role of good leadership is to minimize the possibility of ignoring or misreading important realities that have a direct bearing on the survival and relevance of the organization.

WHAT LEADERS REALLY DO

They don't make plans, they don't solve problems, they don't even organize people. What leaders really do is prepare organizations for change and help them cope as they struggle through it.

How does one set the direction for change? Not by organizing people but aligning them.

(Kotter, 1999)

Systemic Leadership

In this book we focus on the Systemic Leadership Approach. Systemic leaders focus on keeping the organization fine-tuned to new realities. They understand the impact of new realities and change, and help (members of) the organization to work with the value tensions presented, adapt, learn and develop their adaptive capacities.

Systemic Leaders are transformational leaders, concerned with strengthening the organization's capacity for learning. They understand that this will determine its resilience and continued competitive strength. They recognize the consequences of Easter Island myopia.

Understanding the philosophy of Systemic Leadership and the tasks of effective systemic leaders will preoccupy us in the next chapters. One thing Systemic Leaders are good at is inductive as opposed to deductive thinking. Deductive thinking is based on old rules of deduction. Radical change requires new heuristics for framing complex problems.

Inductive Thinking

Understanding new problems requires an inductive rather than a deductive approach. Management focuses mostly on deductive reasoning and decision making. The task of leadership is to embrace **inductive thinking**. Inductive thinking is more complicated and very different from the deductive approach.

Deductive reasoning is about applying rules to circumstances and events. By contrast, inductive reasoning is about looking at circumstances and events and considering what rules may apply to them or finding new rules. The emphasis of inductive thinking lies on identifying and interpreting a variety of data, finding patterns, relationships and linkages that may explain things. Inductive thinking emphasizes questioning. It seeks to draw out specific causes and connections and arrive at inferences that accurately describe reality. Dealing with reality is essential in the case of inductive reasoning, to ensure that inferences drawn stand up to thoughtful scrutiny.

Inductive thinking is an approach we usually neglect – largely because it is time consuming, can be enormously frustrating as we have to find our own answers, and tantalizing when answers seem to allude us. Yet, inductive thinking is enormously powerful and creative when used appropriately. Once again, inductive thinking is not taught much in schools or universities. An organization is left to create its own culture of inductive thought processes and questioning. This endeavor is yet another task we can add to that of leadership as part of the new reality identification and testing process.

EXECUTIVE SUMMARY

Now we have laid out the groundwork of this text on *Leadership and Change Management*. In this first chapter we emphasize that, in order to stay alive, organizations need to respond to the pulse of change. Leadership is about facilitating and directing these change efforts. True change is complex and transformative. Good leadership facilitates transformation and develops the organization's adaptive capacity.

Here are some key points of the chapter:

- Organizations are human systems formed to achieve a predetermined purpose or goal. In order to survive in the longer term, organizations must remain relevant.

- Change arrives by way of new realities. New realities are always arriving and will not disappear.

- The only constant in the world is change. Change challenges existing structures, forms and paradigms. In order for people and organizations to survive meaningfully they need to respond to new realities and adapt.

- New realities are driven by forces in the external environment. Failure to identify the source of new realities can result in the organization responding to the wrong ones.

- Change always creates value tensions. These value tensions represent both gains and losses. Change will always represent loss in some form or another. Identifying value tensions is known as defining the adaptive challenge.

- In order to enhance their adaptive capacity people and organizations need to define the adaptive challenge and then do their adaptive work. These activities enhance their adaptive capacities.

- Adaptive capacity is a function of the organization's ability to deal with the value tensions that change always implies.

- The prime task of leadership is to identify the new realities and to consider the value tensions they imply for various stakeholders.

KEY CONCEPTS

Adaptive capacity
Adaptive challenge
Adaptive work
Entropy
Inductive thinking
Learning organization
New realities
Organizational relevance
Reality testing
Relevance
Resilience
Shift in consciousness
Systemic Leadership
Technical work
Transformation
Value tensions
Virtual world

CASE STUDY
LIFELONG BANK AND TRUST (LLB)

LLB is a community banking institution based in El Paso, on the Texas and New Mexico border. LLB has over fifteen branches in both states. LLB has been in operation for sixty years. Its assets reached $800 million in the mid-1990s, but dropped back to $650 million in 2007. The President, Jack Stock, attributed the decline in assets to a nationwide cooling off of the mortgage banking business. Stock is feeling the pressure to identify and penetrate new markets.

The number of illegal immigrants in both Texas and New Mexico has increased significantly over the last decade. Most illegal immigrants live in the dilapidated parts of town where middle-class families used to live before the loss of many manufacturing operations. The new Latino population that has grown up around El Paso has brought with it Latino folk music, statues of Our Lady of Guadalupe and marisco stands.

To reverse LLB's declining financial position, Stock plans to offer a new mortgage product that will be marketed to illegal immigrants. The Federal Deposit Insurance Commission (FDIC) has maintained there is no federal law requiring banks to verify immigration status of foreign account holders.

Stock realizes that offering mortgage products to illegal immigrants will draw fire from critics. On the other hand it will fulfill the unmet banking needs of a new market and generate a new revenue stream. He believes that offering mortgages to the Latino population and increasing the ownership of homes will result in an improvement in the housing market for all the residents of El Paso.

Stock is preparing to present his strategy to the board of directors for approval. He needs their support to introduce this new innovative policy across the branches of LLB. He hopes to convince the directors of the manifold benefits of his strategy. Entry into the market would give LLB a competitive advantage and a new revenue stream. It would help revitalize parts of El Paso and would grow LLB's balance sheet.

Questions:

1 List the new realities in this case that John Stock is dealing with.

2 Identify the stakeholders affected by John's initiative and identify their value tensions.

3 What would you advocate if you were on LLB's board of directors? What are your reasons?

ORGANIZATIONAL EXERCISE: MALDEN MILLS

Aaron Feuerstein was hailed as a savior when, after a devastating fire in his factory in the depressed area of Lawrence, Massachusetts, in 1995, he continued to pay his workers while his factory was being rebuilt. Now Feuerstein's actions are being questioned. Had he done the right thing in paying his workers even though insurance settlements after the fire were not guaranteed and had not amounted to what he originally thought he would receive? In order to update the factory, Feuerstein spent millions over what he was insured for. Several managers had questioned the scale of the rebuilding; some even thought it was not good practice to rebuild a mill in the Northeast when other textile mills had moved to cheaper labor climates. Feuerstein had overridden these objections, insisting he had an obligation to his workers and to the community to rebuild the operations after the fire.

Malden Mills was founded in 1906 by Henry Feuerstein. After the 1940s many large fabric manufacturers in New England moved south to take advantage of lower labor costs and proximity to cotton growers. Because of this industry shift mill space became cheaper and more available in New England. Aaron Feuerstein, President and grandson of founder Henry, felt it best to keep the mill in New England. At this time Malden Mills began to have its yarns converted to fabric in small outlying plants in Vermont, Maine and New Hampshire, and then dyed, printed and finished these fabrics in its central mill in Lawrence.

Although the mill managed to stay alive, it experienced some rough times, including a declaration of bankruptcy in 1981 when its primary product, fur, abruptly went out of fashion. Feuerstein family members called for Aaron to step down as President, which he resisted. He claimed he had a new solution which entailed drastically restructuring the mill to focus on two new products: Polartec and Polarfleece. Despite warnings from his bankers, Feuerstein persisted, and Polartec became a resounding success, generating sales of $200 million in 1995.

Malden Mills remained the largest textile mill in New England. In other areas in the US companies like Levi Strauss had at the beginning of the 1990s moved their manufacturing operations overseas to cut costs. Wage differentials between American and Mexican or Bangladeshi workers were huge. For example American workers would earn $6.75 per hour versus $1 for Mexicans and 22 cents for Bangladeshi workers. During the early 1990s imports from China and Vietnam increased significantly while US employment and production declined.

The fire of 1995 all but gutted the Malden Mills buildings. Twenty-four workers were injured, thirteen seriously. Despite his managers' skepticism and their suggestion that only the profitable part of the mill be rebuilt, Feuerstein decided to rebuild the entire factory. He also agreed to pay 3,100 Malden Mills employees full pay and benefits for 90 days. He resisted suggestions that new machinery be introduced to reduce manufacturing costs.

The insurance money for the rebuilding was slow to materialize and was less than expected. Malden Mills was forced to borrow significant sums to meet cash flow needs. At this time Feuerstein was hailed as a hero and stories of his generosity to employees and his commitment to Lawrence filled the newspapers. There were guest appearances with President Clinton and he was featured on many major news networks. He received a variety of awards and was named the 'CEO with a difference.'

While all was rosy on the publicity front, relationships between Malden Mills and its other stakeholders were less positive. Buyers were dissatisfied with the quality of certain goods and Feuerstein had to make great efforts to maintain their support. The amount of rebuilding undertaken to restore all parts of Malden Mills, including the less profitable parts, also exhausted the organization's resources.

By 2001 Feuerstein's rebuilding strategy was unable to support itself. Malden Mills had huge loans, had settled a few legal suits out of court, some from injured employees, that cost it several million dollars, and eventually closed a loss-making division after spending $50 million trying to rebuild it. At the same time price competition from other brands continued to increase.

Five years after the fire, in November 2001, Malden Mills filed for Chapter 11 bankruptcy for the second time. Feuerstein was relieved of control of the company by Malden Mills creditors.

Questions:

1 What new realities was Malden Mills facing during the 1990s?

2 What new realities did the outbreak of the fire bring?

3 What strategy did Aaron Feuerstein use to deal with the new realities and what was his rationale?

4 Do you think he exercised effective leadership? If so, why or why not?

FURTHER READING

Ackoff, Russell, L. *Recreating the Corporation: A Design of Organizations for the 21st Century*. New York: Oxford University Press, 1999.

Charan, Ram. *Know-How*. New York: Crown Business, 2007.

Conner, Daryl R. *Leading at the Edge of Chaos: How to Create the Nimble Organization*. New York: John Wiley, 1998.

Diamond, Jared. *Collapse*. New York: Penguin Books, 2005.

Drucker, Peter F. *Management Challenges for the 21st Century*. New York: HarperBusiness, 1999.

Kotter, John P. *Leading Change*. Boston, MA: Harvard Business School Press, 1996.

Senge, Peter, Smith, Bryan, Kruschwitz, Nina, Laur, Joe and Schley, Sara. *The Necessary Revolution*. New York: Doubleday, 2008.

Note

1 *The Economist*, *The World in 2007*, 'After the Bouffant of Pyongyang'. London: *The Economist*, 16 November 2006, p. 43.

2 CRITICAL SYSTEMS THINKING

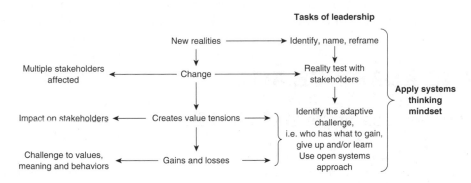

Tasks of leadership

New realities ⟶ Identify, name, reframe

Multiple stakeholders affected ⟵ Change ⟶ Reality test with stakeholders

Impact on stakeholders ⟵ Creates value tensions ⟶ Identify the adaptive challenge, i.e. who has what to gain, give up and/or learn

Challenge to values, meaning and behaviors ⟵ Gains and losses ⟶ Use open systems approach

Apply systems thinking mindset

Figure 2.1

INTRODUCTION

In Chapter 1 we explored the impact of new realities and the value tensions they create. We said that dealing with change is difficult because of the loss it implies. We also discussed how new realities are often complex to identify.

In this chapter we discuss systems, **systems theory** and the importance of having a **systems thinking mindset** if one wants to recognize new realities and be adaptive. New realities are invariably systemic by nature. They are not isolated incidents that only affect a local or small part of a system. The repercussions of new realities reverberate throughout the system. The ripple effect is often subtle and covert, requiring a systems mindset in order to be seen and understood.

Systems theory provides a way of seeing the larger picture without losing the importance of detail. Systems theory advocates understanding the organization as a living system. Since it is a living system, understanding its behavior requires attention to narrative (i.e. its story), patterns of behavior between parts of the system, and interrelationships between those parts. The organization as a living system is treated as a whole, as are its parts. In looking at wholes the systems thinker applies his or her imagination in order to understand the values and roles that systems and their parts represent to one another.

System dynamics, a partner approach to systems theory, provides a method for looking at the reinforcing and non-reinforcing behaviors that either support or challenge system attempts to change. It supports systems analysis especially with regard to the role of feedback. The insights we gain from system dynamics help us better understand how change affects the overall system and where points of resistance might lie.

Even though we may adopt a systems thinking mindset, we know our thinking skills have limitations. Our **mental models** and cognitive maps are limited and biased. The information we perceive and receive is selective, often superficial, and outdated. A systems thinking approach invites us to challenge our mental models and question the rigor of our **critical thinking.** Systems thinking competence and critical thinking skills are the *sine qua non* of good leadership.

THE ADAPTIVE AGE

The Panacea of the Technical Fix

The twentieth century will be remembered for humans' achievements in establishing new frontiers in technical brilliance. It was a century filled with new ideas, new inventions, and the emergence of new paradigms. The result is that it turned us into a **technical fix** society. During that century the emphasis on the technical panacea for all problems reached outrageous proportions. Inventing and designing new technical processes became the principal method for dealing with human problems. Whatever obstacle we encountered we sought solutions in yet another technical fix. The fix might be an aspirin, an abortion clinic, cosmetic surgery, a larger welfare check, weight-reduction tablets, a reorganization, downsizing, or outsourcing. The technical fix supposedly made us feel younger, older, slimmer, safer, smarter, more competitive or more powerful. Do technical fixes really solve our problems or are they just that: short-term technical fixes?

The twenty-first century is challenging us with new problems. Some of these so-called new problems are actually old problems never truly fixed by our previous technical fixes. Our health statistics have not improved; obesity has reached drastic proportions; poverty in real terms is on the increase; and reorganization, downsizing and outsourcing are popular methods for distracting us from our inefficiency and work ethic complacency. To top it all, we are rapidly destroying our environment.

At the time of writing we are facing the humongous mortgage crisis that has exceeded anyone's most pessimistic expectations as it ravages financial centers across the globe. Our technical fixes, new committees, new banking rules and new legislation (for example, the Sarbanes-Oxley Act 2002) have got us nowhere, it seems. Many say we are back to the 1979 world economic crisis, if not even that of 1929. What have we actually learned in thirty years? Are we truly better off? What kind of leadership vision got us here?

In this chapter we discuss the power of systems thinking to get at the root causes of problems and provide us with ways of seeing the world that do not result in quick fix technical solutions.

A New Age

A culture's characteristic way of thinking is embedded in its concept of reality, i.e. its world view. A change of world view brings cultural changes and leads to what historians call a 'change of age' (Ackoff 1999: 4). Today, our world view is changing in fundamental ways. One could say we are undergoing a change of age.

In my previous book, *Leadership through Strategic Planning* (1998), I argued that we are moving into what I called the '**adaptive age.**' The adaptive age will bring a backlash to our customary dependence on technical fixes. There will be a renewed return to values and meaning making and, while technical solutions will remain a significant factor of life, greater emphasis will be placed on the humanistic aspect of systemic issues. In this shift to a more adaptive approach to problem solving, we will recognize the interconnectedness of our planet and its people. We will be forced to pay more attention to our systemic interdependence. We will recognize the need for a systems perspective in order to understand the globalizing world, the problems it faces and their potential solutions. We will grasp that problems cannot be seen or addressed in isolation.

The adaptive age will call for a different type of leadership. Leaders will need to think and respond systemically. They will need to be able to see relationships and patterns as opposed to single issues or events. Leaders will need to recognize that the soft issues are the hard issues and that the power of change lies in the human spirit and not in technical solutions. Above all, we need new leaders with new frames of consciousness.

THE FOURTH WAVE – A CHANGING WORLD

According to Maynard and Mehrtens, authors of *The Fourth Wave*, the hallmarks of a changing world, include:

- a shift in consciousness;
- disenchantment with scientism;
- a focus on inner sources of authority and power;
- re-spiritualization of society;
- a decline of materialism – new definitions of wealth;
- political and economic democratization;
- movement beyond nationality to global citizenship.

(Maynard and Mehrtens, 1993)

A New Mindset

Danah Zohar, in *ReWiring the Corporate Brain* (1997), explains how the 'new sciences' (relativity and **quantum physics**) of the twentieth century is challenging us to rethink our basic categories of perceiving the world. She explains the need for a shift from atomistic thinking towards holism and the emphasis on seeing relationships; from the understanding of parts through fragmentation to seeing parts in integration; from emphasizing the determinate to yielding to the indeterminate, unknowable and uncontrollable.

The **new sciences** teach us that little is certain and predictable. Instead the world moves within ambiguity, uncertainty and infinite possibility. New possibilities are continuously emerging; little can be isolated and controlled; living systems are contextual and self-organizing.

Zohar takes the new realities of the new sciences and illustrates the impact this has on the management of organizations. She claims that understanding the nature of change means being open to all possibilities; that bottom-up leadership is more consonant with the way energy flows in systems; and that imaginative and experimental mindsets are critical in order to respond to changing environments. She advocates that managers become better at asking new and different questions based on new and different assumptions. She points out that the questions we ask determine the answers we get as well as the answers we do not get. She insists that questioning, finding patterns and emphasizing relationships at all levels are requirements of effective leadership.

CRITICAL FINDINGS OF THE NEW SCIENCE

The new sciences relate to the modern physics of relativity and quantum theory.

Relativity relates to Einstein's notion of the relationship between time and space: Mass is nothing but a form of energy (energy E equals mass m times c the speed of light squared) – $E = mc^2$

Quantum theory includes the following ideas:

- Energy is not discrete but comes in small packets of light called quanta.
- At the subatomic level there is no such thing as solid objects.
- Matter comprises both particles and waves; nothing is solid.
- Particles can only be understood in relation to the whole.
- Atomic events have a tendency to occur; there is no certainty.
- Tendencies are probabilities of interconnections; everything is connected with everything else.

- Nothing is an isolated entity.
- There are no building blocks, only a complicated web of relations of the whole.
- The whole includes the observer; the observer is always part of what he or she observes.
- Observations influence results.

(Capra, 1991: 52–84)

Margaret Wheatley, in *Leadership and the New Science* (1994), takes a similar approach to Zohar. Wheatley claims we need new images, new metaphors and new ways of thinking. Organizational leaders and managers need to see the universe as an endless profusion of possibilities, and relationships as bundles of potentiality. Living systems respond to disorder with renewed life, and growth is found in disequilibrium rather than balance.

Wheatley emphasizes the fact that we participate in reality and should give up seeing ourselves as independent observers. Together we are constantly creating the world; we are evoking it rather than discovering it. In light of these realities leaders need to create fields of vision rather than trying to create paths. Orienting one's consciousness to these new realities is essential for embracing the future. Wheatley too advocates 'think living systems.'

THINK SYSTEMS

- Think possibilities not solutions.
- Encourage bottom-up, distributed leadership.
- Focus on new and different questions.
- Challenge existing assumptions.
- Look for patterns and relationships.
- Find new images and metaphors.

WHAT IS A SYSTEM?

A system is a regularly interacting and interdependent group of parts, items or people that form a unified whole with the purpose of establishing a goal. There are numerous types of system. There are for example biological systems (the respiratory system); mechanical systems (air-conditioning systems); ecological systems (plant life); social systems (groups and communities); and economic systems (business organizations).

A system is always embedded in other systems; so any system is always a combination of systems and sub-systems. Arthur Koestler coined the term **holon** to refer to that which is whole in one context, and simultaneously a part in another (Koestler, 1967). Holons are nested within each other. Each holon is nested within the next level of holon, assuring their interconnectedness and interdependence. For example, the nation of the United States is a system and corporate America is a sub-system of that system. A company is both a sub-system of corporate America and a system in its own right where its board of directors is in turn a sub-system of the company. If one thinks about it carefully, the interconnectedness of systems is infinite.

Reality constitutes holons. Holons (wholes) are part of other wholes with no upward or downward limit. Nothing is independent; everything is part of the **holarchy**. The nation is a system, the earth is a system, our galaxy is a system, and the cosmos is a system. All of these systems are interrelated. Quantum physics tells us that these interrelated and interconnected systems affect one another in the most amazing ways even when the parts of the various systems appear to be distant from one another. So for example, women across the world form a system and women in China form a sub-system of that system. Due to the nature of systems, we can know that whatever impacts Chinese women will in some way impact women across the world.

Systems range from simple to complex. The more complex a system, the greater the number of its sub-systems, and the more intricate their operations. Sub-systems are arranged in some form of hierarchy that facilitates achieving the sub-system's goal, which is in service of the larger system's goal. Hierarchy is central to systems theory in that it is the theory of wholeness. Hierarchy derives from hiero, which means sacred or holy, and arch, which means governance or rule. Hierarchy thus means 'sacred governance' (Wilber, 1998: 55). From a systems perspective hierarchy describes an order of increasing holons representing an increasing wholeness and integrative capacity (Waddock, 2006: 56). Each sub-system has its own boundary that contains the inputs, processes, outputs and feedback loops that contribute to the overall system performance and goal (Senge, 1990).

Systems import all kinds of elements from the other systems of which they are part. For example if the larger system is unhealthy or insecure and experiencing fear, the sub-systems will import these emotions into their environments and they will be insecure and fearful too. If the larger system is at war, the sub-systems will become warlike too. If the company as a whole behaves as a corporate bully, its divisions and departments will mirror this kind of behavior. Similarly if the company as a whole lacks rigor, has no checks and balances and behaves recklessly, the board of directors, as a sub-system, will reflect the same attitudes and behaviors. (See macrocosm–microcosm described below.)

LIVING SYSTEMS AND ADAPTATION

The Goal of Living Systems

Quantum physics claims that all matter is in some sense living in that it is in continuous motion. Even rocks are 'alive' and form part of a living ecological system. All systems are therefore living systems. Living systems have one primary purpose or goal and that is 'survival.' Conscious living systems wish for more than survival: they aspire to healthy and prosperous survival. Different types of living systems might construe 'healthy and prosperous' survival differently. For example, family systems might strive for emotional survival; social systems for political survival; economic systems for economic survival. Nevertheless, no matter how it is interpreted or measured, survival is the primary and most immediate goal of every living system.

Let us continue with the previous example. A nation is a system. The goal or purpose of this system is survival. A nation comprises many sub-systems and these sub-systems also have sub-systems. Therefore states, provinces or counties might be one form of sub-system and then there are social communities and economic groups that form another level of sub-system. If we think about these systems, they all have their own individual goals, boundaries and processes aimed at contributing to the overall goal of national healthy and prosperous survival. The social sub-systems contribute political, social, cultural and communal health. The economic systems contribute economic health, and so on. While each sub-system has unique properties and processes, the goals they set out to achieve are always in the service of the goal at the next systemic level. The contribution each sub-system makes to the larger system may be different, but the goal is always the same – to contribute to survival. If we have healthy family systems, we have a healthy community system. If we have healthy community systems, we will have healthy state or county systems and a healthy national system. The opposite is obviously true – unhealthy families lead to an unhealthy national system. If a sub-system is unable to contribute to the survival of the larger system, it loses its relevance and soon dies.

Even though we tend to measure our systemic goals using all kinds of metrics, for example, GDP, birth rates, death rates, infant mortality rates, income levels etc., the ultimate goal living systems seek to achieve is survival, and beyond that 'good' (what I have termed healthy or prosperous) survival.

Adaptive Systems as Open Systems

In order for systems to be healthy and stay alive, they need to be open to external forces and thus be open and responsive to change. Change is reality. Closed systems cannot survive for long as they are in denial, or out of touch with reality. Closed systems that do not change lose their relevance. Living systems stay alive by being open and dynamic (Von Bertalanffy, 1969: 32). This makes them complex to understand and manage. This complexity is exacerbated by the fact that systems resist change as change always implies learning and transformation. Learning and transformation always require giving up something for something else.

As we discussed at length in Chapter 1, this giving up is experienced as loss. Usually this loss relates to a sense of identity and self-worth. A very common example of change and loss in the business organization is the impact of changing technology. Organizations have to keep pace with rapidly changing technology in order to remain competitive. They need to continually forgo old practices in favor of new ones. These changes have implications across the organization. Not only does the overall organization as a system need to change, but the sub-systems need to change and adapt too. The image of the company needs to be honed in tune with the changes, the corporate culture changes as work practices change and employees require continuous retraining to keep apace with change.

Continuous, rapid change demands that a system continuously renews its inputs, processes, outputs and feedback loops to survive. This is no easy task! Systems that adapt well survive. Those that either close their boundaries in order to deny new realities or adapt poorly die. Adapting to new realities is what keeps systems relevant to the larger systemic whole. In Chapter 1 it was pointed out that loss of relevance leads to death!

WHAT IS SYSTEMS THEORY?

General Systems Theory

General Systems Theory developed from the study of biology in the 1920s. This theory centered on the living systems that comprise the natural world and the common laws governing those systems. The major premise that evolved from General Systems Theory is that the common laws that govern natural systems can serve as a conceptual framework for understanding the relationships in any system. Systems theory, the outgrowth of natural systems theory, emphasizes viewing systems as a whole and gaining a perspective on the entire entity before examining its parts (Haines, 1998).

Systems theory provides a different approach to grasping and working with reality. Previously our world view saw reality as comprising many parts that could be put together, taken apart, and studied in isolation. Thanks to quantum physics our world view has now changed. This new understanding of the world is that it comprises an infinite network of living systems (Capra, 2004). Systems theory advocates that in order to understand who we are, what is changing, and what we are faced with we need to think systems. To think systems means to see things as *holons*; that is to look at all things as a part of a system that is part of other systems. We can look at the individual as a system that is part of other systems: the group, the organization, the industry, the community, the nation, the biosphere, all as part of interwoven systems. A systems perspective always treats systems as integrated wholes of subsidiary systems and never as an aggregate of parts.

Applying Systems Theory

Irreducibility of systems

Systems theory develops our understanding of systems by focusing on the structured relationships that form part of any system. The relationships among the parts of a system have certain characteristics that together manifest irreducible characteristics of the system itself. In other words, all systems have properties of their own that are not reducible to the parts. We are aware of this when we think about groups and group dynamics. Groups are systems. We recognize that the group system has a character and a mindset that exists apart from the aggregate characteristics and mindsets of its individual members (Ackoff, 1999). (See Chapter 6 for a discussion of groups as systems.)

Studying the behavior of the whole

By studying systems in their wholeness as systems we can find out things about them: their strengths, weaknesses and how they behave under certain conditions. We can also learn about the role the sub-parts of the system play without having to identify and analyze each individual unit or part. The importance in understanding systems is to identify relationships and situations rather than atomistic facts and events. Frequently our strategy for dealing with complexity is to undertake piecemeal analysis. Given the true nature of things this clearly results in oversimplification. Systems thinking offers us a more adequate method of grasping the complex nature of reality while still remaining relatively simple. The systems thinking approach takes a number of different interacting things and notes their behavior as a whole under diverse influences. Think of the way we observe and analyze teams. We can assess the team as a system at one level in contrast to trying to look at the interactions and responses of each team player. We adopt a similar approach when it comes to organizations. We talk about the culture of the organization, the organization's strategy and its reaction to competition. We do the same with nations and international regions when we talk about the response of 'the Chinese,' 'the Indians' or the 'Asian bloc.'

System characteristics or personality

Clusters, groups or systems appear to have their own personalities or characteristics. Even as individuals join and leave the group, the essential nature of the group stays the same. Changes in membership do not lead to radical changes in group characteristics. Such characteristics of wholes are typical of groups of interacting parts where the parts maintain some basic set of relationships among themselves. The characteristics of groups take on a life of their own that cannot be reduced to the properties of the individual parts. It is a rare circumstance when an individual can make a radical impact on the character of a group, organization or nation. So dealing with wholes provides us with strategies for dealing with infinite numbers of data points or events in a holistic manner (Laszlo 1996). It is what Peter Senge in *The Fifth Discipline* (1990) calls a way of seeing the forest and the trees.

Structure determines behavior

Systems theory tells us that a system's overall behavior depends on its entire structure. Living systems structure themselves in order to optimize their chances of survival. Think of how much time organizations spend on getting the structure right to achieve their strategic goals. The New Science teaches us that systems work best when the parts are allowed to self-organize rather than have structure logically or rationally imposed on them. Alas, we often ignore this reality. (See 'Technical Work' in Chapter 4.)

Dynamic equilibrium

Systems theory also tells us that systems continually strive to attain dynamic equilibrium both internally and with their environment. Systems face persistent threats from both within and without. Striving for dynamic equilibrium means that the system is always in some tension between controlled order and chaos. The key to optimum performance lies in finding the optimum point of tension. The forces that pull for both order and chaos are the energies generated as the system performs its functions while simultaneously renewing and recreating itself in order to adapt to continuously changing new realities. New realities are always arriving and the quest to attain dynamic equilibrium never ends. The system must adapt within the bounds of compatibility with the whole of which it is part. Pursuing dynamic equilibrium and adapting to change stokes system vitality. It is this vitality that stimulates the creative and adaptive forces innate in all living systems.

Systems have an optimum size

There is an optimum size for all systems. This optimum size is intrinsic to the system and is a dynamic concept. What this means is that the system as a whole has an inherent respect for what its optimum size should be: the optimum size is an integral natural feature of the system's make-up. This size can change as the system alters its functions and configuration, but there will always be some limit beyond which the system cannot function effectively or efficiently. Straining this limit places the system's survival at risk. To illustrate this vital point we can turn to the human body. Every person has a cardiac system that suits his or her body. As a person grows and develops, that system will change in size and in function. A heart that is too large or too small will cause heart failure. The right size of heart that makes for effective cardiac functioning will fall within some dynamic range that the system will strive to maintain. The same goes for organizations. Organizations that are too small cannot function economically or competitively. Organizations that are too large become unwieldy, overly bureaucratic, and ultimately ineffective. Survival invariably requires some form of break-up or realignment.

Organic behavior

Systems thinking forces one to think organically; to see relationships rather than people and events; to see patterns rather than isolated incidents; and to think images, metaphors and symbols rather than data, algorithms and building blocks. The fundamental principles of living systems include openness, interrelationship and interdependence.

APPLYING SYSTEMS THEORY

- All systems are alive.
- All systems are interdependent with other systems.
- Systems strive for survival.
- Systems exist within a hierarchy.
- Systems need to be open systems to survive.
- Systems have irreducible characteristics that belong to the system as a whole.
- Sub-systems contribute to the survival of the larger system.
- System behavior depends on the system structure.
- Systems thrive on self-organization.
- Understanding systems means understanding patterns, relationships and roles.
- Systems live in dynamic tension between order and chaos.
- Systems strive to attain dynamic equilibrium.
- The greatest system learning and adaptation occurs at points of disequilibrium.
- There is an optimum size for all systems determined by their inherent nature.

THE MACROCOSM–MICROCOSM PRINCIPLE

An integral part of systems theory is the **macrocosm–microcosm** principle. This principle holds that in a living system the characteristics and force fields that exist in the whole system are recapitulated in every part of its sub-systems. For example, the DNA that makes up the human body is contained in every cell of the body. Scientists need only a scrap of skin or a drop of body fluid to determine the genetic make-up of the entire body. The microcosm reflects the macrocosm and vice versa.

If we transport this concept into the realm of human organizations we observe that the values, attitudes and behaviors of, for example, an industry are reflected in the organizations that make up that industry. A relatively easy example is the financial services industry. Think of how the competitive culture of the industry is mirrored in its various organizations. Similarly, at a more micro level, within the sub-systems of the organization, for example, divisions or departments will reflect the culture and the competitive behavior of the overall organization. Although the emphasis may vary – some departments may mirror the larger system more clearly than others – the same strands of 'DNA' will always be present. By taking a **systems perspective**, adopting the macrocosm–microcosm principle, we find that by researching small systems we can learn a lot about large systems and vice versa.

The macrocosm–microcosm principle can be very helpful when we are considering new realities and the impact of change. With systems thinking we look at the overall picture and its effect on whole systems. This big picture or bird's-eye-view approach gives us hints as to how the new realities will affect the sub-parts of the system. If the larger system is in resistance, it comes as no surprise that the sub-systems will be too. What we observe, however, is that each sub-system will manifest its resistance in a way that is consonant with the functioning of that part. In other words, sub-systems will 'do' their resistance differently. We just need to know how to read the patterns. The challenge for leaders is to develop sensitivity to read these patterns and know how to respond to them. We reserve further discussion on this issue for Chapter 6.

LEADERS NEED COMPETENCE IN SYSTEMS THINKING

The largest gap in the intellectual ability needed for effective leadership in the knowledge age is systems thinking. Without it, leaders can't understand the relation of global forces to local pressures, macro policy to micro implementation, and social character to individual personality. Without it, their organizational vision will lack coherence. When linear thinkers connect the dots, they draw straight lines rather than the dynamic interactive force field that represents the knowledge-age organization.

(Maccoby, 2007: 186)

A SYSTEMS THINKING MINDSET

Big Picture Thinking

Systems thinking is a fundamental disposition and an orientation to life. A systems thinking mindset employs a systems thinking approach to viewing the world and perceiving reality. The basis of systems thinking lies in understanding that all living systems are integrated wholes linked together by a network of relationships. To understand systemically is to understand the nature of relationships. For a systems thinker, understanding the network of relationships and investigating how the relationships contribute to the systemic properties of the system and its sub-systems is critical work. The systems thinker understands that perceiving reality is to perceive a certain network of relationships. Therefore, thinking systems, thinking networks, means thinking relationships.

A systems thinking mindset seeks out patterns and relationships rather than forces and events, and organizes complexity into coherent stories about those relationships. In order to do this, systems thinking not only looks for the bigger picture but also tries to get that bigger picture from a range of viewing points. Seeing the bigger picture provides different information and insights as to the roles of the parts in the whole. Looking at wholes also provides new and different insights into how the parts relate with one another and how these relationships influence the systemic nature of the whole (Laszlo, 1996).

At a simplistic level, a systems thinking mindset is like a movie camera, moving backwards and forwards, looking for the larger perspective and homing in on one detail and then the next, then moving back again to reflect the relationship between the details of a larger vista. The eye of the systems thinker is looking for relationships: existent and potential; strong and weak; significant and irrelevant. The mental models of the systems thinker reflect networks and relationships rather than linear cause and effect processes. These mental models are scenario-driven rather than event-driven, and they deliberately embrace ambiguity, uncertainty and contingency.

A systems thinker realizes that change is constant and that therefore relationships are in continuous flux. Since the structure of the relationships determines the activities and performance of any system, by observing the nature of system relationships and how they are changing, a systems thinker can see and possibly anticipate the changing behavior of the system. This task would be far more difficult and even impossible to carry out if each unit or event of the system or each strand of the network were to be analyzed as it responded to changing circumstances. For example, it is far easier to look at team behavior and map how that changes than to factor in the changes adopted by each individual player. Patterns, movement, change, relationships, system structure and interconnectivity are the lenses of a practised systems thinker.

A NETWORKED WORLD

Albert-Laszlo Barabasi in his book *Linked* (2003), discusses in detail how everything in the world is interconnected. He argues that the world wide web we so readily refer to is not limited to cyberspace and technology. It is manifest throughout the cosmos, in nature, in society and in business. Barabasi argues that networks are ever-present. What we need is an eye for them. Society is a complex social network, which through the six degrees of separation makes the world far smaller than we imagine. He argues that we need to change our cognitive models from linearity to networks and relationships.

Malcolm Gladwell, in his well-known book *Tipping Point* (2002), also discusses how social reality comprises networks. He explains the role of connectors, nodes and links and how they influence what happens in the network by influencing the network outcomes.

As we learn more about how networks in living systems form and operate, we observe that the existence of networks does not signify equality, lack of hierarchy or a level playing field. On the contrary: different points on a network have different capacities, strength and potentials and it is these features and patterns that distinguish one network from another even though they are all interrelated. Living networks are also inherently dynamic. They evolve, break up, reconstruct and change in order to respond to the changing environment and new realities (Barabasi, 2003).

In a living system the activity of each party in a network affects the activities of the other parties at the same time. As all activity is occurring simultaneously, it is exceedingly difficult to isolate not only the timing, but also the sequence of events. A systems thinking approach places emphasis on being in a state of preparedness to respond to a change as a whole, rather than being dependent on devising a series of specific responses to a set of predicted changes.

A SYSTEMS THINKING MINDSET

- Reality is seen as an inter-related network of systemic relationships.
- The network of relationships is infinite and always inviting new possibilities.

- Reality is apprehended through system narratives.
- Narratives place emphasis on values, roles and patterns of changing relationships.
- Reality is explored from multiple competing perspectives.
- Reality is appreciated as comprising multiple competing perspectives.
- Reality is in flux, ambiguous, uncertain and moving toward new possibilities.
- Change occurs simultaneously and not in a linear sequence of cause and effect.
- System components assume roles to advance the survival and health of the greater system.
- Understanding systems requires an interpretation of values, roles and relationships.
- System roles reflect its values, emotions and mindset (beliefs and assumptions).
- Systems can never be totally understood – an element of mystery always exists.

Values and Roles

Now we have looked at a systems thinking mindset in the abstract, let us apply a systems thinking approach to understanding organizations, particularly business organizations. First, let us consider what it is that a systems thinking approach is inviting us to look for when we analyze a system. Essentially our search is for clues as to what a system and its sub-systems represent to one another and to the larger systems in which they are embedded. These representations take the form of values, for example 'competence,' 'safety' and 'integrity,' and roles, for example 'techies,' 'police force,' 'mavericks,' 'heroes,' 'losers' or 'clowns.' These values and roles provide us with information about the network of relationships in the system.

Clearly there are technical tasks and technical roles in our organizational system too. These are the ones we are more familiar with. There is the CEO, the financial controller, HR, the technical team, PR, marketing and sales executives and so on. For every task there is a role. Technical roles are assigned in order to get the technical tasks done. While these tasks and roles are fundamental to the organization achieving its primary goals, from a systems perspective this is not what we are primarily interested in. What we are most concerned with is organizational values and how the psychological and emotional roles assigned to people within the system contribute to its survival and adaptive capacity. For example, every system must have people technically competent, tangibly able to carry out the organization's mission and achieve its tangible goals. We therefore need technically competent people. So with our systems thinking lenses we look at the system as a whole as well as its sub-systems with a view to understanding which parts of the system contribute competence *to the system*. We may find it is not the technical team of PhDs who relate to others with competence. It may not be the financial department that represents accountability, or the HR department that represents caring. Maybe it is the warehouse team or the delivery staff who have assumed the competence role in the system. This observation gives us huge information. Why is, let us say, the warehouse team the carrier of competence in the system? What relationships does the warehouse team have that provide it with competence in our system network? What does the warehouse team do or achieve for the system that endows it with the value of competence and gives it the role of system 'expert' or 'savior' or whatever? The fact that the PhD technical team may deliver its prototypes or new products competently is not the issue. The question is: who does the *system* rely on or lean into for competence? Integrity? Safety? Strength? Stability? Weakness? Corruption? Dysfunction...and so on. These are system-assigned values and roles, and the system has its reasons for assigning those roles! As system thinkers we are interested in uncovering some of those reasons. (Read Chapter 6 for a deeper understanding of how this works in organizations.)

PERSONAL EXERCISE

Think about your favorite organization – 'Greenpeace,' 'Apple,' 'Benetton,' 'Toyota,' 'IKEA.' What values do you associate with it? Maybe it represents values such as caring, excitement, color, elegance. What role does it play in the world as you see it? Advocate, maverick, challenger, ecologist, homebuilder...?

Now select an organization of which you are part. What values and role does this organization represent in its larger system/s? How and why does it manifest these values and play this role? What other systems is it dependent upon to play this role? What could change these relationships? Where are its strengths and weaknesses?

Now consider your department or function. What values and role does it represent to the larger organization? How and why does it manifest these values and play this role? What other sub-systems does it depend on to do this? What have you learned as a result of this analysis?

New Realities

A systems thinking approach looks at the values and roles in the system and the challenge to those roles and values as a result of new realities. Although values and roles may be represented by individuals as well as functions or departments, a systems thinking approach refrains from personalizing issues where possible, preferring to focus on the larger picture.

The values and roles assumed by sub-systems align with the needs of the larger system. As the needs of the larger system change due to new realities and new circumstances, it becomes necessary for values and roles of sub-systems to change accordingly. Failure to respond to the needs of the larger system creates disequilibrium, distress and dissonance. A systems thinking mindset looks at how changing realities place pressure on the system and its sub-systems and observes its efforts at resistance or adaptation.

We explore values and roles in great detail when we discuss organizational behavior, group dynamics and change in Chapter 6. What is important at this juncture is to grasp that systems thinking provides a holistic approach to understanding reality. This approach stresses the composition and configuration of values and roles; how they serve the goal of system survival and how they change in the face of new realities. Imagination and the ability to use metaphors when analyzing and describing the world are essential to a systems thinking mindset, since it is in the subtlety with which things are perceived that one can really grasp a system's dynamics.

THE SYSTEMIC NATURE OF NEW REALITIES

- The source of new realities is the environment, i.e. new realities arrive from the larger system.
- New realities are always systemic – they have an effect across systems.
- They are arrive in patterns and waves, i.e. they are not isolated, unrelated incidents or events.
- They are not necessarily linear in apparent cause–effect impact.
- They always impact several relationships or stakeholders.
- They have a ripple effect across systems – a new reality for one part of the network creates a new reality for another.
- They simultaneously create new realities across networks.
- They are often first recognized intuitively.
- They impact values and roles represented by parts of the system.
- They often change relationships between networks and sub-systems.

NOT SEEING THE WORLD WITH A SYSTEMS MINDSET

Months after the event, it was reported that the animals fled the northern tip of Sumatra days before the massive tsunami hit the Banda Aceh coast in 2004. At the time no one paid heed to the behavior of the animals. They were not reading systems, looking for patterns or seeing relationships. The cost of this oversight was huge! Consider what might have been saved. Instead there was huge devastation and tragic loss of human life.

Now let us reflect on many of the so-called surprise events of our time – Bhopal, Chernobyl, 9/11, Katrina, Kashmir, to name a few. If we had been thinking systems, networks, relationships, and if we had worked with new realities as they arrived and not long after the event, maybe history would look a little different now. Hindsight is a tough teacher.

An Open Systems Approach to Organizational Analysis

Strategic management in organizations is continually striving to find better tools of analysis. The **open systems approach** is slowly gaining more and more enthusiastic adherents. As organizational managers develop in their appreciation and understanding of organizations as living systems, they recognize that the best way to understand them is to treat them as such.

An open systems approach to organizational analysis is based on three major assumptions:

- The only meaningful way to study an organization is to study it as a system.

- Organizations are open systems that exchange matter with the environment.

- Organizations exist in tension with manifold stakeholders who have many competing values and interests. Adaptation requires finding a dynamic point of equilibrium between these changing tensions and new realities in the environment.

The Systemic Leadership approach adopts an open systems approach to understanding how new realities impact the system as a whole and the changing values and roles in the system and in the sub-parts of the system. Here is a step-by-step method for analyzing a system based on the ideas we have explored.

Open system process of analysis

1 Define a conceptual boundary for the system you are going to analyze. Is it the global arena, the nation, a particular industry, or...? In the globalizing world of today your boundary is most likely to be wide, as nations and industries are no longer geographically defined. Be sure not to define the boundary too broadly as the analysis will become too complex to handle. If you define it too narrowly you will of course miss critical issues.

2 Identify key trends and new realities manifest in the macro environment. Here you will need broad horizons since everything is related to everything else. On the other hand, clearly you cannot embrace everything, so thoughtful screening will be necessary.

3 Identify the key systems and sub-systems that make up the larger system you have defined in (1).

4 Establish the systemic properties (values and role) of the larger system.

5 Establish similar properties of the sub-systems of the larger system.

6 Define the organization as a system and establish its values and role in the larger system. Do the same for its sub-systems.

7 Identify key stakeholders in the macro environment; in the organization; in the organization's sub-systems. Identify their most important values and their interrelationships.

8 Consider how new realities are challenging system and sub-system boundaries, values, roles and relationships.

BENEFITS OF SYSTEMS THINKING

A systems thinking approach to perceiving reality and understanding the world and reality has many advantages. Let us look at a few of these advantages from an organizational perspective. It

• helps managers look at organizations from a broader, big picture perspective, something many people avoid or ignore;

• focuses on the interrelatedness of parts and systems and how they work together rather than on isolated events and individuals;

- leads to a more insightful understanding of the environment in which the organization is operating;

- allows for a better understanding of what it means to be in relationship;

- places emphasis on analyzing narratives rather than linear cause and effect events;

- helps uncover the driving forces behind relationships and how relationships play themselves out in reality;

- helps understand the meaning making between the parties of a relationship;

- leads to the identification of new relationships that had not yet been considered;

- results in a better understanding of the stakeholders affected by the actions of the organization;

- uncovers the meaning making and value tensions that arise in systems as they are tested by new realities;

- alerts managers to the multiple activities that occur at any one point in time;

- encourages the identification of patterns – identifying patterns of behavior facilitates seeing how a system is configured; knowing a system's configuration, i.e. its structure, can provide insights into the system's ability to be adaptable and flexible;

- prompts ever subtler questions instead of ending the search with what seem the most expedient answers.

SYSTEMS THINKING EXERCISE

PART 1

We often use metaphors to name the values and roles sub-systems represent within the larger system. The types and variety of these roles and functions are legion. They are only limited by the imagination. In order to grasp these concepts it may help to consider a simple system: your own family system. Take a moment to think about the members that make up your family system. What roles and values do they represent in the system? Use your imagination to define the roles and functions of each person. There may, for example, be an aggressor, an avoider, an enabler, a hero, a savior, or a clown. Now consider the values that can be attached to those roles. The aggressor is associated with the anger in the system; the avoider is associated with fear of conflict; the enabler strives to bring back disequilibrium and establish harmony in the system; the hero demonstrates the courage of the system; the savior ensures survival; and the clown holds laughter and stress release. The family system needs all of these roles, functions and values for 'survival'. Through the interaction of the parts of the system, the family coexists in a dynamic tension that strives for some kind of equilibrium or reasonable harmony. Various family members play their parts to help make this happen. Survival of the system is paramount.

Questions:

1   **What values and roles do different members represent in your family?**
2   **What value and role do you represent?**
3   **How do the values and roles serve the system?**

PART 2

Let us imagine that in our make-believe family the savior in the family dies. This is a sad new reality for each individual member and also a devastating one for the system as a whole. The role of savior was needed by the system. Now the savior, who represented hope and salvation, is gone.

Questions:

1   **Using systems thinking, what will happen to this family system? (Think values, roles and relationships.)**
2   **What is the adaptive challenge to the system? (Refer to Chapter 1.)**
3   **How would you exercise leadership in this situation?**

SYSTEM DYNAMICS

Using an interdisciplinary approach, system dynamics provides an analytical method for learning about the dynamic complexity of systems and especially the role of feedback. Drawing on psychology, economics, mathematics, physics and other social sciences, systems dynamics provides tools to improve and develop the mental models we hold regarding systems (Sterman, 2000).

System dynamics is an aid to systems thinking. It is more rational and logical and less imaginative and intuitive than the approach described above where we analyze the values and roles parts play in a system. System dynamics is concerned with feedback in systems as an impetus to learning. It also looks at the mental models we bring to decision making and provides frameworks and heuristics for testing these mental models.

Importance of Feedback for Learning

What system dynamics teaches us is that the dynamics within systems arise from the interaction of positive or self-reinforcing feedback loops and negative or self-correcting feedback loops. For example, if one organization decides to drop prices to raise demand, very soon competitors will be doing the same. The price war is on. This describes reinforcing behavior that supports the impetus of change. A negative or self-correcting feedback loop describes system behavior that opposes change. For example, if less nicotine is included in cigarettes in order to reduce smoking, smokers will smoke more cigarettes to get the dose they need. These actions challenge the attempt to change the habits of smokers. Hence they are non-reinforcing (Sterman, 2000).

Learning in systems is provided by the feedback process in them. When systems try to change, certain factors support that change (positive feedback) and certain factors counter that change (negative feedback). Two types of learning are typically described. There is single loop learning and double loop learning.

Single loop learning is fairly superficial. Here we simply respond to what we have learned by trying new inputs or new processes. Our way of seeing the world or the system has not changed. For example, the temperature has dropped outside. I need to turn the heating up.

Double loop learning, on the other hand, is where information about the real world alters our decisions within the context of existing frames and decision rules. For example, the temperature has dropped outside. I need to consider the most effective way to warm the house. Besides the heating system, what else can I try? Maybe turn off the heating in unused rooms; close doors to the basement and attic; draw the curtains…and soon invest in solar panels.

Bill Torbert in his book entitled *Action Inquiry* (2004) describes a triple loop feedback that adds another dimension to feedback. Triple loop feedback relates to being self-reflective with respect to the present relationship between our effects on the outside world simultaneous to feedback loops one and two. In other words we obtain feedback on our action(s), our strategies, and our attention and impact at the same time. Triple loop feedback makes us present to ourselves in the now moment, bringing deeper insights into our impact on what we do. For example, I am concerned with the most efficient way to heat my house. Given the cold weather, probably so is everyone else. What is this doing to the demand for energy? How am I contributing to the energy crisis? What are my responsibilities as I try to heat my house efficiently? Which of my actions are responsible, given my concern about the use of energy?

Effective leadership embraces a systems mindset and takes note of the feedback loops that are either reinforcing or countering change in the system. Feedback processes provide information regarding the dynamics of the system. Chapter 6 provides insights on these dynamics.

CHALLENGES TO OUR THINKING PROCESSES

We have seen that identifying and responding to new realities is difficult. It is difficult because new realities are typically complex systemic issues and due to people's tendency to resist change, people prefer to ignore them or to respond to realities of their own choosing. We have also discussed how our abilities to understand the dynamics of systems is limited and that our cause and effect linear mental models do not serve us well in a system-interconnected world. Because clear, thoughtful and rigorous thinking is so important for effective leadership, it might be helpful to reflect on some of the limitations to our thinking and learning processes.

Limitations to Effective Thinking and Decision Making

The real world is complex, dynamic and continuously changing. We selectively screen out some new realities because we cannot pay attention to them all. Nor can we possibly grasp all the interconnections and what they mean. It is impossible to observe all the changes that are going on even if we know that one change in one system has ramifications everywhere else. We do not know and cannot predict with accuracy the time delays between cause and effect across systems. We know many things are occurring at once. We have to accept uncertainty and unforeseen possibilities as the potential results of our actions.

When we receive information **feedback** we exercise selective perception. This perception is based on our own perceptive limitations and biases. Even if 'perfect information' were to exist, our thought processes and projections would distort it in some way or another. We see and hear what we want to see and hear, and we look for information that confirms our opinions. One question is: how might we look for information that challenges our cherished views?

Often the information we receive is inaccurate or incomplete. There is a time delay between the event and the information feedback on an event. This delay renders all information redundant in some way. Information feedback is thus biased, limited and 'old.' We must ask ourselves how we might really participate in new news.

In order to survive we create mental models that are simplistic, easy to use and that confirm our biases and expectations of the world. If we do not make time and devote energy to revising our mental models they become stale and lack rigor. Our challenge is to keep challenging and renewing our mental models.

Our decisions often suffer from poor execution and implementation. The reasons may be perceptual biases, reliance on poor-quality information, or inept mental models. We need to ask ourselves where our greatest limitations lie and how we might overcome them.

PERSONAL EXERCISE

1 Are you aware of your mental models and the critical assumptions on which they are based?
2 Do you regularly challenge those assumptions?
3 Consider the last time you misread or misjudged something. What did you learn about your assumptions and mental models from the experience?
4 When was the last time you explicitly 'changed your mental models'?

To exercise effective leadership requires good thinking skills. At best it requires a systems thinking mindset that is open to all kinds of possibilities. Exercising leadership requires the ability to look at the bigger picture while not losing the detail. It requires triple loop learning and awareness of the limitations to effective thinking and decision making. Systemic leaders are adept at systems thinking and appreciate their own cognitive limitations. This explains their commitment to partnering with others in the reality testing process. This theme is developed in Chapter 4.

DECISION-MAKING COMPLEXITY

- Understanding the dynamic complexity of the world.
- What to take account of and what to ignore.
- Understanding simultaneous action and reaction.
- Timing between stimulus and reaction.
- Knowing what is concurrent and what is sequential.
- Combinatorial complexity of infinite possibilities.
- How feedback creates learning.

EXECUTIVE SUMMARY

This chapter has emphasized the importance of systems thinking and the need for critical thinking skills to stay abreast of new realities. Effective leadership is highly dependent upon the ability to see the larger picture and to understand the interconnectedness of all living systems.

Here are some of the main points discussed:

- Everything is part of a system, and systems are part of systems. There are many types of system. All organizations are a network of systems.

- The primary goal of all systems is survival.

- In order for systems to survive they must be open systems. Closed systems die sooner rather than later.

- A system has characteristics of its own, it is more than its parts, and cannot be reduced to an aggregation of its parts.

- The importance of systems lies in their structure, how the networks and relationships within the system are configured to achieve the system goals.

- Systems are in continual motion. They are continually on the quest for dynamic equilibrium, which is the tension between chaos and order.

- Systems thinking is a mental disposition that sees reality as a series of inter-linked systems. The focus of the systems thinker is on patterns and relationships and how these are affected by new realities.

- A systems thinking mindset looks for the values and roles played by the various parts in the system to better understand how they contribute to the organization's survival.

- A systems thinker realizes that all change is in some way systemic and that responding to new realities requires a systemic approach.

- Systems thinking uses a triple loop feedback approach to learning about the impact of change in the system. Mental models are continually tested and revised so as to limit the natural impediments to critical thinking.

- Our thinking and learning processes are limited. We need to recognize this fact and understand how and why. This reflection helps us embrace ambiguity, uncertainty and change in a constructive way.

KEY CONCEPTS

Adaptive age
Critical thinking
Feedback
Holons
Holarchy, hierarchy
Macrocosm–microcosm
Mental models
New sciences
Open systems approach
System dynamics
Systems perspective
Systems theory
Systems thinking mindset
Technical fix
Quantum physics

CASE STUDY
KILLING THE WRONG DISEASE

In the 1950s the World Health Organization tried to eliminate malaria in northern Borneo by using the pesticide Dieldrin to kill mosquitoes carrying the disease. Initially, the project seemed a great success. Not only did the mosquitoes and malaria disappear but also the villagers were no longer bothered by flies and cockroaches. Then their roofs began falling in on them and they faced the threat of a typhus epidemic.

First hundreds of lizards died from eating the poisoned insects. Then the local cats died from eating the lizards. Without the cats, rats ran rampant through the villages, carrying typhus-infested fleas on their bodies. On top of that, the villagers' thatched roofs were collapsing. The Dieldrin killed wasps and other insects that ordinarily ate the caterpillars that fed on the thatched roofs (Dreher, 2000).

Questions:

1   Using systems thinking, how would you analyze what occurred in this story?

2   What mistakes did the World Health Organization make in trying to eliminate malaria?

3   Is there any incident that has occurred in your organization that has parallels with this story?

4   List in detail what you have learned from this exercise.

ORGANIZATIONAL EXERCISE: ONE CUP OF YOGHURT AT A TIME

The Nobel Prize winner Muhammad Yunus, founder of Grameen Bank in Bangladesh, is a Systemic Leader *par excellence*. A former economics professor at Chittagong University, he chose to study the lives of rural Bangladeshis living in extreme poverty close at hand. The result is the Grameen Bank Group of companies that provide micro credit and other critical services to over 2.5 million poor people in Bangladesh. His insights into the realities of the lives of poor people has inspired others all over the world to engage in various forms of micro lending and micro finance. By understanding the structural barriers that create and perpetuate poverty, he has been able to create new attitudes and new opportunities for poor people around the world.

Yunus's fascinating story begins in 1974 with his identifying forty-two people who owed less than $27 to usurious moneylenders in the village of Jobra. This micro amount of debt (to us, but certainly not to the poor) kept the borrowers enslaved to the rules and demands of those from whom they borrowed. Yunus took over these loans and this began his venture into tiny loans to aid people in self-employment. In 1983 Grameen Bank was born.

In 2005 Yunus entered into a joint venture with Group Danone. Danone is a large French corporation, one of the world leaders in dairy products, known for its nutritious foods and its brand-named Danone yoghurt. Yunus and Danone committed their organizations to creating health foods to improve the rural diet of children in Bangladesh. Millions of the poor in Bangladesh suffer from malnutrition. The challenge for the Grameen–Danone joint venture was how to create a product affordable yet nutritious and accepted by the local people.

The entire approach to the project was carried out using a systems perspective. First the nature of the problem was analyzed by involving as many stakeholders as possible. The poor families were consulted; the local farmers were involved; suppliers of other foodstuffs were investigated; distribution outlets researched and so on.

The final outcome was brilliant. After a huge amount of investigation and research an idea was launched. Yoghurt is a popular food in Bangladesh and Danone has expertise in producing yoghurt. Yoghurt has nutrients that are good for the intestines and help reduce the effects of diarrhea. It was decided that the target market of the yoghurt product would be rural villagers and their children who live on less than $2 per day. The challenge was how to launch a fortified yoghurt product at a price poor people could afford on a regular basis. Further, as there were no refrigeration facilities either in the form of refrigerated trucks or fridges in the villages, there was the challenge of how to get a fresh product to the consumer before it had turned rancid and became inedible. Distribution had to be fast to get the yoghurt into the children's stomachs within forty-eight hours.

The solution was as follows:

- Food production, retailing of the product, and consumption would be as close to one another as possible.

- A micro factory would be built close to the community buying the product.

- Local people would work in the factory.

- Local farmers who had cows, or who borrowed from Grameen Bank to buy cows, would supply milk to the factory.

- Milk prices were guaranteed to the farmers for one year ahead so they could have some certainty regarding their income.

- To provide sufficient sweetness, molasses from date palm trees particular to Bangladesh would be added to the yoghurt.

- Biodegradable corn starch containers, which when discarded would turn to compost, would be used as packaging for the yoghurt.

- 'Grameen ladies,' women who borrow from Grameen Bank and are mothers living in or near the village, would be distributors of the product.

- Distributors would be trained in nutrition and in the value of selling the yoghurt fresh.

- Insulated cooler bags would be provided by the factory to the distributors of the yoghurt.

- Limited supplies would be delivered every day to ensure freshness of the product and minimize the loss of the yoghurt through becoming inedible.

The project has been a huge success. It was a win-win for everyone. Everyone in the system was involved. The local expertise of people was tapped and they have both contributed and gained as a result. The factory is their factory. The health of the project directly relates to the health of their community. New jobs were created; new technologies were tested out; women and men had their part to play as factory laborers, farmers, suppliers and distributors; children had access to nutritional foods; waste was minimized; and the profits generated were plowed back into the community in the form of more money for more poverty-reducing programs.

There was no pressure for growth, profits, or shareholder returns. This small model of development is elegant in its simplicity and sustainable. Here everyone is a leader and everyone is a follower. The network of connections is used to enhance the well-being of the entire system.

Questions:

1 Using the open systems approach, what do you learn about the sustainability of this project?

2 What behaviors are required to ensure this project will sustain a win-win for all stakeholders?

3 What new realities might challenge the viability and future of this project?

FURTHER READING

Ackoff, Russell, L. *Recreating the Corporation: A Design of Organizations for the 21st Century*. New York: Oxford University Press, 1999.

Barabasi, Albert-Laszlo. *Linked*. New York: Penguin, 2003.

Capra, Fritjof. *The Hidden Connections: A Science for Sustainable Living*. New York: First Anchor Books, 2004.

Haines, Stephen G. *The Manager's Pocket Guide to Systems Thinking & Learning*. Amherst, MA: HRD Press, 1998.

Laszlo, Ervin. *The Systems View of the World*. Cresskill, NJ: Hampton Press, 1996.

Maccoby, Michael. *The Leaders We Need: And What Makes Us Follow*. Boston, MA: Harvard Business School Press, 2007.

Senge, Peter. *The Fifth Discipline*. New York: Century Business, 1990.

Senge, Peter. Smith, Bryan, Kruschwitz, Nina, Laur, Joe, Schley, Sara. *The Necessary Revolution*. New York: Doubleday, 2008.

Sterman, John D. *Business Dynamics: Systems Thinking and Modeling for a Complex World*. Boston, MA: Irwin McGraw-Hill, 2000.

Torbert, Bill and Associates. *Action Inquiry*. San Francisco, CA: Berrett-Koehler, 2004.

Von Bertalanffy, Ludwig. *General System Theory*. New York: George Braziller, 1969.

Waddock, Sandra. *Leading Corporate Citizens: Vision, Values, Value Added*. Boston, MA: McGraw-Hill, 2006.

Wheatley, Margaret J. *Leadership and the New Science*. San Francisco, CA: Berrett-Koehler, 1994.

Wilber, Ken. *The Essential Ken Wilbur: An Introductory Reader*. Boston, MA: Shambala, 1998.

Zohar, Danah. *ReWiring the Corporate Brain*. San Francisco, CA: Berrett-Koehler, 1997.

3 PHILOSOPHIES, THEORIES AND STYLES OF LEADERSHIP

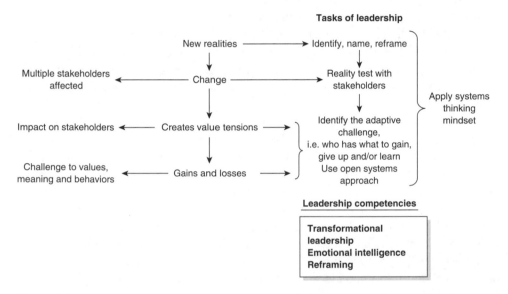

Figure 3.1

INTRODUCTION

The key leadership message of Chapters 1 and 2 concerns the critical importance of new realities and the ability to identify their systemic impact. New realities represent the ceaseless winds of change. These winds arrive more often in high speed gusts than in gentle breezes. However, they are always arriving, and adapting to change requires being able to ride and bend with the winds. To bend and ride effectively requires alertness, openness, mental and emotional adaptability, and courage.

This chapter discusses some of the better-known leadership theories and places them in the context of the **Systemic Leadership** approach we are studying. We begin with a discussion about our preoccupation with leadership as a construct and then critique a general definition of leadership. Thereafter we review the key elements of transformational leadership, followed by the concept of servant leadership and **emotional intelligence**. After discussing the importance of the ability to frame and reframe problems we venture into an initial understanding of the Systemic Leadership approach. We close the chapter with a brief discussion of why we are so fascinated with leaders and the idea of leadership, thereby setting the scene for the next chapter, which takes us into the Systemic Leadership approach in detail.

THE ALLURE OF LEADERSHIP

The history of humankind is replete with stories of leaders leading others (armies, groups, organizations, societies) 'somewhere,' sometimes for good and sometimes for ill. There have been military leaders, social consciousness leaders, technical leaders, organizational leaders, religious leaders and so on. The 'somewhere' may be a geographical place, a new level of social awareness, access to new scientific and technological insights, economic success, or new belief systems and ideologies.

Humans have always been both absorbed and intrigued by the heroic and tragic stories of leaders, and to this day we remain preoccupied and fascinated with the most intimate details of their lives. Yet, despite the close focus on the actions of leaders and the innumerable myths and texts devoted to the stories that describe their characters and the challenges they face, a true understanding of the ingredients that make for both effective and ethical leadership remains elusive. Everyone longs for a magic formula, and there is none!

The topic of leadership continues to preoccupy us in every sphere of life. Whether it is questioning our own capacities for leadership; considering leadership in our family systems; looking at leadership at work; or assessing leadership in the political sphere, the desire to experience 'leadership' in some shape or form is invariably present. Because we are so dependent on leaders and vulnerable to the results of their leadership exploits, it is quite natural that we should want to understand what leadership is all about and which criteria, skills and talents make a good leader.

As we investigate both the concept and reality of leadership we soon come to realize this is a far more challenging task than we might have imagined. For one, the number of leadership theories that exist would be difficult to identify and define. Different theories also approach the concept of leadership quite differently. Some theories focus on the characteristics or personality of the leader; some focus on the capabilities or skills the leader needs or exhibits; some focus on the leader's actions and style of engagement; while others focus on the situation to which the leader is responding.

In our quest to understand the phenomenon of leadership we soon realize that the idea of leadership is both subjective and value-laden. This means different people have different ideas of what leadership represents and what makes a good leader. These ideas are attached to their own values, which they want to see reflected back to them by the person assuming a position of leadership. For example, a large majority of people claim that the prime ability of a leader should be to establish a vision; i.e. leaders should be visionaries. The desire for visionary capabilities in leaders is in reality a desire that they will provide 'hope' or a path to something that is 'hopeful.' Other people may emphasize that leaders need to be master communicators. Here the value attached to communication is the need to be seen and heard; in other words, these adherents want the leader to affirm they are valued.

The fact that our views of leadership are both subjective and value-laden is neither good nor bad. It is quite natural. It is unsurprising that we want to be led by someone who values the same things as we do. The important observation is that we prioritize our core values differently, so our ideas about what constitutes a good leader and makes for effective leadership differs. We discuss the implications of different values associated with leadership at length in later chapters. For now, we simply note that leadership is not one size fits all, nor can there be a definitive blueprint leadership theory to which everyone will subscribe.

Our conceptualization of leadership is also influenced by the times. The idea of leadership is not only a personal construction, but a social one that reflects the social consciousness of the day. For example in times of war we want warriors and heroes, in times of peace we want philosophers and caretakers. In the business arena, at this time of rapid globalization, we want business leaders who have the adventurous spirit and adaptability of Marco Polo; who can reconcile the old with the new; who can help us negotiate the 'Silk Road'; and who will ensure we maintain our cozy lifestyles as we continue to bring riches back from 'East,' namely China and India.

We must also take note that different cultures envision leadership differently. These different views of leadership reflect different expectations of leaders and assign them different roles. For example, in some cultures leaders are expected to be more patriarchal and authoritarian, while in others they are expected to be more like coaches or facilitators.

Whatever view we have or approach we take to leadership, we remain intrigued. We never tire of the topic nor do we cease from exploring new avenues for explaining the leadership phenomenon. Everyone either wants to be a leader or wants to be within the leader's sphere of influence. What does the human spirit need from 'leaders' and why are people prepared to sell their souls to follow potential leaders? What is it about leadership that is so captivating? In this chapter we attempt to answer some of these questions. We also discuss an approach to leadership which focuses on the tasks of leadership rather than on the personality, skills, style or situation of leadership. Let us begin with taking a look at the concept of leadership, broadly defined.

PERSONAL EXERCISE

1   Which values do you think are most important in a leader?
2   Why are they important?
3   Can you identify any effective leaders who do not have those values?
4   Which values do they exhibit? What makes them effective?
5   What can you learn from this difference?

DEFINING LEADERSHIP

In attempting to establish a general definition of leadership there are some basic things most of us would agree leaders do. We know, for example, that leadership is an activity. This activity is a relational one in that the activity is engaging with others called followers.

Since *leading* is the activity, and leading is understood to mean providing guidance or direction, leadership is concerned with providing guidance or direction toward some objective or goal. Providing guidance or direction implies that a goal is in mind. The activity of leadership is thus purposeful, i.e. the objective or goal is not simply random but predetermined, considered or chosen.

To the question 'What is leadership, broadly defined?' we could therefore volunteer this definition:

Leadership is a relational activity where an individual(s) guide(s) or direct(s) others (followers) to attain an objective or goal.

This simple statement provides one of the myriad definitions of leadership that in essence says something about leaders being people who get other people to do or achieve something. The activity of leadership implies movement.

There are clearly several problems with this broad definition. For one we do not know the circumstances the leader and the followers are dealing with that require the activity of leadership. In other words, what type of activity qualifies as an activity of leadership? For example, can one claim that an usher in a movie theater, who directs people to their seats, is a leader? After all, she engages with others and directs or guides them to a goal: their seat. Clearly this is not leadership, and the usher is not acting as a leader. Finding the correct seat in the movie theater, even if it is dark, does not call for the need for leadership. (Refer to the distinction between leadership and authority in Chapter 4.)

The definition above also does not include anything about the required characteristics of a leader or the style of leadership that is most appropriate or effective in guiding followers. Should the guiding or directing be done through influence, charisma, command or coercion? Nor does the definition include any indication of how the predetermined goal to be achieved has been decided upon. Was it the leader's prerogative to establish the goal or direction or did the followers play some role in deciding where they were heading?

When we say leadership is an activity, does that mean a one-off activity or does it mean several activities that build on one another? Here again it depends. In the case of a raging inferno that is threatening to engulf a building and all its inhabitants the brave activity of one or two individuals who get the people out of the building in time could constitute a 'one shot act' of leadership. On the other hand not all situations are sudden, crisis-driven ones. In most situations the leadership activity is drawn out and therefore constitutes a process rather than a one-shot action.

A further question regarding our definition relates to the followers: is there anything about the activity or response of followers that in some way helps define the activity of leadership? For example, are subordinates the same as followers?

Finally, the definition provided above excludes any normative statement as to whether the objective or goal the leader is directing followers to is a realistic or worthwhile one, not to mention an ethically sound one. What if the predetermined goal is trivial, spurious or evil? Can one still classify the activity that leads others in this direction, leadership?

We can see that our definition of leadership above raises several critical questions, namely the following:

1 Are there specific circumstances that require the activity of leadership?

2 Is there something about the person and his or her actions that makes an event or experience one that qualifies as exercising leadership?

3 Does the person need to exhibit any particular style of behavior that will qualify as an act of leadership?

4 Is the act or exercising of leadership a one-off event or a process?

5 Do followers have to respond in any particular way to illustrate they are following a leader? In other words, what makes a follower a follower?

6 Is the leader responsible for setting the goal or direction of the group? Another way of putting this is: is the person who sets the direction of the group the leader?

7 Does the goal to which followers are directed have to be a worthwhile or ethical one to make it an act of leadership?

In the rest of this chapter we discuss an approach to leadership that directly addresses these seven questions and which provides the leadership and change management theory that underpins this book. In Chapter 4, we expand on this even further by explaining in detail the Systemic Leadership approach. First we must cover some of the better-known leadership theories that ground the approach we develop.

LEADERSHIP THEORY, PRACTICE AND PARADIGMS

In this text we do not attempt to summarize the various leadership theories and practices that exist. Two texts to which you may refer for this type of analysis include *Leadership: Theory and Practice* by Peter G. Northouse (2005) and *Understanding Leadership* by Gayle C. Avery (2005).

Northouse's book summarizes some of the well-known leadership theories. It provides a description of the theory, the components that are included under each approach, a summary of the strengths and weaknesses of each approach, as well as some case studies that demonstrate application of the approach. Figure 3.2 opposite, provides a summary of a few of the approaches he describes.

Northouse's book also devotes a brief chapter to the **psychodynamic** approach to leadership.[1] The psychodynamic approach does not assume there are any personality types that are better than any others nor is there a need to match the personality type of the leader with subordinates or the situation. Instead the psychodynamic approach to leadership emphasizes the leader's own insights into his or her psychological make-up and emotional responses to challenge and change as well as encouraging followers to do the same.

A wealth of literature exists that describes the various aspects of the psychodynamic approach. Since the leadership approach we describe in this book has a strong grounding in the psychodynamic approach we explore some of the important literature in greater detail in later chapters (especially Chapter 6). What is important to note here is that effective leadership must include an understanding of the psychodynamics between the leader and the group. Pschodynamics feature in all relationships. Since leadership is a relational activity, psychodynamics will perforce play their part.

Gayle Avery also provides a summary of leadership theories that he gathers under different paradigms. He divides the paradigms into four major eras: Antiquity–1970s; 1970s–mid-1980s; mid-1980s–2000, and the Organic Period beyond 2000. Within each paradigm, Avery analyzes the role of the leader; his or her relationship with followers, and the locus of decision making. His

Trait approach	Skills approach	Style approach	Situational approach	Contingency theory
Leaders have certain profiles. Charisma important. People born as leaders rather than made. **Personality traits:** • intelligence • self-confidence • insight • inspirational • relational • integrity • sociability **Leader focus: personality.**	Describes skills needed. People's abilities can be developed. **3 skill approach:** • technical • human • conceptual. **Skills-based model:** • problem-solving skills • social judgement skills • knowledge. **Leader focus: capabilities.**	Describes behaviors needed. Emphasizes leadership behavior. Task behaviours Relationship behaviours **Blake and Mouton's managerial grid** Concern for production. Concern for people. **Leader focus: style of actions.**	Hersey and Blanchard 3-D management style theory. Different situations require different types of leadership: • delegating • supporting • coaching • directing Leaders look at the situation and respond. **Leader focus: situation.**	Concern with styles and situations. Situational variables prescribe type of leadership needed. **Leader focus: match type of leader to the situation.**

Figure 3.2   Leadership theories – summary from Northouse (2005)

description of Organic Leadership resonates with a number of key components of the Systemic Leadership approach we discuss in this text. Here are some relevant points he makes:

- The management philosophy that underpins Organic Leadership derives from the New Science, which enables the organization to deal with high levels of complexity.

- Organic leadership is based on processes of mutual sense making.

- Leadership is not vested in particular individuals; many people can and do exercise leadership.

- Much of leadership emanates from a shared vision and the core values embedded within the organizational culture.

- Followers are encouraged to be self-leading and self-organizing.

- Power tends to be shared across organization members rather than vested in designated leaders.

As we explore the Systemic Leadership approach the reader will notice the similarities between these components of Organic Leadership and those of Systemic Leadership. One key aspect of both approaches is the focus on the tasks of leadership rather than a prescriptive list of leadership character attributes or capabilities. Even so, there are certain capacities and skills that are important to the Systemic Leadership approach and that directly affect the effectiveness of leadership. We turn to a discussion of these now.

TRANSFORMATIONAL VERSUS TRANSACTIONAL LEADERSHIP

James MacGregor Burns, in his seminal leadership treatise, *Leadership* (1979), introduced the notion of **transformational leadership**. In his book Burns describes transformational leaders as those who inspire others to achieve extraordinary outcomes and in the process develop their own leadership capacity (Burns 1979: 4). Transformational leaders align the genuine needs of followers with the objectives and goals of the leader, the group and the larger organization. Transformational leaders are also credited with seeking to satisfy the higher needs of followers. They attempt to engage the full person; to develop a relationship of mutual stimulation and, as a result, take both parties (followers and leaders) to higher moral ground.

Burns contrasts transformational leadership with **transactional leadership**, which he places at the other end of the leadership spectrum. Transactional leaders tend not to be concerned with the intrinsic motivational or emotional needs of their followers. They are more action and consequence-driven. Transactional leaders are those who lead through some form of exchange. For example, they provide jobs and rewards in return for suitable work performance; they offer safety and security in return for receiving the followers' votes.

Most leadership transactions, Burns claims, are transactional. There is nothing inherently wrong with transactional leadership. At the appropriate time it can be most effective and in fact the only way out of a situation. For example, in the case of that sudden fire in the office building, transactional leadership will be the most effective type of leadership at that time. The person with the appropriate technical skills will be given the power and authority to lead everyone out of the building in exchange for their safety. This will not be a time to negotiate a combined sense of mission or to hold motivating discussions about attaining higher moral ground.

When the number of followers is huge and there are many constituencies, transactional leadership may appear the most pragmatic course of action. There are also cases or situations where followers may deliberately and explicitly prefer not to be mentored or developed. They may simply wish to engage in a transactional relationship with the leader to suit some immediate ends: climbing a mountain, for example. Transactional leadership clearly has its place as a style of leadership.

Transformational leadership has received far more attention than transactional leadership, largely because leadership researchers claim that transformational leadership provides a more effective approach to leading others and achieving higher than expected performance levels. Leadership researchers, Bernard Bass and Ronald Riggio, in their book, *Transformational Leadership* (2006), provide feedback on their research that strongly supports this view. According to them, transformational leaders challenge followers to become innovative problem solvers and help develop their leadership capacities through creating a holding environment that provides both challenge and support.

As a result of their work, Bass and Riggio identify what they consider to be the four critical components of transformational leadership:

1   *Idealized Influence*: Transformational leaders serve as role models for followers. They are admired, respected and trusted and followers want to emulate them. They create a sense of a shared vision, they show persistence and determination, and they demonstrate high standards of ethical and moral conduct.

2   *Inspiration and Motivation*: Transformational leaders motivate and inspire those around them by providing meaning and challenge to their followers' work. They articulate a compelling vision of the future that arouses enthusiasm and optimism.

3   *Intellectual Stimulation*: Transformational leaders stimulate their followers' efforts to be innovative and creative by questioning assumptions, reframing problems, and finding new approaches to solving old problems. Followers are invited to address problems and find solutions.

4   *Individualized Consideration*: Transformational leaders are especially attentive to each follower's needs for achievement and growth. Followers are treated as individuals who have different needs and different strengths. They feel personally cared for and are seen and treated as more than just employees. Transformational leaders act as coaches and mentors. Followers are treated as ends not means to others' ends.

The leadership approach we are going to study takes a transformational approach. While it embraces many of the components identified by Bass and Riggio above, we also deviate from some of them. One of the main differences in our approach lies in the need for the transformational leader not to 'do all the work.' This means that he or she should not be the sole source of admiration, inspiration and motivation. Creating idealized or idolized leaders is highly dangerous to all parties! Our leadership approach does not place the responsibility for creating a vision on the shoulders of the leader. We take the view that vision needs to be co-created in light of new realities – more of which we discuss below.

A further difference from the Bass and Riggio idea of transformational leadership is that the vision co-created with the guiding help of leaders may not be one that arouses 'enthusiasm and optimism.' On the contrary, the vision may be very sobering and challenging; one that calls for sacrifice, personal resilience and determination. The task of leadership is to mobilize others to embrace this vision because it is aligned with reality, regardless of its personal appeal.

The leadership approach we develop in this and the next chapters is a far more **distributed** process than that implied by either Burns or Bass and Riggio. Here leadership lies in enhancing the **adaptive capacity** and thus leadership potential of the group and its members, rather than attributing most of the leadership achievements to one or two individuals.

The next normative theory of leadership we turn to is that of 'servant leadership' pioneered by Robert Greenleaf, a former executive of AT&T.

SERVANT LEADERSHIP

Servant leadership, developed by Robert K. Greenleaf in the 1970s, ushered in a new paradigm in leadership. Contrary to the focus on command and control leadership, still very much in vogue during the 1970s, servant leadership advocates a humble, value-driven and ethical approach that resonates more with spiritual than political or boardroom leadership. Since the 1970s servant leadership has acquired many disciples. The following is a synthesis of some of its major tenets.

Servant leadership has some similarities with transformational leadership in that a servant leader exhibits emotional and moral concern for followers. Servant leadership is understood to be focused primarily on the welfare of others. Servant leaders' orienting value to serve others places them in the position of leadership. They are first and foremost servants whose natural desire is to serve. They are attentive to the needs of others and their aim in serving is that their followers become healthier, wiser, freer and more autonomous. Servant leaders are always questioning whether what they are doing can be done better or differently and if they are truly serving in the most productive and wholesome ways.

According to Greenleaf, one of the key attributes of servant leaders is their prescience: a knowledge of the future that is deeply grounded in the now. They have a tendency to view the past, present and future as one organic entity. This way of being and seeing in the world helps build their intuitive insights and capacities, especially around the primary needs of their followers.

While the leadership approach we are studying does not emphasize servant leadership *per se*, it does concur with the idea that care for followers is essential and that a particular prescience as advocated by Greenleaf is critical to an effective leadership process. (We discuss more of this in Chapter 10.) For our purposes what is most appealing in the servant leadership approach is the focus on the need for mindfulness. Mindfulness of what is happening in the here and now is something we stress in the Systemic Leadership approach.

EMOTIONAL INTELLIGENCE

Daniel Goleman (1995), in his well-known book *Emotional Intelligence*, popularized the idea that effective leaders exhibit high emotional intelligence, or *EI*. Leaders with high **emotional intelligence** or maturity are supposedly better able to develop and maintain constructive relationships with others. This ability to handle relationships effectively is, according to Goleman, derived from the following components:

- Self-knowledge attained by having access to one's own feelings, an ability to discriminate between them and to draw on one's feelings to guide one's behavior.

- Self-awareness and emotional self-management, being the ability to know one's own emotional tendencies and show appropriate emotion that is proportionate to the circumstance.

- Self-motivation, which is the ability to marshal one's emotions to motivate oneself.

- Empathy, which is the ability to step inside others' shoes and to understand their emotions from their perspective.

Emotional intelligence competencies enhance a person's social awareness, and this improves his or her adeptness at grasping the complexity of human situations. Through emotional self-management the emotionally intelligent person is good at creating teamwork and collaboration as well as handling conflict and managing difficult conversations. Goleman and many others insist that without emotional competence, dealing with people, motivating and mobilizing them, influencing and inspiring them is hardly possible.

The leadership approach advocated in this book agrees that emotional intelligence and maturity is an important attribute of effective leadership. Only emotionally mature people can be attentive to their own emotions and those of others, especially in times of challenge and change. Being able to form an emotional connection with followers is critical to get their buy-in and support for change initiatives. Effective leaders have to be able to emphasize and speak to the gains and losses of change, especially the emotional ones. This necessitates both comfort and a facility in dealing with the emotions of others, plus self-confidence in handling one's own.

THE POWER OF REFRAMING

The power of **reframing** is the central theme of *Reframing Organizations*, by Lee G. Bolman and Terrence E. Deal (2003). Here the authors propose that effective problem diagnosis can be assisted by a manager's mental models, maps, mindsets and cognitive lenses being consolidated into four perspectives or frames. The four frames they propose include the:

- structural frame where the organization is viewed as a factory or machine;
- human resource frame where the organization is viewed as a family;
- political frame where the organization is viewed as a jungle;
- symbolic frame where the organization is viewed as a carnival, temple or theater.

Bolman and Deal suggest that by looking at the organization through these various lenses, managers are able to gain different perspectives on the dynamics taking place. By using these lenses strategically, managers can then make suitable interventions and guide employees through the challenges they are facing.

Framing requires an imagination and thoughtfulness that goes beyond simply looking at the technical problems. By taking all four frames together, managers gain a feel for the architecture of the organization, people needs, the competitive characteristics of the culture, and the meaning making, rituals and ceremonies that provide the heart of organizational life. Multiframe thinking helps managers see the multiple realities that exist within the organization. It also provides them with new insights and options in tackling the challenges of change and strategic problem solving.

The ability to reframe problems is a great asset to those wishing to exercise leadership. Often it is in the framing of the problem that people actually get the 'aha' about what is going on. Reframing allows for a problem or issue to be viewed from more than one perspective; always a good thing! Reframing also provides a critically important contribution to the recognition and identification of new realities. It is often in the process of reframing that the essence of the impact of the new reality can be seen.

Let us take an example:

You are a mortgage broker who helps people get mortgages from lending organizations. You have done extremely well in the last five years as house prices have soared.

It is 2008; the sub-prime mortgage crisis has hit across the United States, radically affecting Europe and especially the UK.

New reality: mortgage loans have dried up; there is minimal liquidity in the market; housing inventory is high; few people are selling their homes; some low-income people are forced to sell their homes at low prices.

By framing different questions to establish the impact of the new reality you open up different perspectives and options for dealing with its challenges. For instance...

Are you in the mortgage business?

Are you in the housing business?

Are you in the loan-selling business?

Are you in the credit risk packaging business?

Are you in the investing business?

Are you in the business match-making business?

Are you in the real estate business?

Are you in the home-making business?

By reframing your business and its context in the economy, you might find new and different possibilities for dealing with these new realities. You may be able to use your skills and networks in new ways in new markets. Reframing always helps to provide another window on the world.

The manner in which problems are framed determines the options for their solution and provides opportunities for people with differing mindsets to explore the landscape of the problem from different perspectives. As we discuss in Chapter 4, effective framing of challenges presented by new realities is one of the important tasks of leadership.

THE SYSTEMIC LEADERSHIP APPROACH: AN INTRODUCTION

Now we have reviewed some of the well-known normative theories relevant to Systemic Leadership, let us revisit the questions we raised in challenge to the leadership definition provided at the beginning of this chapter. In response to these questions we introduce some of the key components of the Systemic Leadership approach that we develop further in Chapter 4.

Question 1: Are there specific circumstances that require the activity of leadership?

As stressed in Chapter 1, leaders facilitate and manage the group or organization's response to new realities. New realities herald change. Mobilizing people to engage in change requires leadership. Where there is no need of change, leadership is not required. In dormant or static environments, a designated authority suffices to hold the boundaries, monitor performance and keep the proverbial train on track. The process of change needs leadership, and leaders facilitate and guide others through this process. The circumstance that requires the activity of leadership is therefore the arrival of new realities.

New realities have a systemic impact. To grasp the nature of new realities demands an ability to see the bigger picture, to adopt a systems thinking mindset and to see patterns and relationships. The leadership approach I advocate emphasizes that *true* leadership is primarily and fundamentally concerned with identifying and responding to ever-changing realities.

There is nothing more important, compelling or urgent than the existence of changing realities and wrestling with what that implies for the healthy survival of a system or organization.

Reality, as we discussed in Chapter 1, is always changing. Being in tune with those changes provides the focal point of leadership. Effective leadership continuously holds the organization's attention to the changing nature of reality.

The capabilities or skills that leaders need to identify new realities include the following:

- openness, attentiveness to and curiosity about, a changing global environment;

- strength in systemic thinking;

- an ability to see patterns and relationships;

- good inductive reasoning capabilities.

Question 2: Is there something about a person and his or her actions that makes an event or experience one that qualifies as exercising leadership?

The Systemic Leadership approach does not prescribe or hold as normative any special personality traits or characteristics required of a leader. Leaders may or may not be charismatic; might lean to introversion or extroversion; might have a male orientation or a female orientation. There is no definitive trait that stands out as best or better.

A defining characteristic of a person exercising leadership, however, is a 'prescient' mindfulness about what is transpiring in the system or organization at the present time combined with a tenacity associated with wrestling with new realities and the value tensions they imply (known as identifying the adaptive challenge). This means the actions of those exercising leadership include thoughtful attention to gains and losses that arise as a consequence of change. As we discuss in Chapter 4, the work of leadership includes both adaptive and technical work.

The capabilities or skills that leaders require in order to identify the adaptive challenge and perform both adaptive and technical work include the following:

- intellectual and emotional alertness;

- strong cognitive abilities – the ability to entertain competing mindsets at once;

- emotional intelligence.

Question 3: Does the person need to exhibit any particular style of behavior that will qualify as an act of leadership?

The Systemic Leadership approach does not prescribe any particular style of behavior as a 'best leadership style.' However, since the primary task of leadership is to identify and define new realities, and since new realities are always in some ways threatening, be it at the conscious or unconscious level, some styles of behavior might lend themselves to greater effectiveness than others. For example, when people are in the throes of grappling with the demands of change, domineering or coercive behavior might get short-term superficial results, but certainly no buy-in from followers. Further, since the goal of Systemic Leadership is to enhance the adaptive capacity of the organization and its employees, understanding, empathy, forthrightness and servant leadership-type attitudes will engender greater trust and motivation than will a stern task-oriented style. Mobilizing followers to embrace change, where they realize the necessity and urgency of change from within themselves, requires strong people skills. Those skills include a healthy sense of self and appropriate self-confidence to hold people's feet to the fire when change is needed.

Capabilities and skills that help exercise leadership in the face of change include:

- self-awareness around one's own feelings of change;

- the ability to empathize without faltering on what is required;

- critical thinking skills to understand what is really going on and to follow through with rigor;

- strong conflict management skills.

Question 4: Is the act or exercising of leadership a one-off event or a process?

In reality all acts of leadership comprise a process. There is rarely a one-off event. Sometimes an event might occur in a very short time frame, such as getting everyone out of a burning building, or might be clearly a longer-term process, such as repositioning or restructuring a new division.

Whatever the circumstance, the leadership process always entails recognition of a new reality (burning building), recognizing the value tensions (my life is at stake), framing a needed response (get out now!), finding someone with the required competence/skills to facilitate the response (the fire marshal as leader), ceding one's power to the leader (I will do as you direct me), actually self-mobilizing by responding.

Each one of these elements of the leadership process presents a minefield of cognitive and emotional complexity. Cognitive complexity lies in perceiving the new reality and being able to reality test what is being perceived from multiple perspectives. Emotional complexity lies in being self-aware about one's own emotions regarding the new reality while at the same time being understanding and empathic with others' emotions that may not be in sync with one's own. This is tough stuff and represents the hallmark of adaptive maturity.

Capabilities and skills that enhance effective leadership include:

- high levels of cognitive development;

- process orientation;

- emotional maturity;

- endurance.

Question 5: Do followers have to respond in any particular way to illustrate they are following a leader? In other words, what makes a follower a follower?

An important question for leaders is: what is a follower? Are there any criteria for **followership**? If someone agrees to be guided by someone else or submits to someone else's will, does that make him, or her, a follower? (Check out the discussion on obedience in Chapter 5.)

Simply speaking, one could say yes! Someone leads or provides direction; others follow or take that direction. What we intend by raising this question is to consider the quality of followership. People who agree or acquiesce on the surface may be followers, but probably not for long! Short-term followers provide a dangerous life for leaders and a chaotic existence for the organization.

The Systemic Leadership approach is concerned with the quality of followership. As pointed out in Chapter 1, there is good change and bad change. The quality of followership plays a key role in making changes good or bad.

The goal of Systemic Leadership is not to attract those who agree or acquiesce to a particular direction (blind obedience is to be challenged), but, rather, to create a momentum around the change process that results from others' self-mobilization. The change process is not a linear one where some lead and others follow, but a circular process, where adaptive leaders provide a holding environment that enables the group or the system to integrate the need for change and thereby generate the urgency and energy for that change. Ownership of the change process rests with the followers because the need to change has been made so obvious they realize their choices: change or die!

The capabilities and techniques for creating this process are explored in detail in Chapter 4.

Question 6: Is the leader responsible for setting the goal or direction of the group? Another way of putting this is: is the person who sets the direction of the group the leader?

The prime task of leadership is to orient the group or organization to new realities. We know this is no easy task. It may take several people exercising leadership to get the organization, beginning with senior management, to face new realities. Depending on the nature of the new realities and the threats they represent to the system, this may take time. One important thing leaders must avoid is defining new realities without 'reality testing' them with representatives of the various constituents of the system or organization. Defining reality is tricky since our perceptions of reality are influenced by our world views. It is important to get multiple world views and perspectives to shake out the essence of the new realities. In this sense, then, the group co-creates its goal or direction. It is not simply the prerogative of the leader(s). (Refer to 'The Importance of Vision' in Chapter 4.)

Capabilities and skills that enhance effective leadership include:

- confidence and patience;
- lack of hubris – willing to co-create the future without having to demand all the accolades.

Question 7: Does the goal to which followers are directed have to be a worthwhile or ethical one to make it an act of leadership?

Here the answer is an unequivocal yes! The goal has to be a worthwhile and an ethical one. The idea here is that dealing with new realities is a worthwhile goal and the only worthwhile one! What could be more worthwhile than being in tune with *reality*? Only by being in tune with reality is there any possibility of being relevant; of being empowered; of surviving!

Facing reality as best and honestly as one can, fairly and squarely in the face, is an ethical goal. It means there is no dissembling; no avoidance; no deception; no scapegoating; simply dealing honestly and truly with one's own challenges, one's own real, honest, down-to-earth work. This holds at both the individual and the organizational levels. Ethics is about honestly and courageously dealing with reality.

Capabilities and skills that enhance effective leadership include:

- courage;
- a brave heart;
- and more courage.

BECOMING A SYSTEMIC LEADER

The Systemic Leadership approach specifically shies away from prescribing any essential personality traits and/or capabilities and skills as essential prerequisites. Instead, it advocates that anyone can exercise Systemic Leadership provided that 'in the exercising of leadership' certain tasks are accomplished. To accomplish these tasks, however, requires a certain disposition and the use of certain talents or skills. The person exercising leadership may not habitually display the required disposition, or regularly demonstrate competence in the required skills. Chances are that he or she does indicate a tendency to behave in a certain fashion and hence is able to come to the organization's rescue as a leader when appropriate. At this point, we also need to clarify that leadership can be exercised from a position of informal authority as much as from a position of formal authority (discussed in Chapter 5). Whether the person(s) has formal or informal authority will impact some of his or her actions: how and why we explore later.

While some of the capabilities and techniques useful for leadership are set out in the previous section, here we briefly add a few further thoughts on some of the dispositions, talents and skills that facilitate the exercise of leadership.

Favorable dispositions:

- Self-awareness – being in touch with one's own emotions and how that impacts one's behavior.

- General mindfulness and attentiveness – the capability to be fully present in the present moment.

- Curiosity and the desire to find new levels of thinking.

- Perseverance – the ability to hold steady and push through on difficult problems.

- Self-confidence – appropriate belief in one's own stance in life.

- Genuine care about people.

Talents and skills:

- Ability to see the bigger picture (systems thinking mindset).

- Intellectual thoughtfulness and rigor.

- Patience.

- Strong people skills.

- Ability to hold steady in terms of conflict.

- A capacity for risk taking.

- Vitality and stamina.

PERSONAL EXERCISE

- Are you a transformational or a transactional leader?
- Do your colleagues see you as someone with emotional intelligence?
- How good are you at having difficult conversations?
- Are you able to see the big picture or do you trip up in the details?
- Do others see you as thoughtful and energetic?

THE FASCINATION WITH LEADERS AND LEADERSHIP

We began this chapter with a discussion of the allure of leadership and how the existence of leaders and the concept of leadership persist in capturing our imagination and enthralling us. Why are we so intrigued by leaders? This is no simple question to answer. Here I venture one main idea about why leaders have us so captivated. We discuss the seduction of leadership further in Chapter 7, 'The Shadow Side of Leadership.'

Leaders have power or influence over us and we have both strong and ambivalent feelings about that. On the one hand we cede our power to them, giving them power to use over us. Quite a paradoxical situation! We give them power because we believe they will do what we would do in certain situations, only better. In other words, we see them as mirror images of ourselves only magnified in strength, valor, warmth and possibly integrity. In this way, leaders serve as our *alter egos* writ large. They represent the collective fantasy of ourselves magnified in some way.

On the other hand, we are not sure our chosen leaders are going to reflect back to us that which we wish to see. Our ambivalence tells us there is a chance they will fail us; that we have given the wrong person all that power; or the right person too much.

When our leaders provide us with the mirror image we wish to see, we adore and adulate them (see the discussion on transference, splitting and projection in Chapter 6). They make us feel good about ourselves and this validates our choice of ceding our power to them. On the other hand, when our leaders seem to fail us, we are angry with them. We vilify them, demean them, publicly disgrace them, and even assassinate them. We reject the image we see in the mirror as not ours, and as alien to us.

So we are caught! We are intrigued and captivated by our own image, like Narcissus and we are all narcissistic to some degree. We are fascinated by our own image and struggle to tear ourselves away when we see the beauty of our image reflected back to us. Our fascination includes our fear. Ever vigilant, we try to ensure that our leaders do not surprise us and reflect an image to us that is not beautiful; one we cannot or do not want to accept. Our fascination combined with our vigilance keeps us hooked. Because leaders are mortal, invariably all leaders fail us in some way. Once they do, we abandon them and resume the search for a person with those characteristics that give us the perfect, immortal leader, who will never let us down. We devise new theories, propose new leadership characteristics, new tools and techniques, all in the hope of getting something close to the perfect mirror image. We forget the mirror is just that, a reflection of what is being reflected, and that is us: with all our imperfections and disappointments! Our leaders are a true reflection of ourselves, like it or not.

So...mirror, mirror on the wall...is the most truthful analogy of them all!

EXECUTIVE SUMMARY

This chapter provides some grounding in several of the well-known leadership theories and introduces the reader to the Systemic Leadership approach. It highlights some of the normative leadership theories that are applicable to Systemic Leadership and how they contribute to advancing the adaptive capacity of the organization and its members.

Here are the main points:

- Leadership is a captivating topic; we all want to be a leader or in some way associated with leaders.

- Defining leadership is not an easy task. There are many things to consider when defining an act of leadership.

- There are many leadership theories that focus on different aspects of leadership. Some focus on the personality of the leader and some on the required capabilities and skills of leadership. There is no one size fits all for leadership.

- Transformational leadership as opposed to transactional leadership is a well-known and admired leadership approach. Transformational leaders focus on providing transformative experiences for followers. Transformational leadership is considered by many a more effective way of getting the work of change done.

- Servant leadership, like transformational leadership is another normative leadership theory. Servant leaders' prime orientation is that of serving and improving the overall welfare of followers.

- Emotional intelligence is a form of emotional competence that enhances people's abilities to understand and manage their own emotions and those of others. Emotional intelligence is an important attribute of leadership, since leadership is a relational activity.

- The ability to frame and reframe challenging new realities is a great capability for those who wish to exercise leadership.

- Leadership is a personal and social construct that provides a mirror image of the group, organization or system being led.

KEY CONCEPTS

Emotional intelligence
Followership
Psychodynamic
Reframing
Servant leadership
Systemic Leadership
Transactional leadership
Transformational leadership

CASE STUDY
THE HR DEPARTMENT CHALLENGE

You are the member of a department in AnyoneCan, Inc. AnyoneCan has just merged with Buttercup Fields Homestores, Inc. Both companies consider themselves middle of the road retailers. They do not compete with the discount chains nor with the specialty stores. Buttercup Fields has a few specialty stores as part of its chain.

AnyoneCan, Inc. has been in the retailing business for over 120 years. Buttercup Fields has been operating for the last fifteen years. Due to an aggressive management team Buttercup Fields has demonstrated phenomenal growth over the last ten years. In the last three years it has taken over five smaller store chains. In the merger with AnyoneCan, Buttercup Fields is the financially stronger partner.

The retailing industry has had two long years of recession. Competition is intense and sales are generally lagging all round. The discount retailers have fared the best during the downturn. New technology has radically changed methods of ordering goods, the management of inventories, handling money in the store, as well as new financial reporting procedures both internally and externally.

As a result of the merger, to avoid duplication of activities and to benefit from economies of scale, several administrative departments will be closed. You and several members of your department anticipate that your department will be one of them. Your department has been responsible for all the human resource aspects of AnyoneCan. Corridor gossip is that the new entity, Anyone's Buttercup, plans to outsource all of its HR functions.

You have been told that a committee has been formed to decide which departments will be closed or downsized. The committee will consist of an equal number of representatives from both companies. Both your department and the HR department of Buttercup Fields are at risk.

You and other members of your department feel you want to use your leadership skills to influence the committee to keep the department. Using what you know – new realities, systems thinking, emotional intelligence and so on – how are you going to persuade the committee not to outsource the HR activities and keep your department?

FURTHER READING

Avery, Gayle C. *Understanding Leadership*. Thousand Oaks, CA: Sage Publications, 2005.

Bass, Bernard M. and Ronald E. Riggio. *Transformational Leadership*, Second Edition. Hillsdale, NJ: Lawrence Erlbaum Associates, 2006.

Beach, Lee Roy. *Leadership and the Art of Change: A Practical Guide to Organizational Transformation*. Thousand Oaks, CA: Sage Publications, 2006.

Bennis, Warren, Jagdish Parikh and Ronnie Lessem. *Beyond Leadership*. Cambridge, MA: Basil Blackwell, 1994.

Conger, Jay A. *Learning to Lead: The Art of Transforming Managers into Leaders*. San Francisco, CA: Jossey-Bass, 1992.

De Pree, Max. *Leadership Jazz*. New York: Dell, 1992.

Goleman, Daniel. *Emotional Intelligence: Why It Can Matter More Than IQ*. New York: Bantam Books, 1995.

Goleman, Daniel, Richard, Boyatzis and Annie, McKee. *Primal Leadership: Realizing the Power of Emotional Intelligence*. Boston, MA: Harvard Business School Press, 2002.

Heifetz, Ronald A. *Leadership without Easy Answers*. Cambridge, MA: Belknap Press of Harvard University Press, 1994.

Lakoff, George and Mark Johnson. *Metaphors We Live By*. Chicago, IL: University of Chicago Press, 1980.

Nahavandi, Afsaneh. *The Art and Science of Leadership*, Fifth Edition. Upper Saddle River, NJ: Pearson Prentice Hall, 2006.

Note

1   This chapter in Northouse is written by Emest L. Stech.

4 THE SYSTEMIC LEADERSHIP APPROACH

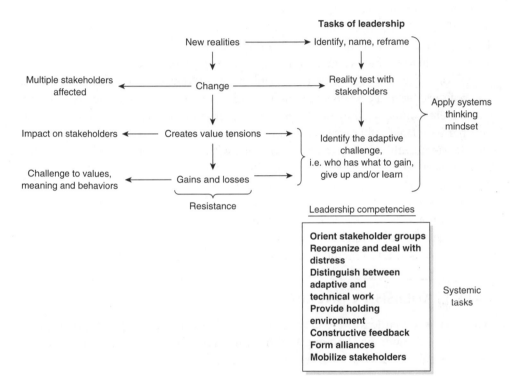

Figure 4.1

INTRODUCTION

This chapter explains the Systemic Leadership approach in depth. We examine the philosophy that underpins Systemic Leadership and discuss how this philosophy translates into practice in getting leadership tasks done.

Chapters 1, 2 and 3 stressed that the fundamental tasks of leadership relate to mobilizing the organization around new realities and change. In Chapter 2 we discussed the systemic nature of new realities and the need for systems thinking to grasp their organizational impact. In Chapter 3, we reviewed some of the normative theories of leadership relevant to Systemic Leadership.

In these next pages, after further developing the concept of Systemic Leadership, we examine some important distinctions that set the Systemic Leadership approach apart from other leadership approaches. These important distinctions include distinguishing between leadership and authority, defining what it means to mobilize others, formulating an understanding of followership, and outlining the critical difference between adaptive and technical work. After a discussion of these important elements of Systemic Leadership, we focus on the specific tasks of leadership and their purpose. At the end of the chapter, the reader should have a good grasp of the notion of Systemic Leadership and some of the challenges leaders face in getting these tasks effectively executed.

The role of leaders is to keep the organization relevant by remaining in tune with new realities. Systemic leaders are continuously alert to new reality signals from the external environment. They need to ensure the organization remains an open system and that its change initiatives respond to real rather than illusory realities. They are also attentive to the patterns and relationships within the systems of which the organization is a part. By tracking new realities, changing patterns and relationships, leaders raise the awareness of others to the new realities that are always arriving. They do this by ensuring there is time and space for discussions concerning new changes on the horizon and by giving people an opportunity to discuss their reactions to these new realities. Systemic leaders are sensitive to the levels of distress in the system and work with organization members to diffuse this distress to optimal limits.

KEY LEADERSHIP CONCEPT

For Systemic Leaders there is nothing more important, compelling or urgent than the existence of changing realities and wrestling with what that implies for the healthy survival of a system or organization.

SYSTEMIC LEADERSHIP – THE CONCEPT

Systemic Leadership is an approach that addresses systemic challenges that arise in a highly interdependent world. These systemic challenges arrive by way of new realities. Identifying these new realities and their complex nature requires systems thinking. It also requires a continuous re-evaluation of existing mental paradigms, assumptions and beliefs, plus a devotion to critical thinking.

The Systemic Leadership approach recognizes that groups, organizations and societies comprise a plurality of stakeholders with competing interests and needs. Due to the growing interconnectivity of nations, cultures, societies and groups, new realities present complex systemic challenges that require recognition of the value tensions that various stakeholder groups experience with their arrival. Systemic Leadership tackles the challenge of change in an integrative and holistic way.

The Systemic Leadership approach:

- embraces systems thinking in order to understand the impact of new realities on stakeholders – Systemic Leaders use a systems mindset to understand the changing nature of reality;

- pays attention to the narratives of systems and observes the changing networks and relationships within a system – this includes giving particular attention to the values and roles different stakeholders take up in the system and its sub-systems;

- understands the dynamism and intricacy of the interconnectedness of systems and promotes a multi-perspective approach to problem solving that includes perspectives in conflict with one another – scenario analysis is an important tool for Systemic Leaders;

- recognizes that what we see depends on our perspective, and that multiple, equally valid, perspectives exist and this plurality of viewing points cannot be suppressed or ignored but must be held in dynamic tension as part of the pulse of a vibrant diverse life (finding common ground among varying perspectives – and therefore realities – is one of the recognized challenges of leadership – no one person or group of people can know all perspectives or hold all aspects of reality);

- focuses on enhancing the **adaptive capacity** of the organization by optimizing its learning potential – Systemic Leaders grasp that adaptive organizations are continuous learning organizations;

- understands the nature of value tensions and the resistance to learning – Systemic Leaders work with these resistances, using them as fodder for the learning process;

- acknowledges that complex problems need the help of the group in order to solve them – no one person has all the answers, and pretending this results in a litany of empty promises;

- sees leadership and followership as '**mirror images**' of one another, rather than as subject and object in a linear engagement of impact and response;

- recognizes that expectations of leaders and leadership vary widely and that one person or one group of people cannot meet all the expectations all the time – there will always be **failed expectations** somewhere;

- understands that everything is not under the leader's control; nor should it be – making progress on complex problems requires co-ownership by group stakeholders, which is a vital motivating force that gets the group to mobilize itself to find optimal solutions;

- distinguishes between **adaptive and technical work** and develops different strategies for each type of work;

- does not assume responsibility for adaptive work, but, rather, gives the work back to the group or organization for them to engage in;

- is concerned with developing people and organizational **capacities** rather than **capabilities**;

- provides constructive feedback that facilitates individual and organizational learning;

- provides a **holding environment** during periods of distress;

- creates a network of alliances across formal and informal authority boundaries to help balance the roles of authority and leadership (as explained in Chapter 5).

THE GOAL OF SYSTEMIC LEADERSHIP

The primary goal of Systemic Leadership is to mobilize people to make progress on challenging and difficult problems that arise as a consequence of new realities and in so doing enhance their adaptive capacity (Beerel, 1998). New realities present adaptive challenges that require adaptive work (see below). Systemic Leaders take the lead in ensuring that the adaptive work is done – something we explore in depth in this chapter.

As discussed in Chapter 1, new realities first and foremost challenge peoples' values and invariably result in a perceived 'loss' of some kind. This reality frequently leads people and organizations to deny or avoid dealing with new realities altogether, as if they did not exist. Rather than deal with actual reality, there is frequently a tendency to create another supposed 'new reality,' one they prefer to consider. The goal of Systemic Leadership is to artfully and strategically hold people's feet to the fire so that they work with real, rather than shadow or imagined, realities. This essential work of leadership is not easy. New realities sometimes present seemingly unpalatable challenges and people's (often) vehement resistance can present itself in a variety of forms; something we discuss in detail in Chapters 5 and 6.

KEY ASSUMPTIONS THAT UNDERPIN THE SYSTEMIC LEADERSHIP APPROACH

Four major assumptions underpin the concept of Systemic Leadership:

- Leadership is defined by the tasks performed rather than the skills or traits of particular individuals.

- Leadership is not something that only those in positions of formal or informal authority are able or expected to do. Therefore, in Systemic Leadership, we refer to 'exercising leadership' rather than referring to 'the leader' or 'the leadership.'

- Anyone can conceivably exercise leadership from anywhere in the organizational hierarchy. Function, discipline or level in the hierarchy should not inhibit the opportunity to exercise leadership.

- The role of leader is distinct from that of authority. Not all people in positions of authority automatically exercise leadership.

MOBILIZING OTHERS

One of the primary goals of Systemic Leadership is to mobilize others. The tasks identified below are carried out in the service of getting people to act or respond to new realities. To mobilize others does not mean to command, coerce, or even influence them in the conventional sense. Mobilizing others requires getting *them* to see why *they* need to act. It implies provoking or stimulating others' self-motivation based on their own insight and realization that action is required. Mobilizing others means getting them to channel their flow of energy, to take responsibility for the challenge of change and to embrace it. Mobilization occurs as a result of learning.

Mobilizing others is not easy. It is easy neither for the person exercising leadership nor for the 'followers.' Why is this so? Well, we know about the fear of loss, the sense of being out of control, and the hard work required to keep apace with change by being adaptive, creative and innovative. People resist change that demands reprioritizing their values, changing their perspectives or world views, establishing new behaviors or forming new relationships. Most people also dislike uncertainty and ambiguity. New realities invariably make these demands and create these conditions.

In order to express their dislike or distress around change, people act out. They deny, avoid, get angry, find a scapegoat, fixate on other issues, lose motivation, rebel, disappear, or sabotage change efforts. There is also the fact that many people prefer to be 'told' what to do. That way they have minimal personal engagement, and they have someone to 'blame' for their actions and their consequences.

Systemic Leadership is about dealing with these psychological and emotional issues as much as it is about dealing with the strategic, technical, procedural and structural issues around change. Systemic Leaders need perspicacity, perseverance and a great deal of energy. Dealing with people's resistance and ambivalence about change requires self-confidence. Creating an environment that fosters self-development and new learning can be an arduous process, especially in an organization where there are many competing stakeholder groups with different interests. The payoff, however, for both the individual and the organization can be huge. We discuss more about the Systemic Leadership tasks in the face of resistance to change below, and especially in Chapter 6.

FOLLOWERS

The discussion of leadership always brings up the discussion of **followership**. It is often said if there are no followers there is no leader. By contrast, the Systemic Leadership concept does not emphasize the word 'followers' as if there is a leader who is leading and guiding and others following his or her lead.

In Systemic Leadership the idea is that exercising leadership occurs from many different vantage points. First, it may occur from a position either with formal authority or without formal authority. It is not just those in formal authority positions who exercise leadership. This means, for example, an insightful janitor, who has no formal leadership responsibilities, can exercise leadership. He may have noticed changing patterns of behavior of the people working on the night shift. He may have some ideas as to what has changed or is changing, and why. By naming this new reality and bringing it to the attention of others, he may indeed exercise leadership.

Second, exercising leadership is more about co-creation than one person defining a reality or vision and others agreeing to follow that lead. The idea behind exercising leadership is to gain widespread ownership of both the challenges the group or organization faces and their solutions. In developing a co-created response to new realities, the Systemic Leadership baton might be passed quite rapidly and frequently among members in the group. The notion therefore of a distinct group of followers does not quite apply. At times someone is a follower of others' guidance or ideas. At other times the same person is the one exercising leadership by holding up new realities or helping the group deal with denial and resistance. The distinction between those exercising leadership and others is 'more fuzzy' and less easily distinguishable than in other leadership philosophies. Those exercising leadership and those following their lead are in a complex relationship with one another. The one needs the other and they both have an impact on one another.

We discuss the idea of '**distributed leadership**' in Chapter 5 where we point out that everyone in the organization needs to act as a change agent. This means everyone is expected to exercise leadership at times while also being a 'follower' at other times when someone else is in the leadership role.

SYSTEMIC LEADERSHIP AS TRANSFORMATIONAL LEADERSHIP

On the transactional–transformational leadership continuum discussed in Chapter 3, Systemic Leadership falls close to the transformational end. Systemic Leadership is less about the exchange between the person exercising leadership and 'followers', and more about developing the leadership capacities both of those exercising leadership, and of others. In line with the definition of transformational leadership, Systemic Leadership advances shared motives and goals, is concerned with the needs of others, and invites participation.

In working with changing realities and in genuinely confronting the value tensions they represent, Systemic Leadership takes stakeholders affected by the new realities to higher moral ground. Tussling with questions around value, meaning and a sense of self is an ethical endeavor that results in greater self-awareness; self-awareness for the individual and self-awareness for the organization and its culture. Heightened self-awareness results in higher levels of morality. Leadership and ethics are discussed in greater detail in Chapter 8.

SYSTEMIC LEADERSHIP AS AN ACTIVITY

Exercising Systemic Leadership means engaging in the tasks that address the adaptive challenges facing the group and helping the group or organization make progress on addressing those challenges. We recall that **adaptive challenges** refers to the value tensions that arise as a result of new realities. Adaptive challenges require us at the individual and the organizational levels to reclarify our values in the light of new perspectives, new situations and new behaviors.

Because the focus of Systemic Leadership is on the activity and not on the person or persons exercising leadership, the style and traits of the person are not focal points. While Systemic Leadership by virtue of its approach may seem to fit some leadership styles more than others, it would be risky to prescribe any hard and fast rules that ensure success. Different situations and different cultures call for different types of Systemic Leadership strategy. As long as the adaptive tasks are effectively undertaken and new realities are directly dealt with, the appropriate leadership style will find its place. In Chapter 3 (p. 78) we reviewed some of the competencies likely to assist someone in being an effective Systemic Leader. The one personal attribute that is undoubtedly helpful is the ability to be attentive to the present and to be able to read the present moment clearly. The present moment reveals the future that is always arriving. If we pay attention to the present, the future will show itself.

SYSTEMIC LEADERSHIP COMPETENCIES

- Systems thinking mindset
- Mindfulness, awareness, attentiveness to present realities
- An ability to frame reality/new realities
- Process orientation
- People skills and emotional intelligence

(Continued)

(Continued)

- Ability to get people to self-mobilize
- Self-effacing disposition
- Self-confidence
- Courage

CAPACITY VERSUS CAPABILITY

Systemic Leadership places greater emphasis on developing people's capacities than advancing their capabilities. The difference between capacity and capability is that the latter (usually) emphasizes technical ability such as intellectual acuity or physical dexterity. It refers to talents or skills that can be learned, changed or enhanced.

Capacity, on the other hand, relates to a power: a power to experience, learn, produce or retain something. Capacity refers to innate *potential*. It is this potential that sets the limits on capability. The greater a person's capacity, the greater his or her potential to learn, grow and understand. People with great capacities can be taught to be very capable. People who have limited capacities will soon reach the limits of their capability. Capacity is therefore the power that defines capability. Capacities grow and recede. Capabilities change or stagnate. Both improve with practice.

Effective leadership can contribute to the development of people's capacities by giving them opportunities to practise and to stretch their limits. Skilled operational management can then channel this capacity into the appropriate technical capabilities. Management's responsibility is to ensure that people's capabilities do not stagnate but remain aligned to changing organizational needs. The greater the capacity of the people in the organization, the more easily this can be achieved. Effective leadership enhances people's adaptive capacities.

THE ROLE OF LEADERSHIP VERSUS THE ROLE OF AUTHORITY

The roles of leadership and authority are often confused. Most people tend to presume that anyone who has a position of formal authority is the leader. For example the president, the CEO, the director, the supervisor and the boss are automatically considered leaders. Particularly senior executives in business organizations are given the title 'leader' regardless of any evidence of their ability to guide the organization through transformative changes. A formal title does not guarantee that the person will be an effective leader. In fact it does not even guarantee that the person will assume the tasks of leadership at all! It is much easier for people to assume the task of authority than leadership. People love to use their power and influence to command the obedience of others. Getting them to change, with all the work that entails, is a different story!

To clarify these assertions let us review how the functions of authority differ from those of leadership. Authority figures are expected to provide direction and protection. They are expected to chart the course and hold boundaries. Those in authority are expected to control conflict, uphold and maintain norms, and generally provide orienting functions regarding group status and physical place. People in authority are expected to solve routine problems, to alleviate distress, to mediate between competing stakeholders or factions and ward off danger. They are expected to have certain answers and to shoulder the responsibility for solving difficult problems (see Chapter 5).

Leadership is about the challenge and process of change. If there is no change there is no need of leaders; authority figures will keep the organization on the straight and narrow. Leaders, however, in their role as facilitators and agents of change, do things that go directly counter to the function of authority. They are supposed to challenge the status quo. They are expected to stimulate shifts in consciousness that create opportunities for learning, that prompt new habits, new norms, different boundaries and new courses of action. Leaders are supposed to allow conflict to emerge, and to engender a certain amount of chaos and disequilibrium in the process of guiding the group or organization to new territory and new ranges of equilibrium.

Clearly the roles of authority and leadership are diametrically opposed. The one fights for order, the other for disorder. The one ensures that existing norms hold, the other strains for new norms. The one focuses on stability, the other on instability (change). The one provides answers and shoulders the responsibility for others, the other (in the case of Systemic Leadership) gives the work of finding solutions back to the group.

Misunderstanding of the nature of leadership often arises as a result of the confusion between authority and leadership. Because people in positions of authority are expected to alleviate the distress of others, to show the way, and to take responsibility for mistakes in the process, people often seek authority rather than leadership. They want those in authority to take away their burdens rather than challenge them to do their part in resolving the issues. Many leaders are not appreciated if they do not wield their power and authority by telling others what to do.

Exercising leadership from a position of formal authority as opposed to from a position with informal or no authority raises different authority and leadership issues. We explore these in detail in Chapter 5, 'Authority, Obedience and Power.'

LEADERSHIP	AUTHORITY
Hold up changing realities	Provide direction
Challenge the status quo	Uphold and maintain norms
Generate creative tension	Control conflict
Set new boundaries	Hold existing boundaries
Identify the adaptive challenge	Chart the planned course
Provide a holding environment	Provide protection
Heighten distress and urgency	Alleviate distress
Mobilize for adaptive work	Solve technical problems
Give the work back	Provide answers
Be open to dissenting voices	Clarify group authority and status

PERSONAL EXERCISE

1   As someone who has a position of authority, do you also exercise leadership? When? How?
2   Select one or two 'leaders' who impress you. Are they good at exercising authority or leadership or both? List your evidence to support your conclusions.
3   Write down the instances when you have tried to exercise leadership but others have wanted you to stay in your role of authority.
4   What can you learn from these reflections?

ADAPTIVE VERSUS TECHNICAL WORK

The distinction between adaptive and technical work is based on the insights of psychiatrist Ronald Heifetz and his work on leadership at the J.F. Kennedy School of Government at Harvard University. Heifetz suggests that the leadership strategies required by the two types of work are different. He observes that adaptive challenges are often inappropriately identified as the need for more technical work. The consequence of this misdiagnosis is ineffective leadership or no real leadership at all. For Heifetz, real leadership is about dealing with difficult questions that challenge the very nature of our meaning and value systems. This, he claims, is the heart of adaptive work.

Adaptive Work

Heifetz's insights are based on his work with highly experienced but burnt-out community leaders. Many of them had lost their jobs or been rendered impotent in their ability to effect change, often for so-called political reasons. While studying their experiences, Heifetz arrived at a new understanding of the issues and challenges facing those who endeavor to exercise leadership. His interpretation of the causes of failed leadership is different from more conventional analyses. The latter tend to focus on the ineptitude or inadequacy of the leader. He or she is usually diagnosed as having failed by having the wrong temperament, selecting the wrong program, lacking political sensibility, lacking appropriate technical or industry experience, demonstrating poor timing or poor strategic skills, or being insufficiently thorough in the actual implementation of change. Consider the many programs, courses and books that have been designed and written to 'fix the leader!'

By contrast Heifetz's approach focuses on the leader's ability to grasp changing realities facing the community or organization and to understand the value tensions they represent. Exercising leadership is not about coming up with easy answers to complex problems, but, rather, about getting the community or members of the organization to face its value tensions and to make practical progress on those value tensions. The real measure of leadership is the ability to mobilize people to work on difficult questions that radically challenge their lives and affect their ways of making meaning. This implies that exercising leadership entails gaining appropriate trust from one's constituents and encouraging them to recognize and deploy their own agency without encouraging moral dependency. Exercising leadership means getting stakeholders to put their own shoulder to the plough in order to effect the adaptive changes the group or organization requires. It does not mean devising a vision on their behalf and then persuading them to be supportive and/or compliant. Leadership is about getting people to do *their own* work in an environment where they are suitably focused, encouraged and supported. Exercising leadership is essentially about encouraging others to do the adaptive work *they* need to do.

Effective leadership is concerned with distinguishing between adaptive and technical work. Adaptive work is concerned with grasping the nature of a new reality and working with the gains and losses it represents. The gains and losses are first and foremost psychological and emotional. An organization that has to recreate or reinvent its technology (which is a continual challenge, given the acceleration of science and technology) has to keep asking the questions, 'Who are we? Who do we want to be? What kind of added value do we bring to our customers?' These are very personal questions as they challenge the very core of an organization's existence. These questions raise important issues about self-definition, competence, and contributing value. They get at whether or not the organization is still really relevant and if so how; and, if not, what it can do about it. These are uncomfortable questions that organizations (and people) would rather not have to ask. Management wants to assume the organization's self-definition has been established, that it is competent, and that of course the organization adds value! How dare anyone challenge or question this!

Effective leadership means getting the organization or group to face these questions and not sidestep them. Effective leadership is about working with others to ensure the adaptive work is done before technical solutions are rushed into. Effective leaders make sure that the adaptive work responds to the new realities, and that it guides and informs the technical response.

Identifying that adaptive work may be required often begins with perceiving that something is discordant between the organization's performance and what is occurring in the environment. A number of signals may indicate that the organization needs to radically reposition itself. These signals must be carefully examined to see what they indicate about the new reality. Regrettably many organizations, like Hunt and Blake (case study below), become distracted and fixate on the symptoms of problems without getting at what lies underneath and behind the problems. Accurately perceiving the true nature of the adaptive challenge is often the most difficult part of adaptive work.

Technical Work

Technical work is a critical part of any organizational activity. Technical work addresses intellectual, procedural and routine problems. The important issue is that it must be appropriate to the problems it is trying to address. The efficacy of technical work lies in the appropriateness of its timing, its congruence with the adaptive work, and of course the skill and efficiency with which it is executed.

Some forms of technical work are more easily identified than others. Every organization in every type of industry has typical types of technical work. Banks upgrade their cash machines, accountants revise their audit manuals, software companies update their software, and retailers revise their purchasing and inventory policies. Most organizations develop strategic plans, create budgets, and develop and refine their policies and procedures. Technical work! Technical work keeps the organizational engine performing, and performing efficiently. While technical work takes care of the functioning body of the organization, adaptive work takes care of its heart and mind. Adaptive work ensures the organization remains relevant through heart–mind engagement that nurtures the organization's energies and passion to be true to its mission. Adaptive work keeps the organization attuned to new realities. Technical work provides the essential follow-through. When technical work replaces adaptive work it has the same effect as rearranging the deckchairs on the *Titanic*!

Performing adaptive work and distinguishing between adaptive and technical work can best be illustrated with the help of examples. Refer to the case study below of Hunt and Blake, a once extremely successful South African business that failed to recognize and meet its adaptive challenges. Instead it favored technical work. The result: Hunt and Blake lost relevance to its customers and was discarded into the dustbin of history. It no longer exists.

THE TASKS OF SYSTEMIC LEADERSHIP

Exercising leadership entails undertaking adaptive work. Several tasks fall under the heading 'adaptive work.' We have already discussed some of these tasks, such as identifying, naming and reality testing new realities, acknowledging value tensions, and identifying the adaptive challenge. Working with adaptive challenges and mobilizing the group to respond to those challenges requires various types of activity that help reframe issues or direct the group to pursue certain actions.

The tasks of Systemic Leadership are summarized below. While these tasks have been outlined as if they follow sequentially, this is misleading. Adaptive work rarely takes place in logical, linear or sequential fashion. It is best to think of the activities of adaptive work as being steps in an improvisational dance. Each activity represents a step or a sequence of steps. So, for example, at one time, there might be two steps forward, three to the side, and possibly one to the back. A little later, the sequence could be entirely different. A step forward might imply that progress is being made. A step to the side might represent turning down the heat. A step back may mean giving space for the group to regress before turning up the heat again. With this image in mind, we can see that the pace of the dance and the sequence of dance steps are determined by the music created by those on the dance floor. Whilst the dance will begin with acknowledging the impact of new realities and the associated adaptive challenges, the rest of the dance will flow from the reaction of the dancers, the anxieties they are experiencing, how these are contained, and the transformative learning taking place.

Systemic Leadership Tasks Outlined

Identify new realities

The primary task of leadership is to get the organization to continuously face new realities as they arrive. Just as sailboats always face the wind, so organizations must always face the winds of change.

Identifying new realities, as we have discussed in Chapters 1 and 2, is not always easy. An important point to note is that exercising leadership does not require any one person to clarify or name the new reality alone. In fact it is preferable if the identification, naming and framing is a group process. This activity in itself generates important learning.

Along with the identification of new realities comes resistance in all its forms – denial, anger, confusion, blaming, scapegoating and so on (see Chapter 6). Working with new realities, therefore, is not a simple cognitive exercise. It affects people's sense of self and their cherished world views, which invariably prompts an emotional reaction. Beware too of those who say they love change. People who fly wherever the wind blows may seem helpful to the process, but may not in fact be doing the deep learning of adaptation. Exercising leadership means holding space for people to reflect on and articulate the value tensions they are experiencing. Even positive new realities deserve time and attention as part of the adaptive process. Rapid acceptance of new realities and change may indicate that the adaptive work has not really been done.

Identify and name the adaptive challenge

New realities most often present new or different values. These create value tensions within organization members or stakeholder groups. Naming the value tensions is known as identifying the adaptive challenge.

Once the adaptive challenge begins to be formulated, further reality testing is required. The best way to do this is to engage system stakeholders (employees, customers, suppliers, members of the community, possibly competitors) in discussions regarding the newly perceived realities and the value tensions they imply. Reality testing is the attempt to grasp the problem fully by repeatedly clarifying the values and current behaviors being challenged and establishing which stakeholder groups are affected and how. (Refer back to the open systems approach in Chapter 2 (p. 48) to help with this step.)

Rushing the reality-testing process, a frequent tendency of those anxious to get on with the more comfortable technical work, will prove detrimental in the long run. Some time (not forever!) is needed to elicit conflicting views or challenging perspectives. Once people engaged in the reality-testing process consider the adaptive challenge has been sufficiently clearly identified and articulated, the adaptive work is well under way.

Orient stakeholder groups to deal with value tensions

Once the adaptive challenge has been identified, the next stage of the adaptive work is to actually shift the organization's attitudes, beliefs and behavior to make it consonant with the values of the new reality. This part of the adaptive work concerns addressing the conflicts between the values that people currently hold and the new values required. It includes mirroring, coaxing, encouraging, challenging and motivating management and employees to embrace the new reality for what it is and what it means to the life of the group or organization.

Dealing with value tensions includes distinguishing between illusion and reality, resolving conflicts, and placing the perceived difficulties of the new reality into perspective. It demands innovation and learning. Often the most difficult part of learning is the unlearning of old values that have served well in the past and no longer serve as well in the changed reality.

Identify who has what to gain and what to give up or lose

Part of the activity of identifying value tensions includes clarifying the stakeholder groups affected by the new realities and what each has to gain and to lose as a result of the value tensions. This aspect of the adaptive work is important as it provides insights into the degree of resistance that can be expected as well as the motivating leverage possible with each stakeholder group.

A stakeholder analysis invariably reveals many more stakeholders than initially imagined. By delving deeper into the needs of various stakeholders and their relative positions of power in the organization, one can observe that different stakeholder groups experience different gains and different losses. Being in tune with the differences between the groups is important. This helps assess where the greatest resistances lie, which stakeholder groups are likely to form alliances and which groups might be in conflict with one another.

In this phase of the adaptive work exercising leadership means helping identify the learning required for adaptation. Based on the effect of change on different stakeholder groups it will become clear that some groups may have to do major repositioning work to remain relevant. This may require a new mindset, new values, and new ways of being competent.

Recognize signals of distress – hold steady and turn up the heat

We know change is always accompanied with some element of distress. Systemic Leadership pays attention to the signals of distress and exhibits sensitivity to what those signals represent. Ignoring people's distress or becoming angry with them is not helpful! On the other hand, giving in to their distress, trying to comfort them by disavowing the true nature of the new reality is not helpful either. Good leaders know how to hold steady in the face of distress by showing understanding without encouraging backsliding into states of unreality. Finding the right balance between patient understanding and holding people's feet to the fire to deal with what is uncomfortable while also instilling an appropriate amount of urgency to deal with the situation is tricky. The likelihood of doing this effectively and sustaining positive momentum is radically enhanced if leadership is distributed. This means that more than one person is holding up the new reality, dealing with the distress and trying to push forward. For a lone leader to take this on single-handedly is not only extremely emotionally demanding, but can also be extremely politically dangerous!

Distinguish between the group's adaptive and technical work

Because people and organizations fundamentally do not like change they try to respond to the demands of change in a technical or functional manner. Rather than take the time or energy to understand the emotional and psychological impacts of the gains and losses associated with change, the tendency is to rush headlong into technical solutions. Most often the technical solutions address the symptoms rather than the root causes of change. For example an organization might be experiencing loss of market share because the new reality is that a new and different technology is luring away traditional customers. Instead of taking the time to understand the nature of the new reality and the need for the organization to reinvent and then reposition itself, it falls into the trap of seeing the loss of market share as a pricing problem or a sales team management problem. In this way the organization avoids doing its adaptive work – adapting to the new reality – by looking for quick fix, rationalist solutions that do not really address the problem. Typically the more elaborate the technical solution, the greater the avoidance of adaptive work.

Think of your own organization. In the face of change how many new technical systems are hastily implemented? New projects and initiatives embarked upon? What about those new positions with elaborate titles that are created? Then there are the new HR bonus schemes, the new procedure manuals and quality control policies. Then of course we must not omit those hundreds of mergers and acquisitions for gazillions of dollars that invariably fail to add any true value at all. Undoubtedly many of these initiatives are technical solutions to adaptive problems! These types of response do not really take the organization forward. They represent examples of 'bad change', as discussed in Chapter 1.

Provide a holding environment or container for the distress

Systemic Leaders help the group or the organization deal with distress caused by change by providing 'release valves' for that distress. If one uses the analogy of the pressure cooker, good leaders can gauge the intensity of the pressure building up in the system and have the ability to help the system let off steam without totally coming off the boil. Good leaders find ways to alleviate the distress by engaging in discussions, encouraging humor, and allowing some escape into technical work so as not to let the system exceed its limits of disequilibrium. Leaders need to listen carefully to what others are saying; they need to be attentive to the behaviors of others; and they need to be aware of the stresses and strains they are experiencing. By keeping their attention on the organizational pulse they are able to read the climate and, with the help of others (see below), keep the system within manageable stress limits. If the stress in the system exceeds tolerable limits, learning will not occur. Chaos can ensue, often resulting in highly dysfunctional behaviors, possibly followed by the ultimate 'demise' of the leader.

Make constructive interventions to keep people on track

Exercising leadership includes continuously bringing the organization back to the task of doing adaptive work around new realities. This requires constructive feedback to stakeholder groups or organization members in an effort to keep them oriented to adaptation and learning. This attentive feedback ensures the goal of change is not lost and that progress continues to be made at a pace the organization or group can tolerate while still responding appropriately to the urgency of the new reality.

Get on the balcony to gain new perspectives

To retain effectiveness leaders need to find ways in which they can distance themselves from the day-to-day demands of organizational and group dynamics. They need to develop strategies to enable them to take a step back so they can remove themselves from the dance of organizational life and have an opportunity to observe it without being caught up in it.

The idea of getting on the balcony (another important Heifetz concept), forces the leader to try to take the role of 'observer' and thereby see the larger picture of what is truly going on in the organization. This respite from the daily needs of others provides opportunities to gain new insights and new viewing points of how the organization is truly functioning, to see points of harmony and disharmony, and to understand changing patterns and new relationships that are evolving or dissolving. Being able to get on the balcony aids systems thinking and is essential for a deeper understanding of organizational life.

Give the work back

When the going gets rough, people like to look to those in positions of authority, or to those who are willing to assume the role of leadership, for answers. Rather than wrestle with their own challenges or assume responsibility for their own decisions, they prefer to turn to someone who will assume the responsibility for telling them what to do. Particularly when people have to face tough questions that require tough answers they hope that someone else will do their work for them and thus lessen the discomfort or personal sacrifice. This is a very seductive situation for leaders. Because people want to depend on them, the leaders are made to feel omnipotent, wanted and needed, and excessively competent. This fatal attraction between people and erstwhile leaders is more often than not doomed to failure. Leaders cannot and should not assume responsibility for the adaptive work of others. Not only is it misleading and irresponsible, it is also unethical (something we discuss in later chapters).

Effective leadership is about giving adaptive work back to those to whom it belongs. Part and parcel of good leadership is the ability not to be seduced into believing one can assume the adaptive work of others. Good leadership is about reflecting or deflecting the 'savior' projections back to the people who are doing the projecting and getting them to assume responsibility for their own work. This does not mean that good leaders should lack interest or concern for the challenges that others face. On the contrary, they are aware and supportive of the stresses and strains of adaptive work, and they assist by providing a holding environment that helps contain the distress and discomfort being experienced.

A key role of leaders is to help others frame the challenges they are facing and to inject perspicacious questions into discussions. Their challenge is not to become providers of answers and solutions but, rather, to become a resource for good questions and for assistance in wrestling with the truth. The act of giving the work back to others is one of the most challenging for all leaders and for all of us. We love to be seen as experts, as people who have answers, and as problem solvers. Regrettably we do not realize that providing solutions for others seldom provides real solutions at all! It is often self-serving without showing any real care for the other.

As mentioned earlier, Systemic Leadership is best classified as transformational leadership. The transformational leadership approach focuses on the transformation of others. By getting people to take ownership of their own adaptive work, you develop their adaptive capacities. Although the experience of adaptive work is frequently distressing, finding the inner strength and confidence to take up one's own agency has huge personal benefits. Developing individual and organizational adaptive capacities is the hallmark of effective leadership.

Form alliances across group factions and constituencies

As we have discussed, it is difficult to exercise leadership alone. Lone warriors and saviors seldom survive. Systemic leadership understands that mobilizing people from various constituencies toward a common goal requires distributed leadership – a leadership that is shared with representatives from different groups who can help reality test the new vision prompted by change and who can represent the multiple perspectives that each group brings to any change initiative. Effective leaders are able to form strategic partnerships and alliances across stakeholder groups that assist in mobilizing others to embrace change with understanding, energy and commitment.

Mobilize resources

Ultimately the role of leaders is to mobilize others to embrace their value tensions around change and then take up their own autonomy by self-mobilization. The Systemic Leadership approach prefers the term mobilize to lead, influence, convince or direct. Mobilizing people means freeing them up to move. Systemic leadership frees people up by helping them untangle the knots that immobilize them, such as unresolved value tensions, distress and fear. We discuss this further in Chapter 6.

THE TASKS OF SYSTEMIC LEADERSHIP

1 Identify new realities.
2 Identify and name the adaptive challenge.
3 Orient stakeholder groups to deal with value tensions.
4 Identify who has what to gain and what to give up or lose.
5 Recognize signals of distress.
6 Distinguish between the group/organization's adaptive and technical work.

7 Provide a holding environment or container for the distress.
8 Make constructive interventions to keep people on track.
9 Get on the balcony to gain new perspectives.
10 Give the work back.
11 Form alliances across group factions and constituencies.
12 Mobilize resources.

CASE STUDY
OLD COLLEGE UNIVERSITY

Old College University is celebrating its 100th anniversary and is faced with a 'new reality' it has been avoiding for some time. The new reality is that its Business School requires special accreditation in order to make it academically on a par with competing business schools. The accreditation it requires places emphasis on scholarship and research. Under these standards all faculty members are expected to possess a doctorate and to carry out research and publish books and articles in scholarly journals. This emphasis has a major impact on the curriculum of the school and on the workload of faculty. Further, it means that faculty members need to have an interest in and the aptitude to carry out research and write.

Old College University Business School has hitherto placed high emphasis on teaching. Faculty members have been attracted to the school because of the low pressure for scholarship in favor of high teaching loads and intensive classroom interaction. Students who are attracted to Old College University are also those who are interested in pragmatic, down-to-earth learning with less emphasis on scholarly rigor. The accreditation 'new reality' creates considerable value tensions for Old College University. It also presents major adaptive challenges to several stakeholder groups. The challenge for Old College University Business School is how to mobilize its various stakeholder groups to embrace this new reality.

Let us work through the Systemic Leadership tasks:

Step 1: Identify New Realities

Old reality	New reality
A culture of easygoing pragmatic learning.	A culture with an emphasis on scholarly excellence.
Little competition between faculty for status.	Increased competition between faculty for status.
High teaching load.	Lower teaching load with emphasis on scholarship.

Classroom ratings matter most.	Scholarship matters most.
Pragmatic, hands-on faculty favored.	Scholarly faculty favored.
Middle of the road students attracted .	More intellectually demanding students attracted.
Senior management competence based on collegiality and accessibility.	Senior management competence based on ability to inspire scholarship and research.

Step 2: Identify Adaptive Challenge of Old College University

How to transition from a friendly, low-key teaching university to a more intellectually rigorous, demanding and competitive scholarly university? How to inject different types of rigor into faculty and increase the intellectual 'quality' of students?

Step 3: Orient Stakeholder Groups to Deal with Value Tensions

Some key value tensions:

• pragmatism, hands on, easygoing *versus* intellectual, scholarly, performance-driven;

• classroom popularity *versus* publications success;

• friendly, non-threatening culture *versus* intellectually challenging/threatening culture;

• low entry-level requirements for students *versus* more demanding entry-level requirements;

• new business model: low-end fees, more students *versus* higher fees, fewer students.

New value orientation required:

• new culture of scholarly focus and competition;

• new values important to get ahead;

• changing expectations of students;

• new leadership style and competencies required.

One can see from this analysis why Old College University has been delaying acknowledging the accreditation reality for some time. The implications of embracing this reality are enormous and resistance from both the leadership and many faculty members is understandably high.

Step 4: Identify Who Has What to Gain and What to Give up or Lose

Old College University stakeholders include:

- the university as a system;

- current Dean of the Business School;

- faculty members with PhDs;

- faculty members without PhDs;

- faculty members who have an aptitude and enjoy scholarship;

- faculty members who do not have an aptitude or do not enjoy scholarship;

- faculty who have been at Old College for many years;

- relatively new faculty;

- brand new faculty;

- administrative staff;

- existing students;

- potential new students;

- alumni;

- other university services.

As we can see, the new reality of accreditation for Old College provides a mixed bag. Some stakeholders have more to gain and some more to lose than others. That is often the case with new realities. Dealing with the 'losses' that arise for those who cannot do scholarship or who are not adept at writing books and articles is of course challenging. The art of exercising leadership is helping stakeholders understand their losses and gains, and helping them see gains even in the most challenging circumstances.

For example, a sixty-year-old faculty member at Old College University who does not have a PhD and/or does not wish to engage in scholarly pursuits will conceivably have to look for another job. This could seem a huge loss. Maybe he has been there for twenty years and he sees himself being forced into early retirement. Consider his anger and sense of humiliation or being unappreciated. Providing creative alternatives can be challenging. This is some of the work the group needs to do. It is not the responsibility of the leadership to provide the answers.

On the other hand, a younger faculty member, without a PhD may decide he or she is prepared to get that extra degree so that he or she may continue teaching at Old College Business School. Here the discussion would center on how this faculty member might be assisted during the transition.

There will also be mixed reactions from various student groups. Some existing students may be displeased with higher standards while others might like them. Potential new students may feel more or less attracted to Old College University, depending upon their own interest in education.

A detailed stakeholder analysis would reveal many stakeholder groups in conflicting positions – some with far more to gain or lose than others in this situation. We can imagine this new reality would raise the anxiety and tension across the university and create a great deal of pressure on the senior administration.

Step 5: Recognize Signals of Distress

The Old College Business School new reality certainly presents many challenges to the entire system and all of the sub-systems. Fear and anxiety about the future of the school and the professional careers of the faculty are likely to be uppermost in their minds. This will have an impact on the quality of teaching at the university and the experience of the students. All kinds of emotional behavior will likely be displayed, both overtly and covertly across the campus. Exercising leadership will mean recognizing behavior as a signal of distress and working with that distress while not deflecting from the new reality. We discuss dealing with distress in great detail in Chapter 6.

Step 6: Distinguish between Adaptive and Technical Work

Old College Business School has a great deal of adaptive work to do around the new accreditation reality. Those who engage in exercising leadership around this issue will pay attention to discussing the value tensions different stakeholder groups are experiencing and what they have to 'learn' in order to adapt. This will not be easy as people find it difficult to discuss their feelings concerning their self-esteem and sense of competence. Groups would far rather do technical work as this makes them feel less vulnerable and they feel they are getting something done. The challenge for leadership here, as always, will be to get the timing right about doing the adaptive work before moving into the technical work. Examples of technical work in this situation include assigning new titles to people or departments, creating new classroom assignments, new curricula or new outcomes assessments. While these all have their place, the adaptive work needs to be engaged in first in order to speed up the adoption of change and heighten its chance of success.

Step 7: Provide a Holding Environment or Container for the Distress

Exercising leadership will require monitoring the levels of distress in the system and ensuring it does not reach untenable levels. If the distress is too high, Old College Business School will cease to function effectively and will devolve into destructive in-fighting, heightened inter-stakeholder conflict, scapegoating and all kinds of other regressive and dysfunctional behaviors (see Chapter 6). The emotional life of the organization will require support and succor without misleading organizational members into the false belief that the new reality has disappeared. Managing the tension optimally will require time, empathy from management, and open discussions across stakeholder groups. These will have to be well managed so that space for emotions is provided without the sense of urgency about change being lost. This is not an easy task and requires patience and steadiness on the part of both those in authority roles and those exercising leadership.

Step 8: Make Constructive Interventions to Keep People on Track

Exercising leadership will mean continuously intervening in positive ways when the momentum toward the goal of embracing the new reality is lost. At times, constructive intervention, comments or feedback may simply alleviate distress or allow for some emotional give around the discomfort of the new reality. As mentioned earlier, there may be a 'dance' in that not every action will seem as if things are moving forward and this could be very frustrating to some who just 'want to get on with it.' Finding the optimum balance between give and pushing forward is part of this dance.

Step 9: Get on the Balcony to Gain New Perspectives

To understand the group dynamics likely to take place at Old College Business School requires taking a step back and getting out of the fray. Getting on the balcony can take many forms. It may mean staying away from some meetings; it may require changing one's role in meetings; it could include engaging in discussions with others more peripheral to the immediate Business School system; or it may mean just taking a few days off for self-renewal. Any activity that enhances the ability to engage in systems thinking invariably provides new insights.

Step 10: Give the Work Back

One of the major leadership challenges in any change initiative is finding how to avoid being responsible for the emotional remedies and the technical solutions. Systemic Leadership, which aims at enhancing the adaptive capacity of others, is an approach that invites those engaged in the change process to devise their own remedies and solutions. This means in the case of Old College Business School that various stakeholder groups need to get together to discuss 'the problem.' They need to talk to one another about what it means to them; what they believe they are gaining and losing; what they think they can do to alleviate the discomfort and move things forward. They should be encouraged to come up with ideas and suggestions and given some room to test these out. All the while leadership requires holding their feet to the fire, maintaining a sense of urgency, yet containing the levels of distress.

Step 11: Form Alliances across Group Factions and Constituencies

Exercising leadership alone can be a burdensome and dangerous endeavor. It can be burdensome in that the psychological and emotional work required to deal with multiple stakeholders' responses to change can be huge, frustrating and tiresome.

In the case of Old University Business School, exercising leadership would require dealing with the reactions of frightened faculty members who know they have to educate themselves further or lose their jobs, with frightened deans who do not know how to create a culture of scholarly excellence, and with anxious students (existing and potential) who are afraid they will no longer have the competence to perform adequately at the

Business School. There will also be the anxious university treasurer who has to chart the university through financial challenges as the university alters its business model.

These examples simply scratch the surface of all the dynamics likely to be taking place at Old College University. Taking this on alone is frankly suicidal! Effective leadership will depend upon an alliance of people across the university and the Business School engaged in dealing with both the adaptive and the technical work. Some members of the alliance will focus on the adaptive work and some on the technical. Some members will assist in holding people's feet to the fire around the new realities, while others will focus on alleviating distress and creating a holding environment. The adaptive work should be well under way before any type of technical work is embarked upon. Also members of the alliance should engage in discussions on progress being made.

Step 12: Mobilize Resources

In order for Old College University Business School to adapt to the new reality it will need to mobilize its resources to embrace change as openly and constructively as possible. While there will always be stakeholders who will not be able to get on board with the demands of change, Old College will need to mobilize a critical mass in order to survive the new demands.

Part of the leadership challenge at Old College is to hold up to faculty in the Business School the new reality that the new accreditation standards present a new reality to *all* business school faculty at any respectable college and that if they do not face it at Old College they are most likely to face it somewhere else. The writing is on the wall that faculty members without PhDs who do not publish and carry out research are going to find it more and more difficult to get jobs even in average universities.

Postscript: Alas, Old School University found the resistance to the new accreditation standards too high and the adaptive work too complex. The president and senior administration blamed their reluctance to embrace the new reality on the cost associated with changing the culture of the Business School. Sadly, Old School University will continue to struggle along as yet another mediocre educational institution desperately trying to balance its budget on tuition dollars. How long will it survive?

THE IMPORTANCE OF VISION

Leadership research results reflect an almost universal expectation by people that leaders are those able to create a compelling **vision**. People want inspiring, enthusiastic and hopeful visions. These are the types of vision they value and want to align with. Alas, this is so often Alice in Wonderland thinking. New realities need to underpin all visions. A vision for the future that does not respond to the realities the group or organization is facing is simply pie in the sky. Enthusiastic, optimistic vision statements can be dangerous. New realities may deliver hard, even brutal news. Any visioning of the future must be a realistic, sober statement of what is true and really possible in light of that truth. Desirable or idealistic vision statements invite extreme caution.

A vision statement developed in isolation by the CEO with the aid of her senior management team is far from the ideal. The process of creating a vision for the group or organization should be something that evolves from the adaptive work described above. Adaptive work is distributed work; it requires participation across the organization. If the vision statement and the adaptive work are not in sync, the vision statement will lack coherence and traction in the life of the organization. It will simply become an intellectual document to which people pay lip service. Part of the reason for giving the work back to the group or people in the organization is for them to devise a vision that reflects the values and real-world tensions that exist and they can own. Giving anyone a vision statement they are expected to comply with will hardly motivate or mobilize them.

The future vision of the organization needs to be co-created by the group as they grapple with new realities and engage in adaptive work. Co-creation will create buy-in and will also provide reality testing as people question, challenge, disagree, or present different visions. Peter Senge, in *The Fifth Discipline* (1990), asserts that shared visions emerge from personal visions and that it does not work just to establish an official vision. Senge also suggests that the role of the leader, rather than espousing a vision for others, is to hold the tension between the group's visions and the world's reality, thereby facilitating others to work toward closing this gap (Senge, 1990: 226). Senge's ideas resonate with the Systemic Leadership approach.

EXECUTIVE SUMMARY

The prime function of Systemic Leadership is to orient the organization to new realities and to hold up the value tensions being created. Systemic Leadership requires both insight and foresight in reading the changing environment and translating its effects into the mission, values and core competencies of the business. New realities set the agenda for the adaptive work required to align the work of the organization with the requirements of new realities.

1   Systemic Leadership focuses on new realities a system is facing.

2   New realities affect different stakeholder groups differently. These differences need to be identified.

3 A critical part of Systemic Leadership is to identify the value tensions that each stakeholder group faces. Sometimes the value tensions may be similar and sometimes they may be different. Identifying the value tensions is not easy. Either they may not be obvious and/or people try to hide their distress by denying or even disavowing the value tensions they are experiencing.

4 Systemic Leaders help the system reality test value tensions that various stakeholder groups are experiencing. Reality testing means talking with people about their losses and gains. It means understanding their struggle around what they have to give up and helping them to see what they have to learn in order to adapt. Being adaptive means understanding the loss–gain tension and working with it in a conscious way.

5 The next task of Systemic Leadership is to help people deal with their distress. This will come in the form of denial, anger, blaming, scapegoating, passive-aggressive behavior and fleeing into technical work. Part of the task of leadership around distress is trying to understand its cause and its intensity. The higher the distress, the greater the tendency to turn to technical work – hire new people, give new titles, change the benefits system, move the car park – do anything other than deal with new realities. Observe how rapidly senior management can move into technical mode long before they have really grasped the impact of the change.

6 Systemic Leaders are adept at holding people's feet to the fire to do their adaptive work. This too is not easy, as they will resist. The person exercising leadership has to be careful that he or she does not become the issue and attract the blame, anger and so on.

7 Exercising Systemic Leadership means leading with oneself. One has to model one's own adaptive capacity and one's own ability to deal with one's adaptive work before one has a chance of mobilizing others.

8 A critical task of Systemic Leadership is to give the work back. This means mobilizing others to do their work. They will resist. They do not want to do adaptive work. They prefer someone else to take responsibility for this work.

9 Systemic Leadership mobilizes others to embrace change in an energetic and committed way. This is the true measure of effective leadership.

KEY CONCEPTS

Adaptive capacity
Adaptive challenge
Adaptive and technical work
Capacities, capabilities

Distributed leadership
Failed expectations
Followership
Holding environment
Mirror images
Vision

CASE STUDY
HUNT VS. BLAKE

Hunt and Blake, a well-established timber and building products business, had branches throughout South Africa. It had been in operation for over a hundred years and boasted a list of loyal customers. Its main market was the farms and small towns or rural areas. Hunt and Blake had served its customers with care and concern for many years. Its strategy had been good friendly service, high inventory levels so that customers rarely had to wait for stock, and a very lenient credit policy. It claimed to be a values-driven company, and made every effort to be a socially responsible corporation and a good employer. Its employees were loyal, content, and considered Hunt and Blake to be their lifetime employers.

By the late 1980s, Hunt and Blake managed more than eighty outlets, spread hundreds of miles apart. It purchased timber products directly from plantations and, once purchased, these products were hauled to other locations to be cut, treated or processed. Most of Hunt and Blake's timber products required very basic carpentry skills in order to be installed. Its other building products were purchased direct ex-factory from three or four regular suppliers.

Hunt and Blake's turnover exceeded R500 million. Its board and senior management comprised family members, all descendants of the founding partners. Middle management was selected from the local community and the criteria for selection were based on the ability to communicate Hunt and Blake's friendly, family values.

During the early 1990s, Hunt and Blake began to face what, according to it, was unexpected competition. Competing outlets appeared in some of its major selling areas. All of these competing suppliers were owned by the same large timber company whose original market had been limited to supplying railways, mines, and other large construction projects. Little by little, Hunt and Blake's customer base was eroded. Soon it began to lose its most loyal customers. Investigation revealed that the competition offered lower prices a greater range of products, and more DIY assembly items. Over a period of three years, Hunt and Blake's turnover dropped slightly and then stagnated, despite several price increases. In contrast, the competitors' businesses appeared to be booming, as they opened new, bigger outlets in the larger towns.

Hunt and Blake's management team decided to engage consultants to help diagnose the problem and to advise on how to stem the tide of deserting clients. After several months of analysis, the consultants made three key strategic suggestions. These were:

- more modern, easy assemble products be stocked for resale;

- lower levels of inventory be held, incorporating a wider range of items; and

- a more stringent credit policy be introduced to reduce accounts receivable from an average of 90 days outstanding to a more tolerable level of 45 days.

The rationale for these suggestions was that Hunt and Blake was unable to be price competitive with such high inventory holding costs and the long delays in collecting cash from its customers. The consultants claimed that the competitive prices of the other firms were the critical reason for the decrease in sales and loss of market share.

With support of the board and senior-level management Hunt and Blake strove to implement these changes. It invested in a new inventory management computer system and appointed a new director of purchasing. It hired a number of credit control staff to monitor the levels of accounts receivable and set new inventory holding levels. It revised its pricing structure, lowering the prices on some of the most successful product lines. Despite all of these efforts, the organization was unable to stem the loss of customers, which was followed soon by the resignation of disgruntled employees. After the fifth year of falling profits, the reluctant families sold their stockholdings to the competitors. Hunt and Blake, the faithful, honorable building supplier, was no longer in existence.

This story is a typical example of an organization and its consultants failing to understand the nature of new realities and adaptive challenges. Struggling managers and quick-fix consultants so often focus on symptoms rather than on underlying causes of problems and then seek relief in technical solutions to what is actually an adaptive problem.

The new reality for Hunt and Blake was that the values of the world were changing. Even farms and small country towns were progressing to a modern world. In a modern world, the traditional values of family and loyalty find it difficult to compete with the rationality of the marketplace. The company's adaptive challenge was to recognize the new reality and the ensuing value tensions. Customers now wanted to shop in modern, efficient, price-competitive stores, with a wide range of comparable products. The new reality included a world of increasing customer sophistication, where customers want to have choices so they can consciously exercise their buying power. Instead of loyalty, price and comparability have become the greatest purchasing discriminators. In the past, people may have appreciated wood products that require at least some basic carpentry skills to install. Modern people do not have the time, and/or no longer wish to make the time to develop their carpentry skills. The traditional approach to doing business (concerned, friendly and familial), is also perceived as anachronistic in its ways, especially if it fails to clearly communicate that it has embraced modernity.

Hunt and Blake was facing an adaptive challenge of major proportions. The culture of the surrounding society had changed from one which held traditional values to one in which, modernity dictated, new marketplace values be held. As an organization in that society, it would be expected to reflect those same values. Its founding values, based on a traditional culture, were no longer the key values held by its customers. Its staff members, chosen for their sympathy with the traditional values, were caught in the culture clash. They had identified with the organization's value system, and resisted new modern ideas and systems. Their values, attitudes and behavior remained embedded in the old ways. They feared that the company was becoming like their non-caring, money-grabbing competitors, but they also realized that modernity was an inevitable trend. Over time, many of them were modernizing their values too. Not knowing how to bridge the gulf between old and new values, the distress was too much. Many of them left the firm.

Hunt and Blake and its consultants did not begin by identifying the 'new reality' and the values at stake. What makes identifying the adaptive challenge so different from the other techniques of analysis is the emphasis on values and meaning making. This approach rests on the belief that the first work to do is to identify value conflicts and tensions and to clarify the value changes that are needed. To proceed with technical work (e.g. introducing new systems without re-examining values) is, at best, premature. The value analysis may reveal that systems are not the critical issue anyway.

Hunt and Blake needed to orient the organization to the changing world. Management and staff should have been challenged to adapt their values to the new values of society. This required the exercise of a kind of leadership that the Hunt and Blake management team did not perform. Management and staff should have been included in the discussions of the 'new world out there' and what it meant for their business. Everyone should have been engaged in discussions about how they might bring their values of family and friendly, long-standing commitment to the new world of modernity, price competitiveness and efficiency. There should have been discussions on what they, as an organization with united goals, had to learn and what compromises they could and should make. Management and staff should have been encouraged to be innovative in coming up with a strategic solution which would still give them unique meaning, purpose while developing a sustainable business model. Without this emphasis on value analysis and meaning making an organization is tinkering with superficial, short-lived quick fixes.

Identifying the adaptive challenge is the heart of any work on strategic change and is prior to strategic analysis. It is critical to the achievement of an effective transition from the old to the new. Hunt and Blake resisted doing its adaptive work and fell into the trap of chasing technical solutions to solve adaptive problems. The demise was inevitable.

Exercise: Work through the Systemic Leadership tasks (see p. 101) to see how one might act as a consultant to Hunt and Blake to do its adaptive work.

ORGANIZATIONAL EXERCISE: MIND THE GAP

It could be argued that parts of the recent history of The Gap retail group reflect a lamentable story of market opportunities thwarted by complacency on the part of its leadership. In the last 10 years, the merchandise group that owns more than 3,100 stores under the Gap, Old Navy and Banana Republic brands, has lost literally billions in shareholder value.

Don Fisher and his wife opened the first Gap store in San Francisco over forty years ago. They began by selling Levi Strauss jeans and a large assortment of gramophone records. By 1998, the Gap had developed a distinctive brand of jean that reflected a classic American style of clothing. The huge success of the Gap clothing brand was credited to Mickey Pressler, formerly from the Ann Taylor store chain.

The Fisher family is deeply steeped, some might say obsessed, with tradition. Don Fisher and his wife of fifty-four years, Doris, and their three sons, Bob, Bill and John, all live within a few blocks of one another. All three sons attended Princeton and Stanford Business School and all three sons have worked for the family business. This tightly knit San Franciscan family still holds a significant percentage of the Gap's stock and three of the twelve board seats.

In 1976 the Gap faced the first big new reality when the Federal Trade Commission accused Levi's of price fixing. It soon became clear that discounted jeans would flood the market. The Gap's fortunes declined and Don Fisher was challenged to formulate a new concept. One attempt was to try to partner with Ralph Lauren. This failed as the organization was unable to manufacture clothes to fit Lauren's specifications.

In another attempt to shore up sales, Fisher purchased the Pottery Barn. This purchase proved a disaster and he sold it several months later at a $14 million loss. Around the same time he bought a small chain of safari wear stores known as Banana Republic.

In 1983, Fisher appointed Mickey Drexler to take over merchandising. Drexler made huge changes to the Gap formula. He brought in natural fiber clothes that were stylish, comfortable and long lasting. Gap's fortunes returned; the company grew to 2,428 stores by 1999 and the stock split eight times and returned over 46,000 percent. Mickey created a new and exciting Gap culture. The acquisition of Old Navy proved another feather in Mickey's cap as its sales soared rapidly to over $1 billion.

In 1995 Drexler was officially appointed CEO. Don Fisher moved over to be chairman of the board that comprised many childhood and college friends. Fisher and Drexler were often at odds and over time things between them deteriorated. Family ties inevitably got in the way of Drexler's future at Gap. Don's two sons, Bob and Bill both worked for the company. The elder son, Bob, who headed the Gap brand stores, had no real interest in retail. His work ambivalence, added to a lack of management decisiveness, contributed to his quitting his position in 1999. Don took this hard as his other son, Bill, had quit a year earlier. Relations between Don and Drexler soured. Soon after Bob left, Drexler invested in certain fashions becoming trendy; an investment which was never returned. During this period Don engaged in huge store expansion, signing deals for over a thousand stores in a two-and-a-half year period.

It could be argued that the timing of such confidence precipitated disaster. As Gap merchandise ceased being competitive in a highly competitive retail market, Don was faced with closing a great number of stores, some of them only recently opened under the new expansion. Debt ballooned, store sales slumped for ten straight quarters and the stock price collapsed from over $50 to $8. Fisher fired Drexler and after months of research appointed Paul Pressler of Walt Disney Parks & Resorts as the new merchandiser. Paul and Fisher had similar personalities. They may have been seen as overly rational, penny pinching and lacking in creative and intuitive flair.

On being appointed Pressler soon got to work, reduced debt and increased store sales. Fisher decided he could now relax. He appointed son Bob as chairman of the board while he remained on the board as director intending to take a back seat. Meanwhile Pressler changed the entrepreneurial culture of Gap to one obsessed with rational calculations and financial returns. Creative people in the organization quit and morale plummeted. After the initial improvement, sales continued to fall and in 2006 Fisher fired Pressler. Bob, the eldest son, was appointed interim CEO. He tried to boost morale and entice creative people back to Gap, with minimal success. At the same time Bob and Don began pushing forward on a plan to remodel eighty of Gap's existing stores.

The search for the new leader was not easy and took more time than anticipated. Finally in July 2007, Gap announced it had appointed veteran food and drug retailer Glenn Murphy as its new CEO to succeed son Bob Fisher. Glenn, a Canadian, claims two decades of retailing experience in grocery stores and book retailing. He is credited with turning around the Canadian store Shoppers Drug Mart.

When the board committee first launched its search it insisted it was going to find an apparel merchant as its new leader. Its plan was to attract someone who understands the creative process and who can execute strategies in complex environments. After an exhaustive search, the board hiring committee appointed Glenn Murphy insisting he is just the right man for the job!

In April 2008, after less than a year at the helm, Glenn Murphy was awarded a $39.1 million compensation package, most of it in stock grants. The award is intended to give him an added incentive to help the company recover some of the $32 billion in shareholder wealth that has disappeared over the past decade.

According to *The New York Times*, Gap also paid Murphy $2.1 million in bonuses, including $1 million for taking the job, to supplement his salary of $755, 769 for a half a year's work. He received miscellaneous compensation of $363, 593 including $50,000 to pay the lawyers who negotiated the contract, and $182,301 for personal usage of a company plane. Because his family still lives in Toronto, Gap will spend $400,000 during the current year to cover air travel.

Gaps profits and stock price have improved since Murphy's arrival, but its sales continue to slip. Murphy has warned that the weak economy will make it difficult to revive sales this year (2008/2009).

Questions:

1 What new realities has Gap been avoiding?

2 Is Don Fisher a Systemic Leader? Whatever your perspective, how do you support your reasoning?

3 What technical work did Gap engage in, in the face of change?

4 If you were to exercise Systemic Leadership, what advice would you give Don Fisher and his board?

FURTHER READING

Beerel, Annabel. *Leadership through Strategic Planning*. London: International Thomson Business Press, 1998.

Heifetz, Ronald A. *Leadership without Easy Answers*. Cambridge, MA: Belknap Press of Harvard University Press, 1994.

Heifetz, Ronald A. and Donald L. Laurie. "The Work of Leadership", *Harvard Business Review*, January–February 1997.

Heifetz, Ronald A. and Marty, Linsky. *Leadership on the Line*. Boston, MA: Harvard Business School Press, 2002.

Parks, Sharon Daloz. *Leadership Can Be Taught*. Boston, MA: Harvard Business School Press, 2005.

William, Dean. *Real Leadership*. San Francisco, CA: Berrett-Koehler, 2005.

5 AUTHORITY, OBEDIENCE AND POWER

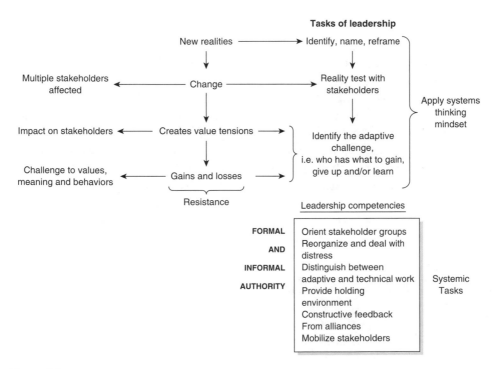

Tasks of leadership

New realities ⟶ Identify, name, reframe ⟍

Multiple stakeholders affected ⟵ Change ⟶ Reality test with stakeholders

Apply systems thinking mindset

Impact on stakeholders ⟵ Creates value tensions ⟶ Identify the adaptive challenge, i.e. who has what to gain, give up and/or learn

Challenge to values, meaning and behaviors ⟵ Gains and losses ⟶

Resistance

Leadership competencies

FORMAL AND INFORMAL AUTHORITY

Orient stakeholder groups
Reorganize and deal with distress
Distinguish between adaptive and technical work
Provide holding environment
Constructive feedback
From alliances
Mobilize stakeholders

Systemic Tasks

Figure 5.1

INTRODUCTION

Leadership and authority partner in regulating social life. Leadership cannot function effectively without its fellow partner, authority, whereas authority can exist (not for long) without the activities of leadership. This chapter explores the pervasive and dominant role of authority in our lives. Whether it is our parents, school, the Church, government, or a political party, interpersonal relations are largely dependent on authority structures and our obedience or conformity to their demands. One of the first things we learn in life is 'who is in charge,' 'why' and 'the need to obey.' We also learn of the dark and abusive side of authority and how much that can influence our actions. On the brighter side, we learn the extent of our own authority in the different spheres of our lives and how that authority helps us get what we want.

The notion of leadership is often confused with that of authority. People in positions of authority are not automatically leaders. They have to exercise leadership to earn that title. Many people claim they desire to be leaders, whereas what they really want is the power and status that come with a formal authority position.

As we discussed in Chapter 4, the roles of leadership and authority are different. An organization needs both roles for optimum effectiveness. The issue of authority is a hugely important matter of concern for erstwhile leaders. Leaders need authority to influence, motivate and mobilize others. However, authority is a slippery master that brings all kinds of obstacles along with its benefits.

This chapter sets out the role of authority and the many expectations associated with that role. We explore the psychological and emotional issues triggered by authority and discuss how these factors contribute to or block the process of change. We discuss the challenges associated with exercising leadership from a position of formal authority as opposed to a position of informal authority. Also, we reflect on the changing nature of authority in organizations and the impact it is having on the workforce. Finally we provide some ideas on how those in leadership roles can navigate their way by using their authority optimally.

DEFINING AUTHORITY

Authority, according to *The Concise Oxford Dictionary*, means the 'the power or right to enforce obedience.' It is also the noun for a person or body having authority, such as the Water or Transport Authority or 'the Church.' Authorizing someone to do something means conferring the power of authority on them so they can command the obedience of others.

What our authority definition does not make explicit is that those awarded positions of authority have some performance obligation linked to the power vested in them. Acquiring authority, therefore, is a process of exchange. Ronald Heifetz provides a simple definition of this: 'authority is conferred power to perform a service' (Heifetz, 1994: 57). For example a king has duties associated with reigning. In order to reign effectively, he needs certain powers. Since 'reigning' is a highly complex endeavor, and affects a huge number of stakeholders, those who reign are granted a great deal of power. The king is thus in some countries the highest authority in the land as he has the most power. A traffic official, however, is supposed to ensure the smooth flow of traffic and to monitor certain roads for delinquent drivers. In turn the traffic official is granted certain powers to facilitate the achievement of those functions. The traffic official is thus the highest authority on certain roads as she has most power there. Similarly, parents have certain performance obligations and certain powers, making them the highest authority in the home. The concept 'authority,' therefore, implies a direct relationship between the complexity of tasks to be carried out, the significance of their impact on others and the power vested in the authority role.

THE ROLE OF AUTHORITY IN OUR LIVES

In every sphere of life there are those who have authority over us; who tell us what and what not to do; who establish the rules and who hold us to them; who reward us and who punish us; who seemingly give us breaks (a great new job) and take them away (lay us off). We are never free from the influence or sphere of authority figures. There is no escape!

No matter how high up we are in a system, any system, we always have to account to some authority. How we understand the role and power of authority and our feelings about being obedient to those in authority condition the way we respond to them. Our understanding and experience of authority influences the way we take up our own authority, how we use our power and how we exact obedience from others. As we discuss later in this chapter, our ability to exercise leadership is influenced by how we handle authority; our own and that of others.

Exposure to the power of authority begins at a very early age and influences much of our behavior for the rest of our lives. Our first and foundational encounter with authority begins with our parents. The first lessons of life teach us that someone with authority takes charge; protects us; nourishes us; sets rules of engagement; commands obedience; punishes us; loves us; and rewards us. These early experiences shape our understanding of authority; provide signals of the potential for love and benevolence; and an authority's capacity for danger and abuse.

From early on we begin to grapple with who has authority and why. We are taught to obey authority and to tread carefully when challenging its legitimacy. Authority figures can be dangerous! As subordinates to others who have power, when we seemingly have none, we focus on being safe and being obedient. In our youth we are less attuned to whether or not the authority figure is meeting his or her performance obligations. We are more focused on the power he or she wields.

As we grow older we become more discerning as to whether or not those in authority deserve the power they have. We begin to question the nature of authority, we question whether or not certain people are worthy of being vested with authority, and we question the power an authority might have over us. Our ideas about authority, including our respect and fear of those in authority, are reinforced or challenged by our experiences with authority figures other than our parents.

By the time we are in our mid-teens we have created a mental construct about the trustworthiness of authority figures ('authority figures are only out for themselves'). We have also developed an emotional response pattern that guides our reaction to them ('challenge them whenever possible'). Our mental construct and emotional response pattern increase in intractability as we grow older. We use our mental construct to test the trustworthiness, likeability, effectiveness and benevolence of new authority figures we encounter. We deploy a variety of response strategies to negotiate our way and ensure survival in the face of those who have more authority than we do. Coping with authority – teachers, coaches, priests, policemen, traffic officials, principals, bosses, tax collectors – is part of everyday life. In fact, if you think about it, a huge part of daily living is devoted to responding to the demands of those who have authority over us. No wonder we have strong feelings about authority!

ENGAGING WITH AUTHORITY

From our early years we recognize the vast influence of authority on our lives. Even though we may wish to avoid them, and even though we may resent having to be obedient to them, we learn pretty quickly that we need people in authority to help us get what we want. Authority figures, by meeting their **performance obligations** (e.g. being thoughtful, diligent and concerned bosses), use their power to protect us from others, to help us advance in our careers, and to legitimize our ideas. If we play our cards correctly, those in authority confer some of their power on us and authorize us to do things we might not otherwise have been able to do. We also need to be sure we handle those in authority carefully. We must not challenge their authority unduly or tactlessly. We must not undermine them. We must be appropriately obedient, although weak authority figures will expect us to be sycophants, and we must certainly demonstrate loyalty. Failure to obey these rules can have dire consequences. Regrettably, most of us have many tales to tell of authority figures who have 'turned on us' or have abused their powers in destructive ways.

From those early years, when we first became conscious of the power of authority and its potential for giving or taking away, we developed coping or response strategies. We use these response strategies in our efforts to get what we want while minimizing the potential for danger.

Typical authority response strategies include the following:

- fight them – challenge their authority; try to make them earn our obedience.

- flee from them – avoid them at all costs; try to remain invisible or mute.

- seduce them – flirt with them; ingratiate yourself with them; try to manipulate them.

- partner with them – pretend we are on equal ground and act as if we are collaborating with them to make things happen; try to encourage collegiality.

- ignore them – act with indifference to them as if they did not really exist; pretend they do not matter.

- negotiate with them – engage in continuous interaction with them, always trying to alter or renegotiate any terms of engagement.
- be a 'Yes' person – if they say jump, we ask how high.

PERSONAL EXERCISE

As you read this list, where do you see yourself? Which responses do you use and when? Does the gender of the person in authority make a difference to your response? What about race or ethnicity? Does that affect your response? How does the situation alter the response strategy you typically use? Are there any other strategies you use that are not on this list? What about your employees? How do they respond to you? When and how might they change under different circumstances? How aware are you of your response strategies and of those of others?

The effectiveness of different response strategies to authority figures varies. Clearly effectiveness depends on the people involved and the situation. The important issue is not to place a judgment on the response strategy itself but to ask questions:

1 Is it effective, does it serve me well?

2 Is it subtle or is it blatantly transparent?

3 Does it stereotype me in any way?

If it is either not effective or blatantly transparent and it does tend to stereotype you, maybe it is time to develop some new and alternative strategies.

OBEDIENCE AND AUTHORITY

From a leadership and change management perspective we need to understand how we respond to those in authority. Why are we prepared to obey someone or some authoritarian rule or injunction and why not? What are our motivations and our reasoning processes? Awareness of our own behaviors towards authority will provide us with insights into the behavior of others. Since one of the important goals of leadership is to mobilize others, i.e. get them to do things, it is important that we have an appreciation of when and why others obey authority and when and why they do not.

Obedience is a complex psychological phenomenon, as revealed by psychologist Stanley Milgram, in his now famous experiments. In his experiments, people from the general public were invited to participate in a study of memory and learning. Some of the participants were designated 'teachers' and some 'learners.'

The experimenter explained to participants that the study was concerned with the effects of punishment on learning. In the experiment the learner is strapped to a chair and an electrode attached to his wrist. He is told he has to learn a list of word pairs. Whenever he makes an error, the teacher is to administer shocks of increasing intensity.

The real focus of the experiment is on the teacher (the subject). After watching the learner being strapped into place, the teacher is taken into an experimental room and seated before a shock generator. The shock generator has a line of thirty switches, ranging from 15 volts to 450 volts, in 15 volt increments. There are also indicators ranging from Slight Shock to Danger to Severe Shock. The experimenter explains to the teacher that he has to administer the learning test to the man in the other room strapped to the chair. When the learner answers correctly, the teacher moves on to the next item. When the learner gives an incorrect answer, the teacher is to give him an electric shock. He must start at the lowest shock level of 15 volts and increase the level each time the man makes an error.

The teacher is a genuinely naïve participant in the experiment. The learner is an actor who actually receives no shock at all. The goal of the experiment is to see how far a person will proceed in administering pain to a protesting victim when he is ordered to do so.

As the shocks escalate, the victim (actor) increases his protests until he demands to be released from the experiment. Conflict arises for the teacher, who sees the suffering of the learner and is pressed to quit. The experimenter, the authority in this case, orders the teacher to continue. To extricate himself from the situation, the teacher must clearly challenge the authority and break off his engagement with him. The aim of the investigation is to see when and how people will defy authority in the face of a clear moral imperative.

The results of the Milgram experiments (several hundred people participated in a variety of experiments similar to that described), is literally 'shocking,' to say the least. Many 'teachers' obeyed the experimenter no matter how vehement the pleading of the person being shocked and no matter how painful or dangerous the shocks seemed to be. A significant percentage of participants (in some cases 65 percent of subjects) administered the highest level of shock possible (450 volts!), regardless of the consequences for the 'learner' or victim. Few if any people did not agree to participate in the experiment once they learned that shocks had to be administered. The results for experiments that included women deviated little from those of men.

In his book describing these experiments, Milgram analyzes the behavior of and the rationalizations provided by the obedient participants. He describes how a variety of inhibitions against disobeying authority come into play, preventing the person from breaking with authority and thus keeping him in his place.

Here are some of Milgram's findings and interpretations of the results:

- In general subjects found it difficult to break with the authority figure even though he (the experimenter) had little authority over them. The experimenter was simply a Yale professor engaged in an experiment. There were no consequences for the subject if he pulled out of the experiment.

- People justified their remaining in the experiment out of a sense of obligation or duty to the experimenter. They claimed they had a commitment to the experimenter and it would be awkward to withdraw.

- People were unable to realize their values in action. They found themselves continuing in the experiment even though they disagreed with what they were doing.

- Some became so engaged in the technical task (pressing the correct switch) that it helped them ignore the larger consequences of their actions.

- Participants did not see themselves as responsible for their own actions. They were doing what they were told to do. Some claimed, 'I would not have done it by myself. It was what I was told to do.' Responsibility for the act and the consequences belonged to the authority.

- Moral concern for the victim was shifted to how well the subject was living up to expectations of authority. People looked to the experimenter for approval of their performance.

- The experiment acquired an impersonal momentum of its own. A mindset developed in the subject that 'it has got to go on.' The experiment became larger than the people in it.

- Some blamed the victim, claiming the punishment he received was inevitable due to his deficiencies in intellect and character.

- The results of the experiment were worse when a third person, other than the teacher, administered the shock. Distancing the person from the effects of his actions resulted in even less concern for the victim.

The findings of Milgram's experiments do not do much for boosting faith in the goodness of human nature. However, we need to understand his findings in the context of the powerful (sometimes frightening) influence of authority we experience at an early age when we are at our most vulnerable. Further, our education rarely provides explicit opportunities for us to learn about and develop mature strategies for dealing with those in authority. Leadership training usually excludes any attention to 'working with authority.' The self-alienation factor revealed by Milgram's experiments, where a person renounces responsibility for his or her actions, claiming he or she was 'told to do it,' has severe implications for organizational behavior in general.

What Milgram's study of authority and obedience teaches us is that obedience does not automatically imply:

- support

- agreement or assent

- loyalty

- affection

- commitment

- understanding

- respect

- future imitation

- learning or adaptation

- conformity

- consistency

- an ethical disposition.

Obedient behavior simply conveys compliance. Any further motivation for obedience requires deeper exploration. From a leadership (and ethical) perspective, why people obey is as important as whether they do or do not. Getting people to obey, even with a smile on their face, does not mean they are taking ownership of their actions, adapting or learning. When people obey without feeling responsible, without developing their adaptive capacity, and without a sense of having learned something they are no better than robots. In fact, in some sense, robots are better; they at least obey and execute instructions consistently.

Many people obey authority out of fear. They fear the power authority has and they fear the consequences of disobedience. A great deal of obedience results from fear. Fear of losing the relationship with the authority; fear of the consequences of not obeying; fear of being seen as an outsider in the group; fear of having to take responsibility for one's own actions; fear of not having an alternative, so why not go with this one? And so on. Authority brings out people's fear. Milgram does not really dwell on the fear factor in his book, but he does illustrate how, in the face of an order from an authority figure, the line of least resistance is obedience. We discuss fear and its significance for leadership in Chapter 7, 'The Shadow Side of Leadership.'

THE MORAL FORCE OF AUTHORITY

The results of Milgram's experiments provide some powerful reminders of the moral force of authority. Early childhood lessons taught us to obey authority and that those in authority are 'right.' The person in authority knows the 'right' thing to do, and the 'right' thing for us to do is to obey. Those in power make the rules! Obey has become associated with moral rightness. Obedience to authority, the boss, the President or the *Führer*, is considered doing one's moral duty.

Doing one's duty, according to the Enlightenment philosopher Immanuel Kant, defines moral behavior. Consequences of our actions do not matter. The sole moral requirement of any person is to do their God-given duty. According to Kant, reason (rational thinking), determines the nature of one's duty. As we can see from Milgram's experiments (and the other atrocities that have taken place in the name of nationalism, e.g. Nazism, ethnic cleansing, Abu Ghraib), people defer reasoning to those in authority. Hence the common belief and practice that authority figures are to be obeyed not only for the power they wield but also because obeying them is fulfilling one's moral duty.

Effective authority figures and those who wish to exercise leadership understand the moral significance of the dynamic just described. Manipulating people's undue (and sometimes misplaced) sense of obedience, their desire to be dutiful and their fear of challenging authority is at best thoughtless, certainly self-serving, and at worst reprehensible. People who have earned positions of authority, either formal or informal (see below), have an ethical responsibility to understand the regressive forces of authority on individual behavior and to avoid using those forces to their advantage. Alas, paragons of virtue in this regard are few and far between.

THE CONCEPT OF TRANSFERENCE

Michael Maccoby, in his book *The Leaders We Need* (2007), provides some other insights as to why we follow leaders and why we willingly follow bad leaders. (Maccoby uses the roles of leaders and authority figures interchangeably. These are distinguished in the present text.) He explains an important psychological phenomenon known as 'transference.' He uses transference to explain why we follow people and why we select certain authority figures or leaders and give them power over us, sometimes totally indiscriminately.

Maccoby explains that often we are driven by unconscious, irrational motivations when we follow people. These motivations are rooted in emotional attitudes formed in early life based on the impact our parents had on us. In selecting our leaders, we transfer strong images and emotions from past relationships onto our relationships with people who have power over us. These images and emotions are both positive and negative, resulting in positive or negative transference. For example, if we had a warm, loving and strong father, who was thoughtful and understanding, we would project these feelings onto male authority figures who remind us of our father. If, on the other hand, we had a strict, uncompromising, punishing father, male authority figures would be seen as demanding and dangerous. In projecting these images both conscious and unconscious factors come into play.

The trouble with transference is that it distorts objectivity. It prevents us from seeing people as they really are. It also impacts our response to the authority figure. For example, in the case of the loving father, where we have such a positive transference, we will respond to the person like the admiring daughter. As the admiring daughter we will be less discerning of our 'father's' behavior and we will become the 'obedient little girl' again. The authority figure in turn will take on the role of father figure (known as counter-transference) and treat us as the adoring, compliant daughter. This dynamic, claims Maccoby, is the reason why we so often get the leaders we want (the perception of a strong, loving father) and not the leaders we need – someone who makes wise judgments and decisions (Maccoby, 2007: 93). The result is that everyone is a loser. The people in transference cede their power (or in the case of negative transference withhold it) to someone who is not, according to objective criteria, the best person for the job. They lose their perspective and autonomy, causing them to obey (or dissent) without rational assessment or thoughtful moral reasoning. The organization loses as the authority figure (leader) is neither performing optimally nor called to account appropriately, and those in transference do not wish to challenge the status quo. The authority figure is also in a bind. If he rejects the role of father figure projected onto him, he will be seen as a poor leader and will lose support. He is therefore caught up in the projection. Fear of breaking the transference dynamic holds the system in stasis, ultimately causing a destructive break of some sort.

The role of transference affects most of us, more or less. The tendency to transfer our images and emotions to those in authority plays a key role in how and why we develop the response strategies described in 'Engaging with Authority' above.

PERSONAL EXERCISE

1   What criteria or principles influence your obedience to authority?
2   How easily do you challenge authority and usually on what grounds?
3   When do you expect others to be obedient to your authority?
4   What kinds of transference do you project on authority figures?
5   What kinds of transference have you noticed people project on to you?
6   How do projections on you help or hinder your leadership effectiveness? And how have they helped or hindered you in the past?

MAX WEBER AND AUTHORITY

The great early twentieth-century sociologist Max Weber was particularly interested in the role of authority in human relations and in its creation of bureaucracy. In his classic text, *The Theory of Social and Economic Organization* (1964), Weber classified various types of authority based on the authority's claim to legitimacy. He identified authority as a form of control that commanded either voluntary or involuntary submission. He was also interested in where authority came from: whether authority existed by virtue of the role or office or it was vested in the person, and in both cases what made them legitimate.

Legitimacy

According to Weber, for something or someone to have any claim to authority, it or they require some form of legitimacy; legitimacy being associated with at least one of the following:

- being lawful;
- being in accordance with established or accepted patterns and standards (conforming to accepted tradition);
- being reasonable (logically valid);
- being genuine (the real thing);
- being in some way associated with a hereditary right (the rightful heir).

Legitimacy in no way implies being appropriate, superior or ethical.

Without a legitimate grounding or source any claim to authority is bogus, suspect or trivial. No one wields authoritarian power for any length of time if (sufficient) others do not recognize the validity of the source of that power. Authority depends on the support of others. Like leadership, authority is a relational concept.

Weber identified three main aspects that make authority legitimate: rational belief; tradition; and the existence of special characteristics in a person. Based on these forms of legitimacy, Weber identified what he considered to be three pure types of authority: **rational authority**, **traditional authority**, and **charismatic authority**. All other types of authority, he argued, stem from these three essential forms. In order to understand the differences between the three pure forms of authority and their variations, Weber used four aspects as the basis of his analysis:

- the type of legitimacy claimed;
- the type of obedience required by the authority;
- how obedience to authority is enforced;
- how authority is exercised.

Rational Authority

Rational authority Weber associated with legal authority. He also extended the idea of rational authority to bureaucratic authority, particularly that exercised by corporations. Rational authority is authority associated with a specific office or role to which power is ascribed. (I refer to this as 'formal authority' below.) Rational authority is arrived at by agreement, is expedient and rational, and the scope of the law (or specific rules) sets the sphere of authority.

Rational authority is also bureaucratic authority where bureaucracy is achieved through a hierarchical structure of administrative staff. It is impersonal and rational; there are technical rules or norms; rules are clearly defined; special training is required for one's position in the hierarchy; professional behavior and values are distinct from personal; appointment is made by a free contract (one can leave the hierarchy); performance is rewarded, usually by money. Good examples are the Catholic Church, the Army, and business corporations. Control is exercised on the basis of knowledge. Specialized knowledge is withheld from those lower in the hierarchy.

Traditional Authority

Traditional authority is intrinsic to all social systems. Here tradition (customs and beliefs handed down for posterity) is considered the legitimate world order and defines what is normative. Tradition exacts obedience by arousing primitive fears of penalties for challenging the 'natural law' and being ostracized from the group. The group has absolute claim to authority to uphold tradition. Traditional authority commands loyalty to established values, attitudes and behaviors. Conformity to norms is of the utmost value.

Charismatic Authority

Charisma comes from the Greek word meaning gift of grace. Charismatic authority (defined as informal authority below) is based on the characteristics of the individual person who has exceptional powers or qualities. Here authority is freely given. There is no formal or explicit appointment. The authority given is not part of a rational system, nor is it impersonal. On the contrary, it is highly personal and affective. Legitimacy is based on recognition.

Weber's analysis provides helpful insights into the different claims of different types of authority. Exercising leadership most effectively requires a combination of at least rational and charismatic authority to gain the greatest buy-in and to achieve most effectiveness. One important matter to note is that

Table 5.1 Weber's authority schema

	Rational authority	Traditional authority	Charismatic authority
Legitimacy	Rational agreement	Traditional status	Recognition
Obedience	By agreement	Personal loyalty	Voluntary
Enforcement	Law, rules	Use of censure and psychic coercion	Freely given and withdrawn
Exercise of authority	Control of knowledge	Loyalty to values, attitudes and behaviors	Through personal character

traditional authority is likely to be the one most challenged during the change process. Leaders need to recognize this possibility and demonstrate sensitivity to the fact that traditional authority, because it commands personal loyalty and carries with it all kinds of psychic 'baggage,' presents the greatest source of resistance.

FORMAL AND INFORMAL AUTHORITY

Here we look at authority in a slightly different way from Max Weber, with a special focus on business organizations. We distinguish between two types of authority – role-related and attribute-related, where role-related authority is aligned with Weber's rational and traditional authority, and attribute-related is akin to his charismatic authority.

Formal Authority – Role-related Authority

Role-related authority refers to the formal assignment of authority to a person in a particular institutional role, for example the President, magistrate, or financial controller. Different institutions have different types of authority roles. Institutions designate these different roles in order to achieve their mission and goals most efficiently. Certain types of role define the institution. A chief surgeon will be found in a hospital; a magistrate in the judiciary; a priest in a church; a teacher in a school; and a croupier in a casino. Some roles are common across institutions. For example there is the ubiquitous financial controller, the ever-needed computer help desk, and the head of facilities management. Each role, usually given a formal title such as foreman or plant manager, invests its holder with certain performance obligations as well as certain powers.

Let us look at the range of the performance obligations of those in positions of **formal authority**:

- to establish goals in conformity with the institution's mission and strategic plan;

- to establish and reinforce the rules of engagement between designated parties;

- to set boundaries or limits;

- to define and confirm the roles of others;

- to assign performance obligations to others;

- to establish the system of punishment and rewards for a group, organization or a society;

- to provide protection for subordinates;

- to authorize others to do something;

- to accept or reject new group or organization members;

- to establish the rules or criteria for the acceptance or rejection of a person, project or plan;

- to prescribe the rules and customs of acceptable behavior (set the moral code);

- to enforce laws;

- to judge or evaluate the performance of others.

As we can see, the expanse of tasks assigned to those in authority is wide and pervades every activity of organizational existence. As we have discussed, those in authority are given certain resources (capital, materials, equipment, know-how and people) to help achieve their set tasks. Their power gives them the right to exact and enforce obedience from others in carrying out those tasks.

Now we ask: who confers this authority or formal power on others? The system. Which system? The system that participants have explicitly and implicitly agreed to support as a way of getting important tasks accomplished. Who are the system participants? We are! There is the political system, the social system, the cultural system, the economic system and so on. We are part of these systems and to some degree more or less support the authority relationships that make up those systems. All these systems are part of larger systems (remember systems theory in Chapter 2), and in turn are made up of an infinite number of sub-systems. We recall that all living systems are inherently hierarchical. In our tangible and practical world, which aims to get things done, authority structures hold these systems together.

Since this is essentially a business book, we are interested in the economic system so we continue our authority discussion with respect to business organizations as part of the economic system. One feature of business organizations is their hierarchical (bureaucratic see p. 135 below) nature. Formal authority designation is a power and control mechanism integral to the efficient functioning of hierarchical institutions. A hierarchy is a system in which those in authority are ranked one above the other; the person with the greater authority being higher up in the hierarchy. The higher up one is in the hierarchy, the greater one's performance obligations but also the greater the power one has to command the obedience of others in the system.

Hierarchies are designed to be orderly and efficient through the delegation of power downwards by means of a tiered system of different authority rankings. Specialization of task and performance along with delegation of power are ways that humans have organized themselves since the beginning of recorded history. The notion of authority, obligation and power is deeply etched in our individual and collective consciousness and while it might contribute to efficient performance it also brings a lot of emotional baggage with it, hence our tendency toward transference, and sometimes thoughtless obedience.

Informal Authority – Attribute-related Authority

Attribute-related authority is based on a characteristic quality ascribed to a particular person regardless of his or her official organizational role. This quality could be some special know-how, emotional or technical competence, special experience, connections in high places, or a particular charisma. Here a person is seen as having certain competencies or qualities that are useful and attractive to others. Where the organization has not formally recognized these attributes, peers, indirect subordinates, and even superiors might invest this person with informal, as opposed to formal, authority. People in the organization freely cede their power to this person (invest their personal authority) in return for benefiting from his or her advice, technical skill, network relationships, or proximity to his or her aura. The person has no organizationally defined power (formal authority) but benefits from the confidence and authority granted by others in the system.

While those who enjoy **informal authority** may not have the sanction of those in formal authority, they hold a great deal of sway in organizations. Besides the fact that the person in question clearly has an attribute that others admire, an important factor is that the informal authority they have acquired is freely given. This means that those who recognize the informal authority figure willingly obey his or her requests and commands. There is usually a form of positive transference on this individual that makes getting things done a lot easier. Resistance to authority is usually less and the feeling of 'them versus us' diminished.

Formal authority	Informal authority
Part of hierarchical system structure.	Informal part of system.
Authority transmitted by rational agreement.	Authority transmitted by recognition.
Authority impersonal – part of role.	Authority highly personal.

Role-related.	Attribute-related.
Power attached to role.	Power given by others, can vary.
Involuntary submission by subordinates.	Voluntary submission by anyone.
Rules and norms clearly defined.	No formal rules and norms.
Seen as appointed from above.	Seen as appointed from below.
Obedience enforced.	Obedience voluntarily given.

Exercising leadership can occur from both a position of formal and informal authority. However, exercising leadership from a position of formal authority has different challenges from those of informal authority. It is important to take these different challenges into account when trying to mobilize others in the change process.

Challenges facing those leading change from a position of formal authority

- Formal authority should ensure plans are achieved; change requires plans to be changed.

- Formal authority should uphold order; change requires a certain amount of disorder.

- Formal authority should respect precedence (tradition); change requires a break from precedence.

- Formal authority should enforce rules; change requires new rules.

- A high percentage of people resist formal authority, thus increasing resistance to change efforts.

- People are afraid to challenge formal authority, leading to uncommitted obedience.

Challenges facing those leading change from a position of informal authority

- People can withdraw their support without organizational recourse.

- Those in formal authority can undermine the actions of those in informal authority.

- The attraction of the informal authority can change if circumstances change – e.g. a person's technical competence suddenly becomes redundant.

- The informal authority can present a threat to formal authority, thus creating organizational tension.

- The informal authority may have insufficient authority to mobilize a sufficient number of others to change.

Both formal and informal authority roles are needed to make the change process effective. Formal authority helps hold the boundaries and provides a container for the anxiety and stresses around change. Informal authority helps make change part of the 'we are all in it' culture, as power has been freely given or volunteered. Informal authority can also more easily test out change strategies without committing to them until an optimal approach is found. Formal authority has less flexibility in the eyes of others. If it does too much 'testing' it is likely to be criticized for being confused and indecisive. Optimal change processes always include some form of partnering between those in formal and informal authority.

PERSONAL EXERCISE

1 What kinds of authority do you hold – formal or informal or both?
2 In the case of informal authority, what is the source (reason) for your authority (e.g. technical competence)?
3 How effectively do you connect or partner with those who have more formal authority than you do?
4 How effectively do you create strategic relationships with other people who have informal authority?

EXTERNAL AND INTERNAL AUTHORITY

Given the enormous role authority plays in our lives, each one of us is challenged with critical existential questions. Who determines our fate? Are we forced to surrender to indomitable forces? Is all authority for our actions external to us? Do external powers determine the consequences of the way we live? Are we victims of circumstances?

If we consider the results of the Milgram experiments described earlier we note that potentially horrendous acts (shocking people to death) derive from simple obedience to a banal authority, not even a potentially harmful one! Seemingly ordinary and otherwise good people knuckle under to the demands of authority and perform callous and severe actions. Are we solely driven by forces external to us? Is there any authority, particularly moral authority, that we have of our own that transcends external demands? The fact that an authority may have some legitimacy does not mean it is ethical, despite our tendency to consider **obedience** a moral imperative. The values espoused or practised by those in authority might also contradict our own. How do we cope with this tension?

The concept of **locus of control** was introduced by psychologist Julian Rotter in 1966. The locus of control assessment he devised provides an indicator of an individual's sense of control over the environment and external events. The locus of control assessment comprises questions pertaining to one's sense of mastery over one's fate and the role of external causes in influencing the outcome of events. People with a high score on the scale are considered to have a high internal locus of control. They feel relatively in control of their lives and the consequences of their decisions. They attribute their successes and failures to the results of their own actions. Some research findings show that people with a high internal locus of control are inclined to be more proactive, take more risks, and be more energetic and self-confident. 'Internals' are less anxious when harder goals are set and are conform less to authority. They demonstrate the motivation, confidence and energy often considered leadership traits.

By contrast, people with a low score on the scale are considered to have a high external locus of control. They attribute events in their lives to external forces acting on them. They look to factors such as luck, other powerful people, and faith as great influencers in their lives. 'Externals' are less confident in their intelligence and ability. They tend to be more reactive to events and less able to rebound from stressful situations. They rely on others' judgments and conform to authority. Where they are in positions of power, they use more coercive power as they project their sense of insecurity onto others. In general they feel less secure and less in control of their lives.

Several studies have explored the link between leadership and locus of control. Although somewhat limited, the pattern of research results consistently indicates that internals are more likely to emerge as group leaders, and that groups headed by internals perform more successfully than those headed by externals. Clearly there are other considerations that need to be taken into account when considering effective leadership. As people interested in exercising leadership, it is important that we consider our own locus of control. How do we view authority and to what extent do we believe external forces rule our behavior and our lives? Handling group dynamics and the many types of resistance to change, including personal challenges to one's leadership, requires a strong sense of self and a strong sense of internal control otherwise we will be victims blowing with the wind.

CHANGING NATURE OF AUTHORITY IN ORGANIZATIONS

All organizations are to some degree hierarchically arranged. Formal authority roles are established in a hierarchical manner, with the highest authority at the top and less and less authority delegated downward. Managers and supervisors act as controllers of the hierarchy, making the idea of hierarchy manifest in reality. However, hierarchy is not simply a series of structured roles subordinated to other roles. It is also a structure of 'boundaries in the mind' (Hirschhorn, 1997: 116) and has a highly emotional content. There is a picture of hierarchy people carry in their heads that is affected by the feelings of pleasure and pain associated with the earliest hierarchy experienced, namely that of the family system. We often overlook this emotional aspect when we examine hierarchies and treat them simply as rational constructs. The existence of hierarchy itself conjures up authority and obedience issues for the individual, triggering any positive and/or negative transference she or he has with authority, along with safety and reward expectations.

Skill, knowledge and wisdom are supposed to increase as one goes up the hierarchy, along with increased power and safety. Knowledge and information is aggressively guarded the higher up one moves, thereby providing an imaginary safety net from the arbitrariness of authoritarian power experienced by those in the lower echelons. In turn, the hierarchy with its system of authority roles provides safety and containment for those in the middle and lower management roles and for those who have no managerial functions whatsoever. 'The boss' defines the work; sets the pace; prescribes the needed skills; negotiates across functions; decides right from wrong; sets the benchmarks of performance; protects insiders from outsiders; and lays out expectations, rewards and punishments.

Well, we have a new reality! Institutions are being literally turned upside down amidst the turbulence of change. The hierarchy–authority paradigm just outlined is undergoing huge change. With the growth of mind and knowledge work and the rapid changes in technology, work is no longer as set and bounded as before. More options for customers make work more decision intensive. Customer responsiveness requires those decisions to be made at the point of customer contact. Work is far less structured; tasks are not that clearly delineated; decision making is far more interdisciplinary; skills require continuous development; performance benchmarks and expectations have to be established by the worker; and responsibility for moral behavior is devolved downwards. For organizational employees, grasping this changing situation requires a restructuring of the mind.

For most workers the relationship with organizational authority has now changed or is changing. Transference and projections onto authority are becoming less and less effective. People are pressured to take up their own authority to get the work done. Waiting for the boss won't do it. Hierarchy and classical authority no longer exist in bureaucratic form. Predictability and protection behind roles and rules are no longer possible. Workers are experiencing new pressures and new vulnerabilities. They have to work out what is expected of them in a world of rapidly changing arrangements. In order to perform effectively they need to be more psychologically resourceful and more psychologically present. Simply 'doing your job' no longer suffices. There is a new pressure to keep pace, to remain competent, to take risks, and to participate in charting the course. Not only has the world flattened, but hierarchies have flattened. There is no time to wait for long drawn out delegation of authority or handovers. Everything is on the move! Everyone in the organization has to see themselves as a change agent.

This changing reality raises the personal stakes in organizations. Not only are employees less guided and less protected, rules and procedures are less clear and less stable than before. People are expected to find their own authority and to assess what needs to be done. Good judgment, strategic relationships and self-authorization is the new currency for survival. People's response to this changing world of work varies. While bringing out their creative and entrepreneurial skills and inviting more personal commitment and accountability, it also brings up people's fear and anger. Typical reactions include: 'What are the rules of the game now? What is expected of me? How will I know whether I am getting ahead? What are the rules for advancement? I never signed on for this type of work. How am I expected to know what the right thing is to do? I never wanted to be more than a 9-to-5 person. I am expected to take charge but no one tells me what that means.' These sentiments reflect some of people's fear and resentment about losing the **holding environment** provided by the original bureaucratic and hierarchical organization. People now have to rework their authority relations both with others and with themselves. This is not easy to do and requires a different kind of leadership. Systemic Leadership, the main focus of this text, provides an optimal approach for dealing with a rapidly changing environment with ever more new realities and new ground rules for employee engagement.

AUTHORITY, POWER, LEADERSHIP AND GROUP DYNAMICS

To understand organizational behavior requires recognizing that at any point in time the organizational system is dealing simultaneously with three dynamic issues:

1 Power – who has it, who wants it, to whom will it be given, from whom will it be taken away?

2 Authority – who has it, is it legitimate, is it serving the system, is power being used effectively?

3 Leadership – who is exercising leadership, is it from a position of formal or informal authority, who supports the leader, who does not, who wishes to take over leadership?

Power is the common currency of both authority and leadership. To exercise either authority or leadership requires power. The political struggle in organizations always centers on acquiring power; acquiring it to be in charge (make the rules and control others), and/or to lead (initiate and facilitate change). The struggle for power we call competition. People in an organization, any organization, are always engaged in competition. Sometimes competition is exceedingly overt, and sometimes disarmingly covert. Most often both overt and covert processes are occurring simultaneously. Competition can be excessively brutal, and other times more contained. Competition always exists; it is the life force at work in the organization.

We name the power–competition dynamic 'workplace politics.' Many claim to 'hate' the politics they experience in their organizations. They want to have nothing to do with it. They want to work in an organization where it does not exist. Well, they are going to be looking for that organization for a very long time. There will always be competition or workplace politics! The question is not, 'Will it disappear?' but 'Is it healthy competition? Does the internal rivalry for power serve the best interests of the organization? Does the competition keep the organization on its toes and contribute to its adaptive capacity? *Also* most importantly, 'Do the power dynamics in the organization contribute towards facilitating good change?' (as defined in Chapter 1).

Power

Power is an ever-present reality essential to all living things. Without power we die, both biologically and psychologically. We need power to take care of ourselves physically. Also we need power to be able to affirm ourselves in the world and build self-esteem. Power makes us interpersonally significant, i.e. it makes us someone to be considered in the world and by others. Power gives us the capacity to assert ourselves and to make meaning out of life. Power facilitates both self-realization and self-actualization (May, 1972: 20). Power makes us relevant, something we discussed in Chapter 1. Individuals and organizations need to be relevant to survive.

We cannot see or touch power (like electricity) but we can observe its manifestations. Not only do we need power, but we want it. We want it because with it we are able to determine the actions of others in the direction of our own ends.

Different descriptions of the potential of power

- Power is the ability to get what one wants (Parenti, 1978).

- Power is the ability to influence others in ways that further one's own interests (Parenti 1978).

- Power is the ability to get things done (Moss Kanter, 1977).

- Power is the potential ability to influence behavior, to change the course of events, to overcome resistance, to get people to do things they would not otherwise do. Politics and influence are the processes, the actions, the behaviors through which the potential power is utilized and realized (Pfeffer 1994: 30).

- Power is the ability to cause or prevent change (May, 1972).

Power with respect to others is always related in some way to their interests. For example A only has power with respect to B if B wants something A can give him, e.g. affection, safety, a job, freedom, etc. Once B's interests are no longer served by A, A's power is diminished. One way of looking at the source of power is to consider the interest being served (Parenti, 1978: 9). Power relationships can be changed if interests are redefined.

From both authority and leadership perspectives (remember we distinguish between the two roles), understanding the changing nature of the power–interest relationship is important. If due to new realities peoples' interests shift, this might result in the loss of power or influence.

Positional Power

Formal or **positional power** is a temporary entitlement that comes with a job, an appointment, an office, a position. One thing we know: positions are not permanent. They are given or ascribed; they are transient and usually on loan. Positions can be removed, lost, or taken away at any time. Herein lies the shadow side of positional power: those in positional power are invariably drawn into a catch-22. The very condition of having positional power creates the fear of losing it, and losing it is inevitable. The more positional power one has, the more one has to lose. Unsurprisingly this fear of loss leads to the desire for more and more positional power.

Understanding the transitory nature of positional power is critical to finding an empowered professional life. There is no question, we all need some positional power. The secret is learning how to get it, how to hold onto it and how not to disempower ourselves.

Personal Power

The power that is essential to leadership is **personal power**. Personal power comes from the inside, it inheres in our being. Personal power belongs to us. It cannot be taken away. It can only be given away. One way of giving away our personal power is to get caught up in the catch-22 mentioned above. Let us take a closer look at the meaning of personal power.

Personal power is an inner capacity. A 'capacity' describes an ability to receive, hold, absorb, retain, produce, make or create something. It describes the maximum possible amount or the innate potential for development or accomplishment of something. Personal power, therefore, is the capacity to adapt, the capacity to learn, the capacity to cope with uncertainty, the capacity to grow, the capacity to serve, and the capacity to be flexible without abandoning one's self or one's principles. Personal power is the capacity to integrate our inner and outer worlds; the capacity to integrate the past and the future; the capacity to adapt to uncertain circumstances; and the capacity to respond and engage with new realities.

The inner capacity that resides in each one of us has infinite potential. Once we come to know and trust this enormous inner personal potential we become less vulnerable to the lure of ever more positional power, to the divisive power plays that dominate corporate cultures, and to the culture of fear that embraces the world.

Effective leaders have a strong sense of personal power. They know and rely on their inner capacities. They do not depend on positional power for status and influence. Leaders who are addicted to positional power live out their shadow side – something we explore at length in Chapter 7.

AUTHORITY AND NEW REALITIES

A major challenge facing organizations is the willingness and ability of those in authority to relinquish the right to identify and name new realities. In the past it has been the practice of executive or senior management to identify the changes necessary to respond to the external environment. As highlighted in 'Changing Nature of Authority in Organizations', p. 134, this practice is changing. Authority to name, frame and identify new realities must be distributed throughout the organization. Anyone and everyone should be encouraged to participate in identifying the winds of change.

Creating an environment where someone in authority is not in charge of reality may demand a huge culture shift. The burden does not only fall on senior management who may have to give up some of their authority. Many individuals know no other reality than that defined by someone else (low locus of control). In their world this reduces their own risk of failure, reduces accountability for their actions, and allows for a lack of intellectual or psychological engagement. These individuals prefer to have someone tell them how it is and what to do next. Neither a power hungry authority figure who closets information for his own purposes or disengaged employees, reluctant to engage actively in the changing world of the organization, can expect to cling to these behaviors for any length of time. As we discussed in Chapter 1, new realities are always arriving, and arriving faster than ever. All hands are needed on deck! There is no time to wait for the captain to officially declare the reality of the next tidal wave. Everyone on board is expected to be continuously vigilant; to help anticipate it, meet it, and ensure the ship survives 'shipshape.' Lower-level managers need to be empowered to get things done without waiting for official sanction. Initiative and risk taking should be encouraged and rewarded regardless of a person's position in the hierarchy. The earlier new realities are identified, the greater the power and opportunity available to the organization has to respond thoughtfully and to its own optimal advantage.

LEADING WITH OR WITHOUT AUTHORITY

'Is one ever liked for oneself?' Queen Elizabeth I asks (in the film *The Virgin Queen*). 'Or am I only liked for what I can get done or for the favors I can bestow on others? Oh, the royal cloak is hard to shed!'

Positions of authority, though enticing, can be a great burden. One never really knows if loyalty is to the role or the person. Even though people may obey one's commands, one may not have their loyalty or attention.

The position of authority also attracts all kinds of projections and expectations, along with envy and fear. The stakes of authority are high. Meeting performance obligations or expectations can be frustrated by disobedient and dissenting subordinates. Because one has authority, people expect one to understand the problems and have the answers. When one does not know the answers, one is deemed incompetent. When one does have the answers, many won't like them and one is challenged. One is expected to outperform to stay on top and at the same time watch one's back.

Exercising leadership requires authority (either formal or informal) and the power that goes with it to mobilize others. As highlighted in the discussion of formal and informal authority earlier, there are challenges to exercising leadership either with or without authority. Having formal authority might possibly provide more formal resources (e.g. an identified budget and dedicated people) than without authority, but not necessarily so. The quality of people's commitment might be better when leading from a position of informal authority. There are no hard and fast rules – bar this one: whether a person is exercising leadership with or without formal authority, he or she will gain greatly by partnering with other people in positions both of formal authority and of informal authority. Partnering across different authority boundaries will provide far greater support for the change effort; less fear of the potential coercive nature of formal authority; less vulnerability to changing interests; and a spread of the risks associated with change. Exercising leadership as the Lone Ranger is rarely an optimal strategy. Creating a network of support with people with varying sources of power and legitimacy provides a stabilizing effect.

Important authority aspects for exercising leadership

- Be sensitive to coercive aspects of authority.
- Be aware of own response strategies to those in authority and to the response of others.
- Remember obedience can be a double-edged sword.
- Refrain from generating mindless followers.
- Be attentive to appropriate and inappropriate dependency.
- Beware of transference and counter-transference.
- Charismatic authority holds its own dangers.
- The changing nature of organizations devolves authority downwards.
- Strive to develop an internal locus of control.
- Strengthen personal power.
- Use power as a resource not an entitlement.
- Do not inspire fear or dependency or just a winning attitude – focus on learning and adaptation.
- Inspire self-affirmation, excitement, hope.
- Beware the abusive aspects of power.
- Keep one's eye on new realities.
- Above all – exercise leadership with non-attachment to the devotion of others. The goal of leadership is not popularity, respect, fame or appreciation. The goal of exercising leadership is to engage with reality, with what is real, what is true, with what will affect our lives whether we like it or not.

EXECUTIVE SUMMARY

The issue of authority is a complex one. It affects every aspect of people's lives in one way or another. People have a lot of emotion around this issue. Effective leaders have an understanding of the impact of authority on both themselves and others. They know that some form of authority is required to get things done. Using authority wisely is critical to the success of change efforts.

Key considerations regarding the role of authority:

- Authority is a power conferred to achieve something. Power enables the holder to command the obedience of others.

- People have different mental constructs that influence their response strategies to those in positions of authority. It is important to know this about oneself and to be able to read these behaviors in others.

- Authority frightens people into obedience and compliance. Leaders need to understand that compliance does not translate into adaptation or learning.

- Obeying those in authority is frequently referred to as doing one's moral duty. The power of authority implies a moral obligation to others. This is not necessarily a good or healthy phenomenon. Leaders need to understand and not abuse this dynamic.

- Because people have so many emotions around authority, it triggers all kinds of irrational behaviors that entrap both those in authority and others. Sidestepping these behaviors takes self-discipline and insight.

- Max Weber devised a schema for understanding various types of authority and the grounds that give these types legitimacy. It is helpful for leaders to understand the source and legitimacy of their authority.

- Leadership can be exercised from a position of formal or informal authority. Different strategies are required in each case.

- Research results seem to indicate that leaders with an internal locus of control are likely to be more effective than those with an external locus of control.

- The changing nature of organizations has devolved authority and responsibility downwards, requiring members of organizations to become more self-authorizing.

- Organizational life is always taken up with power, leadership and authority issues. The common denominator is power – who has it, why, how are they using it and who will take it away?

- It is important that organizations do not rely on those in positions of authority to define reality for others. Members across the organization should be involved in defining the changing new realities of the system.

KEY CONCEPTS

Charismatic authority
Formal authority
Holding environment
Informal authority

Locus of control
Obedience
Performance obligations
Personal power
Positional power
Rational authority
Traditional authority

CASE STUDY
FLIGHT RISK

Samuel Hardcase, an engineer at Jameson Engineering Inc., willingly broke the law, admitted his guilt, and was willing to accept punishment in order to bring to the public's notice the inadequate attention to public safety.

In December 2004, just at the beginning of the Christmas season, Hardcase planted box cutters, bleach, modeling clay, a ten-inch knife, and matches on three different domestic airliners. Immediately after his action he e-mailed the Transportation Security Administration (TSA), identifying himself and giving exact details of dates and flight numbers. In one of the airliners the items were not discovered until after Hardcase's hearing. In another airliner, the items were discovered after three weeks. In the third airliner, during the third week, a passenger found the ten-inch knife, which had worked its way loose from behind the panel in one of the toilet sections of the plane. The passenger had emerged from the toilet brandishing the weapon out of fear rather than with the intention to use it. Agitated flight attendants overwhelmed him and had him handcuffed to a rear seat of the plane until the end of the flight. Thereafter he was arrested. He was released after explaining his innocence.

Hardcase's misplaced e-mail was eventually found in the TSA's information system. Hardcase's contention that security screening of passengers and planes is inadequate and that the TSA is inefficient and blundering seemed to have been supported.

In the fourth week Hardcase was arrested. He acknowledged his actions, understanding that there would be penalties. In June a judge accepted his guilty plea to a misdemeanor charge of violating security requirements at San Diego airport. Hardcase initially faced one count of carrying a concealed dangerous weapon aboard an airliner, a felony that carries up to one year in prison. A plea deal for two years' probation and a hundred hours of community service was later established.

California Attorney Frank Bell said, 'The government believes that the appropriate resolution of this case is a guilty plea to a misdemeanor rather than a felony because of the defendant's extensive cooperation with federal authorities.' Bell stated that Hardcase's age, clean criminal record and 'motivations for misguided conduct' were factors in the government's decision to reduce the charge against him.

Legal issues aside, many still question Hardcase's behavior. Was he gaming the system at high risk to others, or was he justified in acting out of social responsibility by pointing out flaws in the law? Was he behaving as a responsible citizen?

Questions

1   List the formal and informal authority issues in this case.

2   What was the source of Hardcase's authority? Was it legitimate?

3   How might Hardcase have used his authority differently?

FURTHER READING

Heifetz, Ronald A. *Leadership without Easy Answers*. Cambridge, MA: Belknap Press of Harvard University Press, 1994.

Hirschhorn, Larry. *Reworking Authority: Leading and Following in the Post-Modern Organization*. Cambridge, MA: MIT Press, 1997.

May, Rollo. *Power and Innocence: A Search for the Sources of Violence*. New York: Dell, 1972.

Milgram, Stanley. *Obedience to Authority*. London: Pinter & Martin Classics, 2004.

O'Hagberg, Janet. *Real Power: Stages of Personal Power in Organizations*, Third Edition. Salem, WI: Sheffield, 2003.

Parenti, Michael. *Power and the Powerless*. New York: St Martin's Press, 1978.

Pfeffer, Jeffrey. *Managing with Power: Politics and Influence in Organizations*. Boston, MA: Harvard Business School Press, 1994.

Shapiro, Edward R. and A. Wesley Carr. *Lost in Familiar Places*. New Haven, CT: Yale University Press, 1991.

6 ORGANIZATIONAL BEHAVIOR, GROUP DYNAMICS AND CHANGE

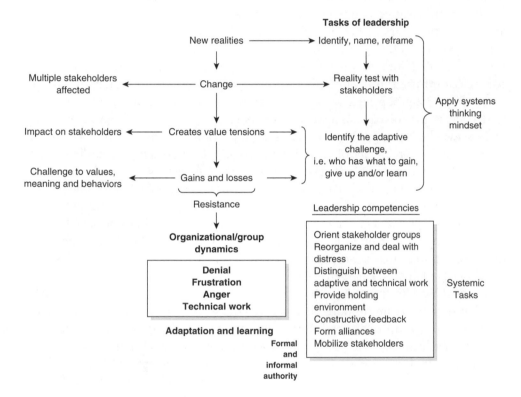

Figure 6.1

INTRODUCTION

Chapter 1 introduced the concept of new realities. New realities signal change, and change is challenging. Change creates anxiety. This chapter explains why organizations exist in continuous tension around a variety of existential anxieties that are ever present. Change, especially radical change, causes organizational anxiety to escalate. Organizational behavior and group dynamics reflect organization members' ability to deal with the distress caused by managing the various anxieties they experience.

We adopt the **group relations** approach to organizational behavior to provide a framework for understanding the emotional undertow of organizations and the tensions that exist. The group relations approach is a psychodynamic approach that focuses on the **conscious and unconscious processes** of group behavior. It includes a systems approach by analyzing the organization and its parts (groups or departments) as whole systems. The emphasis is thus placed on patterns of behavior, interrelationships and roles taken up rather than on the behavior of specific individuals.

The group relations approach emphasizes the importance of containing the anxiety of members in the organization. To be effective in containing anxiety requires some understanding of the sources of that anxiety. The emotions and relational behaviors of members of the organization are treated as crucial sources of information concerning the anxieties inherent in organizational life.

Based on the group relations approach to organizational behavior a key task for leadership is that of **containment**. Leaders need to know how to read the group, understand the basis of their anxieties and find creative methods for their containment. Lack of containment or excessive anxiety in the organization radically impacts its ability to be adaptive and achieve its primary goals. Achieving optimal levels of tension in the organization (some must exist for healthy functioning) is considered one of the most important functions of leadership at this time. The framework we discuss in this chapter provides guiding ideas on how containment might be achieved.

This chapter is not intended to equip the reader with all the skills of an organizational psychologist or psychoanalyst. Although many of the terms and concepts explained clearly emerge from the discipline of psychology, and may seem to some like 'psycho-babble,' they are concepts that have more recently crept into mainstream thinking. If you find yourself shying away from these concepts, in true group relations fashion, you are asked to consider why. What do these terms bring up for you? Like it or not, people genuinely interested in human behavior require a rudimentary understanding of important psychological ideas since human behavior stems largely from the psyche. Systemic Leadership places a great deal of emphasis on reverence for the mystery of the psyche.

This chapter is linked in particular with our discussion on systems and systems thinking in Chapter 2. It may be helpful to refer back to that chapter at various points in our discussion here.

SYSTEMS THINKING

In Chapter 2 we discussed systems thinking and its relationship with new realities. As we recall, systems thinking means viewing the world as composed of one large system or whole as well as a series of infinite smaller systems or wholes. Within these wholes patterns are recognizable and all parts of these systems are in some relationship with one another (Laszlo, 2002). A systems thinking approach is essential to grasp both the impact of new realities on any system as well as to understand people's rational and irrational **defenses** against the new realities and change it implies (Huffington et al., 2004).

An organization is a living system participating in the life and activities of many other systems. As we discussed, it is also the sub-system of many systems: the industry, the economy, the nation and so on. The organization too comprises many sub-systems designed to help achieve the overall organizational task.

In order to understand the behavior of the organization under the pressure of change, systems thinking is best applied at three levels: the organization as a whole; the groups that make up the organization, i.e. each group as a whole; and the individual as a whole. We approach organizational behavior by focusing primarily on group behavior and the 'group-as-a-whole.' Our investigation covers both the conscious and unconscious behaviors of the group with respect to change. While we do not ignore the role of the individual in group behavior, it is not our central focus.

In our attempt to uncover the group dynamics in the system (we can never be sure we have totally uncovered everything), we look at the patterns of behaviors exhibited by the group as well as the existing and changing relationships within the group. These behaviors provide indicators of the group's capacity to adapt and learn. We can use what we learn about group behavior and apply it to the organization as a whole.

Understanding group dynamics is no easy task. Not only are people's behaviors overt and covert, conscious and unconscious; the motivations that underlie the behaviors require interpretation. In our efforts to grasp it all we are sure to experience some ambiguity, uncertainty and confusion. We will never be absolutely sure that we have understood all that is going on and that our interpretations are close to the mark. Even though practice in awareness and interpretation can improve one's sensitivity to organizational dynamics, it is important to acknowledge that there will always be an element of mystery. Surrendering to that mystery keeps our ego in check and allows for a healthy respect for the power of the group.

NEW REALITIES AND THE IMPACT OF CHANGE

In Chapter 1 we discussed how new realities invariably signal the winds of change. Change, for good or ill, presents all kinds of challenges. Enduring change demands adaptation. The adaptive process is always a learning and transformative process. For all kinds of reasons people resist change. They fear the inevitable loss that change always implies, they fear the challenge of learning, especially unlearning or learning something they cannot presently identify with, and they fear having to embrace reality in all its complexities.

Loss and Value Tensions

Change introduces value tensions (see Chapter 1). Value tensions relate to the experience of having to change or reprioritize our values and having to alter familiar behaviors. For example, I am an educator who thrives on classroom and student engagement. Now I have to include online classes in my syllabus. I am resistant. What will this do to the quality of my class? I have to learn more advanced computer skills. My students are better at computers than I am; how will I keep up? How will they get to see what a great teacher I am when part of their experience is via the computer? Online systems denigrate the quality of teaching…and so on. My self-esteem is at stake. My values are challenged and I have to change my behaviors by sitting at the keyboard instead of engaging in the classroom.

The Challenge of Learning

Integrating new realities effectively in our lives requires adaptation. Adaptation refers to the ability to integrate new realities into one's world view and to consciously work with the changes and value tensions these present. Adaptation requires learning. This learning usually has two elements: a cognitive or mindset change followed by a specific skill change. In the example mentioned above, I have to 'change my mind' about the way education will be delivered in the future. Whether I like it or not, the new reality is that online education will become increasingly popular and acceptable. I do not have to like it, but I have to accept it, work with it and include the reality in my approach to teaching. I also have to take on some skills training to become more proficient with the computer. Until now, I have not minded computers. Since I am going to have to use them even more than in the past, I'd better do more than 'not mind them'! Here again I have to 'change my mind' so that I can actually enjoy my computer work and my online teaching. If I wish to remain a good and relevant teacher (remember Chapter 1) I must adapt – not just accept, not comply, not cope; ADAPT!

The Challenge of Reality

The changing world we are currently experiencing is bringing with it 'catastrophic' changes rather than incremental shifts. At this time nothing appears sacred. Everything is subject to change. New technology, new materials, new processes, new organizational relationships, new business models, new products, new services; you name it. New ideas challenge our existing paradigms of thought at an alarming rate.

Under this bombardment of new realities we need to free ourselves from outdated conceptualizations of the world. New reality is chaotic, unpredictable and irreverent. Not only does this of course present excitement – anything is possible – but it also increases our anxiety. Our ability to perceive reality is defined by our psychic limits.

To try to grasp it all leaves most of us with a sense of fear and a feeling of being overwhelmed. Can we survive this turbulence, this chaotic upheaval? Will we be able to keep up? One way of coping is to screen out that which we cannot handle. Another is to simplify our world views into those aspects we 'like' and can deal with and those 'we don't like', which we assign others to deal with. The bottom line remains that we try to 'cherry pick' our grasp of reality to suit our purposes and suppress what is beyond our psychic limits into a submerged tank of subliminal anxiety. Containing this anxiety keeps us close to the edge.

The anxieties just described exist as tension in the **psyche** of the individual. This tension is made manifest in the individual's behavior and, along with the tensions that arise in group life, manifests itself in the collective group behavior. While these tensions will never be totally eradicated, they require some containment to enable the group to do its work effectively. Containment of anxiety is one of the most important functions of both authority and leadership.

Before we delve into the complexities and paradoxes of group life we discuss an important element of human psychological make-up that has significant implications for both the individual and group life.

EMBRACING THE SHADOW

As young children, first our family, then our friends, and then society inculcate in us certain values that set the terms of our self-acceptance. We learn from these influences the 'definition' of 'good,' that which warrants approval, and 'bad,' that which warrants rebuke. Needing love of others and a sense of self-esteem we spend our lives cultivating what is rewarded as 'good' and exclude from our behavior or self-image that which is disapproved of or deemed 'bad.' From early on we are thus taught to split between good and bad.

The well-known psychiatrist Carl Jung developed some profound theories (or insights) with respect to what happens to the rejected part of our humanness – the so-called badness. Because we choose to identify with 'good' or 'light' (communal values and approval) we banish from conscious awareness those parts of us we do not want as part of us. The disowned part of our nature Jung named the **shadow**.

The shadow includes both primitive and undeveloped parts of us that have never been conscious as well as those parts rejected by the ego. The **ego** is the conscious part of the psyche that directly controls thoughts and behavior, and that is most aware of external reality. For self-esteem the ego aligns with the values of the collective, community or group with which it identifies. To satisfy our ego we shove into the dark cavern of our unconscious our hatred, rage, jealousy, greed, competition, lust and shame. We also include those behaviors denounced by our culture – addiction, laziness, aggression and dependency. The shadow also includes our unlived life: those positive qualities we are afraid to realize, and that part of us that from a young age we were discouraged from showing. These aspects might be our creativity; for women it might be their strength, and for men it might be their sensitivity.

Jung explains how this internal splitting between the acceptable and non-acceptable parts of ourselves has dire consequences. Banished from conscious awareness and control, our shadow self gains autonomous and often destructive power. Despite what we might think, whatever lies in our shadow is alive and well and waiting for expression.

Think of a time when you, with little provocation, expressed exceeding outrage and anger. Afterwards you may have said to yourself 'I don't know what made me so mad. I just lost it!' That could have been your shadow side at work, longing to express suppressed intense anger about something else. Suddenly this suppressed anger had an opportunity for expression even though the specific situation did not warrant it, but there it was, activated without your conscious permission. Our shadow side can sabotage us at the most inconvenient times!

> Our psyche is an incomprehensible wonder, an object of abiding perplexity – a feature it shares with all of nature's secrets. (Jung, 1990: 25)

Due to the processes just explained, according to Jung, two psychic systems are formed in the personality, one of which remains unconscious, the shadow, while the other receives active support from the ego and the conscious mind, **the façade personality**. The façade personality or persona is the mask that conceals our real individual nature. It is our visible sign of agreement with the values of the collective, community or group with whom we identify. Jung explains how the ego forgets it possesses aspects that run counter to the persona (those unacceptable parts of ourselves), and imagines itself to be in harmony with the values of the collective. In order to do this the ego both suppresses and represses the shadow side. **Suppression** is the conscious pushing aside of thoughts, feelings, desires and motivations in an attempt to live up to the ethical ideal of the collective. **Repression** occurs when thoughts, feelings, desires, and motivations are withdrawn from the control of consciousness and function independently of it. Repression is the more dangerous of the two as the forces and contents that are repressed change and become regressive, causing more primitive behaviors to be mobilized. These repressed parts of us lead an active underground life of their own, which can, especially during times of stress, result in destructive behaviors at both the individual and collective levels.

Jung also explains that not only does the individual have a shadow side but so does a group. The group has a collective conscious and unconscious (we expand on this later in the chapter); the collective unconscious harbors those feelings the group considers unacceptable and does not feel free to express; for example the group's fear, shame or incompetence. In times of intense change, where anxiety about keeping up and being competent is at a peak, the group shadow can loom large. Exercising leadership effectively requires heightened awareness of the organization's (and particular groups') shadow side. Even if feelings relegated to the shadow remain lurking there, they will influence the adaptive capacity of the group. Part of adaptation is embracing the shadow side. How does one do that? By making time and space for unconscious issues to surface. This is part of the secondary task of the organization (see p. 153) and one of the containing functions of leadership.

A Shadow Tale

An example of the shadow in both the individual and the group might be helpful. I recently held a seminar for executives entitled 'Leading People: Leading Change'. The goal of the seminar was to study the integration of power, leadership and authority and their effects on group dynamics. Twelve people attended, five of whom were women. Of the twelve, eleven people had MBAs and two people with MBAs were company presidents. The age group ranged from thirty-eight to over sixty. The oldest member of the group, a woman, in her early sixties, did not have an MBA or any other executive experience. She had come as a result of her boss's insistence that she be exposed to some leadership training.

In the afternoon of the first day the group of twelve was divided into three groups of four and given an exercise. Until this time the group had been together studying group dynamics and group behavior in 'real time.' The older woman, let us call her Susan, had not uttered one word throughout these sessions. Her sense of anxiety, intimidation and of being overwhelmed in the presence of the other group members was palpable. In turn, the rest of the group ignored her, talking across her, not inviting her opinion and apparently not even noticing her silence and discomfort.

The goal of the afternoon exercise was for group members to practise systems thinking. In order to practise systems thinking each group was given a relationship to explore. One group was asked to consider the relationship between the corporate scandals and suicide bombers. Another group was asked to consider the relationship between the war in Iraq and the tsunami off the coast of Indonesia. Groups were given thirty minutes to discuss whether, how and why relationships between the events they were given to consider existed. At the end of the exercise the small groups reconvened as one large group to discuss their findings. As people drew up their chairs to resume the large group seminar format the oldest male of the group said, 'And so Annabel, if everything is related to everything else, who is the suicide bomber in this room?' I replied, 'Interesting question!' Dead silence ensued. Obviously people were taken aback and uncomfortable with the prospect of a suicide bomber in their midst, if only in metaphorical form. Suddenly, without warning, Susan threw herself forward, leaning far across the table and said: 'Oh well, let me commit suicide and then you can all get on with it!' No one responded to Susan's outburst. Her action and her comment were totally ignored. Other members of the group began openly speculating who the suicide bomber might be, several of them suggesting that the most likely suspect was me. As you can imagine, the afternoon debriefing session was lively!

It is not easy to try to interpret or totally understand the conscious and unconscious dynamics of this vignette. One explanation for Susan's behavior is that her conscious need to escape from the group led to her unconscious offering of herself as a martyr for the group's cause. After all, if someone has to die, why not her? She is the 'old crone' who sees herself and is seen by others as 'worthless' to a world of executive MBAs. In fact she is so 'worthless' that no one has noticed, or cared about her existence. Neither did they comment on her action. No one said, 'Susan, what are you doing?' or, 'What do you mean?' Susan had become invisible to the group. Another possible explanation is that the only way she could give meaning to the group, and to herself, was by dying; by martyring herself for the group's cause. In this way she had more to give than anyone else. A third consideration is that Susan was scapegoated by the group (see p. 161) to alleviate their tensions about having a suicide bomber in their midst.

So who do *you* think was the suicide bomber?

PERSONAL EXERCISE

1 Consider your own ego or façade personality. Which values and attributes keep you most aligned with your most important reference group, e.g. your family, your church community or your organization?
2 Which values and which parts of your personality do you consciously suppress to remain aligned to your important referent group?
3 What important aspects of your personality do you feel get least expression in your life? E.g. your love of music; your spirituality; your longing for solitude...?
4 Which part of your shadow side do you think you bring to the groups with whom you engage? (A tough one.)
5 Have you observed the organization's shadow side at work? When? How? What can you learn from this?

THE TASKS OF ORGANIZATIONS

Every organization is a social system. Leading and managing the organization as a social system entails the execution of two tasks: a primary task and a secondary task.

The **primary task** centers on the organization achieving its main objective or goal. The main objective is usually found in the organization's mission statement and strategic plans. Effectively carrying out the primary task of the organization serves as the ballast that ensures its survival. An essential part of the primary task includes managing the achievement of the organization's goals, the execution of its plans, and providing appropriate direction to employees. Fulfilling the primary task effectively is dependent on the organization keeping abreast of new realities and being adept at change.

The **secondary task** of the organization is to take care of the emotional life of the people in the system. To survive, organizations (like people) need emotional health. Emotional health determines the system's ability to adapt to new realities. If the system is too open to the environment, reacting impetuously to changes and swinging between one strategy and another, it will surely fail. If the system is too closed, too resistant to change, denies or ignores new realities, it too will fail. Healthy adaptation to new realities requires thoughtful assessment, good judgment and an appropriately rapid response. An emotionally healthy system is one where anxiety about new realities and change is contained to the point where sufficient anxiety exists to keep people awake, engaged and on their toes, but there is not so much anxiety that fear overwhelms and overpowers their willingness and ability to learn.

Although we refer to it as the 'secondary task,' the emotional health of the organization reflects its adaptive capacity and determines its ability to be creative, innovative and responsive. The primary task remains the central work of the organization; however, its efficacy relies on how well the secondary task is executed. If excessive attention is paid to the primary task at the expense of the secondary task, the emotional health of the organization will suffer. If the secondary task becomes the primary preoccupation of both management and employees, the primary task will suffer. A careful balance of the two tasks is required. Management's role in achieving this balance lies in its ability to contain both the conscious and unconscious anxieties of the people in the system (Huffington et al., 2004).

Change affects both the primary and the secondary task. Exercising leadership requires paying attention to both simultaneously. Just as leadership requires attention to mission, vision, strategies, etc., it also has to consider the effects of change on the emotional life of the organization. Effective leaders understand that human emotions are not a waste of time; they are an important source of information. Being in tune with the emotional life of the organization requires both a systems mindset and emotional intelligence. The latter we discussed in Chapter 3.

Group dynamics refers to the interaction between people in the organization at the emotional level. Group dynamics can either hinder or help an organization's ability to change. Exercising leadership demands sensitive attention to group dynamics to ensure it does not torpedo execution of the primary task. This is not easy to do, especially in a world of radical change. Mushy leaders lose sight of the primary task and wallow in the emotional life of the organization. Overly tough leaders ignore the emotional life of the organization to the detriment of the organization's long-term survival.

GROUP RELATIONS APPROACH

The field of organizational behavior is *huge*. The multitude of theorists in the field approach understanding organizations from many different perspectives, for example political, social, economic, cultural framing, and psychological, in order to provide a window into the world of people at work. The perspective we are going to take in this text is known as the group relations approach. The reasons for adopting this approach, as opposed to any other, is that in my experience it is the most powerful method for developing provocative insights into organizational dynamics. It also provides creative and challenging ideas for exercising leadership and facilitating the change process.

Group relations is a study of human organizations in the **Tavistock tradition**. The foundations of the Tavistock paradigm of human behavior lie in Wilfred Bion's experimental work with the reactions and responses of members of leaderless groups. The theories Bion developed over years of observation form the groundwork of the group relations field, which has since expanded enormously. After explaining some of the key theories, insights and approaches of group relations in relation to understanding human behavior (it is impossible to cover the whole field in any one text), we apply this theory to leadership and change management.

The group relations approach is essentially psychodynamics based. The **psychodynamics** aspect emphasizes the conscious and unconscious emotional, relational and political processes and dynamics involved in organizing people (French and Vince, 1999: 5). The group relations approach provides a means to explore the **projection**s and defenses of the individual in relation to the group and to look at the impact on the emerging dynamics of a system as a result (ibid.).

This approach can particularly help us to learn about organizational learning and change. It recognizes that the management of change is always accompanied by anxiety, which often results in people's defensiveness and work avoidance. It points us to both the rational and **irrational behaviors** of people and provides insights into people's defenses and what they might be defending against. The group relations approach makes the emotional and unconscious processes created within and between systems visible, thus providing important information on what is going on beneath the surface.

The aim of group relations is organizational transformation by enhanced understanding of the connection between the emotional and relational dynamics of the individual and the organization. Contrary to the emphasis of most learning, which is placed in an individual context, group relations highlights the importance of the collective experience and action as a source of learning. The focus on the collective, the group-as-a-whole, is directed at enhancing our understanding of what is inhibiting healthy organizational development, change, learning, communication and action. Its approach is to look at the institutional aspect of collective experience, resistances and defenses. While humans gain fulfillment by being part of a group, they also experience anxiety. They use their roles to mediate this anxiety and maintain cohesiveness with the group.

Group relations also introduces a new understanding of leadership where the emphasis is on containment rather than control. The question it raises for leadership is how most effectively to contain emotion, especially anxiety, in the organization. If anxiety is insufficiently well managed it can become an organizational way of life that blocks creativity and change. The organization's capacity for learning is a crucial factor in the ability of individuals, teams or organizations to generate lasting change.

Finally the focus of group relations is on the system. (Review Chapter 2 for a reminder of systems thinking.) It provides an approach for looking at the interactions of the individual, the group and the broader systems of which they are part. Although, in our discussions we will use the group as a unit of analysis, we need to cast our learning of what is going on in the group into the broader organizational system context – something we discuss later in the chapter.

GROUP RELATIONS APPROACH

- A study of human behavior.
- Psychodynamic basis where attention is given to both conscious and unconscious processes.
- Explores the projections and defenses of the individual in relation to the group.
- Emotions are treated as important information.
- Emphasis is on organization transformation and learning in the face of change.
- Focus is on collective learning experience.
- Uses systems thinking for analysis.
- Emphasizes leadership role of containment.

GROUP RELATIONS THEORIES IN ACTION

Description of Groups

The definition we will use for the purposes of studying group dynamics in organizations is the following: 'A group exists when two or more people are engaged in an activity or task that requires mutual collaboration.'

A group, like an organization, is a social system characterized by wholeness and interdependence. A group possesses an identity of its own apart from the identities of the individual members (co-actors) of the group. The productive efforts of the group create a synergistic effect, which belongs to the group as a whole. The 'whole' of the group is greater than the sum of its parts.

A group has a culture that establishes norms of behavior; has an identity to assist the group in making meaning out of its existence; has a 'personality' (persona) that reflects the collective conscious and unconscious disposition of its members (e.g. a fun group); and has a shadow side (often the opposite of its revealed persona).

Controlling a group is almost impossible, contrary to what many would like to believe or pretend. If the group is an integrated system, no single component can control the rest. One component, however, can have an impact on the whole system.

Successful group decision making results when individuals are well integrated into the group. Effective integration means a level of reciprocity among group members with respect to self-disclosure, trust and risk taking. A well integrated group is an 'emotionally healthy' one, able to sustain a fine balance between achieving its tasks and maintaining social cohesiveness. Emotional health means the group's anxieties are optimally contained.

What we Learn from Bion

Wilfred Bion's intensive work with small groups provides us with some interesting insights into the unconscious processes of groups.

Bion distinguished between two simultaneous mental planes on which a group operates: one plane is associated with the task or work of the group (termed **work-group** mentality) intent on achieving the primary task. The other mental plane, often unconscious, is the tendency to avoid work on the primary task. He termed this basic assumption group or **basic assumption mentality** (Obholzer and Roberts, 1994: 20). The reciprocal relationship between these two levels of mentality can be seen as the group working with reality and avoiding it.

In work-group mentality the group members are caught up in achieving their set tasks and are interested in their effectiveness. In basic assumption mentality the group is caught up in reducing anxiety and internal conflicts among its members based on certain underlying assumptions. According to Bion much of the irrational behavior we observe in groups stems from this basic assumption mentality. Bion distinguished between three basic assumptions: basic assumption dependency, basic assumption fight–flight and basic assumption pairing.

- A group in basic assumption dependency is totally taken up with taking care of its members. The leader is supposed to take care of the group, protect them, make them feel good and provide solutions to any problems. The pathological dependency on the leader stultifies the group, inhibits growth, development and change.

- A group in basic assumption fight–flight looks to the leader to suggest some action to deal with an identified danger or enemy who should be fled from or fought. Engaging in fight or flight distracts the group from facing reality and doing its real work.

- A group in basic assumption pairing holds a collective and unconscious belief that whatever actual problems currently exist, a future event will somehow solve them. The group has some fantasy that a 'pairing' will occur, resulting in salvation. For example the leader and a person within or external to the organization will in unison devise a saving plan or creation that will deliver the group from present discomfort. In this mode the group acts as if it is oblivious of present challenges and lives in hope for the future.

When the group is under the sway of basic assumption mentality, if loses touch with reality. It ignores the pressures of achieving the primary task and instead dwells on trivial matters as if they are life and death (Gillette and McCollom, 1990). Quick fix solutions are grabbed at and all forms of technical work are used as a distraction from real work. The group tends to close itself to external events and smothers any conflict or challenge. When embroiled in basic assumption mode the group is terrified of change and resists it at all costs. Getting the group to do real work or mobilizing the group to adapt to new realities presents a huge challenge.

Exercising leadership when the group is in basic assumption mode is extremely difficult. First, the group will pressure the leader to collude in its dependencies. If the leader succumbs, he or she is stuck in role while trying to challenge the group to face reality. If he or she resists collusion, the group will seek out another leader who is more likely to satisfy its needs.

Assuming the group manages to sustain a state of basic assumption mentality, on the one hand there will be some relief since its anxiety will be contained and responsibility for solving real-world problems diminished. On the other hand, group members' sense of self around their creativity, competence and potential for achievement will be stifled. The group will be in conflict one way or another!

The task of leadership is identifying and framing new realities and facilitating the process of change. One new reality might be the shift of balance between a group (or the organization's) work-group mentality and basic assumption mentality. Being aware and attentive to the effective balance of the two is part of balancing the primary and secondary tasks of the organization. Achieving this balance is a difficult feat in times of radical change. Sometimes the group will seem to do its damndest just to act out!

Group Survival

We know from our discussions of systems that a primary goal of the system is to ensure its survival. Sub-systems serve the larger system by contributing to its likelihood of survival. Living systems of course aspire to more than just survival: they hope for a happy and prosperous one (see Chapter 2, p. 37).

It comes as no surprise that Bion points out another common basic assumption of groups is people come together for the purpose of preserving the group (Bion, 1961: 63). This unchecked assumption can lead to a group mentality that holds the group must survive for its own sake at all costs. Given that members both love and hate the group, at times they will both fight for its survival and attempt to sabotage its existence. The greater the anxiety of the group, the more it will close ranks and the emphasis on group survival will become paramount regardless of the call of reality. Challenging the group's survival at these times can be foolhardy and result in scapegoating or 'assassination.'

Large Groups

Group member anxiety escalates when the group size exceeds twenty-five people (Huffington et al., 2004: 2). At an unconscious level individuals experience 'terror' at the overwhelming nature and potential of a large group to create complex relationships and to annihilate them. In an attempt to dispel any notion that there are difficulties, threats or conflicts within the group, group members can take flight from intense paranoid anxiety and aggression and withdraw their psychological presence from the group in an attempt to hold onto a sense of self. This is what Turquet calls 'basic assumption oneness,' meaning that the basic operating assumption is that each individual is alone and has to fare alone to survive (Turquet, 1974).

It is rare that organizations have groups of twenty-five people or more. However, it is as well to note that large groups often include many psychologically absentee members. This has enormous implications for the group dynamic. Absentee members indirectly endorse the actions of others without committing to whatever they are doing. The results we often see as mindless mob behavior. From the organizational stance, psychologically absent members will certainly not be adaptive to change, nor will they be engaged in the collective learning of the group.

Splitting

Bion (and others) assert that the central issue for individuals when joining or participating in a group is the tension created by their unconscious fear of being engulfed, overwhelmed or obliterated by the group at one extreme and becoming estranged or separated from the group at the other (Gillette and McCollom, 1990: 56). This tension causes simultaneous love–hate feelings toward the group. These ambivalent feelings, Bion and other psychologists tell us, remind us of the ambivalence we had as infants towards our mothers when we feared total fusion or immersion on the one hand or separation or abandonment on the other. Since having both love and hate feelings at the same time in the same object, our mothers, this caused life-threatening anxiety and as infants we develop coping strategies (defenses). The coping strategies we use to restore psychological equilibrium are known as **splitting** and **projective identification**.

Splitting, as discussed earlier in the section on the shadow, is where we disown parts of the self (or someone else) that are undesirable; for example, 'I am never angry.' Projective identification is where we unconsciously identify with a person or an attitude by projecting those disowned parts of ourselves (or someone else) onto them: 'Boy, is he an angry man!' (Klein, 1952). Organizations engage in splitting when they assign the emotional life of the organization to the Human Resources function, assuming that anything and everything 'emotional' or 'relational' is their problem to solve.

Groups elicit strong, ambivalent feelings from their members. The group is needed yet resented; it provides hope and despair, succour and dread. The ambivalence we have toward groups, therefore, causes us to re-engage our infantile coping strategies – something we term **regression**. The splitting and projective identification we use in group life holds the group together in an unconscious alliance where members allow one another to express split parts of themselves.

Projective Identification

Projective identification is a psychological process whereby we project disowned parts of ourselves or others onto an external object (Klein, 1952). As a child we only wanted a good mother, so the 'bad' parts of her we might have projected onto a 'bad' father, thus creating a good mother/bad father syndrome.

In the case of our own adult projections, we unconsciously identify with the object onto which we have projected parts of our self. This unconscious defense enables us to, among other things, experience vicariously the activity and feelings of the object. For example: 'I am rarely angry because John is angry for both of us' or, 'I need never show my anger as John will do that for me.' At an unconscious level John and I are in cahoots.

Bion and others assert that splitting and projective identification not only help group members deal unconsciously with their ambivalence about the group, but also each group member becomes a receptacle for the projected parts of others in the group (Gillette and McCollom, 1990: 64). An added covert group process is that each group member elicits certain types of projection, resulting in their representing certain roles for the group, e.g. the angry person, the seductress, the clown and so on. Group members are recruited into taking up roles 'given' by the group in the service of group cohesiveness. This entire dynamic creates an unconscious alliance among group members, thereby mediating their anxiety about being part of the group and enabling them to express their full selves through others. The unconscious alliance formed through these combined unconscious processes bonds the group together and reinforces the essentiality of survival of the group at all costs.

In times of change, when anxiety in the organization and within groups is at a peak, group member defense strategies in the form of splitting and projective identification become exaggerated. The danger of excessive defensive behavior of this nature is that individuals are thrust into rigid roles that reduce group effectiveness and can lead to all kinds of scapegoating.

Role Specialization

Another aspect of the splitting/projection dynamic is role specialization. Role specialization occurs when a person takes on the projected material from several or all group members. We can all think of people we know who appear always to play the same role in a group situation. There is the pacifier, the emotional one, the devil's advocate, the clown, the challenger, the cheerleader, the idealist and the pragmatist, to name a few. As individuals, our tendency to collude with these dynamics and the role we typically take on (for which we have a propensity) is known as valency. For example I might have a valency to be a pacifier since that is the role I have played in my family since I was a child. The unconscious collective of the group detects my valency for this role and recruits me to take on this role on behalf of the group. I then become the stereotyped pacifier for the group.

An individual's demographic characteristics (race, age, gender, ethnicity), also affect the roles the group assigns them. Individuals unconsciously collude in taking on a role by agreeing to sacrifice or suppress some part of themselves in order to express or develop others. For example, if there is a challenger in the group I do not have to participate in challenging, I can remain in my role as pacifier. This unconscious give and take provides group solidarity. The result is that no one person is fully who he or she is in the group. The group collectively holds all the parts of all the group members.

The power of roles in a group means that when a person playing a role acts, it is as though everyone has acted, because the part each member has projected onto that person has been given expression (Smith et al., 1987: 71). The differentiated roles assigned to group members serve to manage the anxiety, defend against being engulfed or estranged, provide vitality to the group, facilitate getting work done and simplify emotional life. Understanding group dynamics requires seeing individual roles amidst the constellation of roles in the group. Roles serve meaningful and purposeful functions in groups and protect individuals from anxiety and ambivalence. Through roles members can be used to dramatize conflicts of the collectivity while other members participate vicariously in this dramatization. Effective leadership requires working with this dynamic. For example, if John is always the challenger, and leads the group's resistance to change, it would be ineffective to simply remove or fire John from the group. Exercising leadership in this instance would entail working with the *group's* resistance to change by recognizing the group's *voice* through John's actions.

> ## INDIVIDUALS BEHAVE ON BEHALF OF THE GROUP AS A WHOLE
>
> Group-level analysis assumes that when a co-actor acts, he or she is acting not only on his or her own behalf, but on behalf of the group or parts of the group. Co-actor behavior from a group-level perspective cannot be simply examined by assuming that the motivation and genesis of the co-actor is merely a function of his or her idiosyncrasies. It must be viewed as a synthesis of and interaction with the group's life and mentality. Simply stated, the co-actor is seen as a vehicle through which the group expresses its life. (Gillette and McCollom, 1990: 54)
>

Scapegoating

The origin of **scapegoating** lies in the myths and legends of human history. Scapegoats have been used by tribes and groups to carry their disowned sins or evil spirits and are then killed or banished from existence. The tribe is cleansed through this sacrificial act. Organizations and groups appoint scapegoats all the time. They are selected to represent the group's badness or weakness. This could be the group's fear of failure, sense of incompetence, vulnerability to exposure, anger at authority, guilt about non-performance, or anxiety related to new realities (Colman, 1995).

When group members experience excessive aggression, frustration or fear, they will unconsciously seek someone to take responsibility for their anxiety. A member of the group will be recruited into the scapegoating role to represent the unwanted parts of the group. In some cases the scapegoat role may be given to a small group or sub-unit of the organization. Because the group cannot stand to see itself in the scapegoat he, she or they will be 'killed off' or driven into the wilderness. The group will deny any responsibility for its actions. It will callously isolate the scapegoat(s), wanting to have nothing to do with this disowned part of itself.

Scapegoating is an especially destructive form of role differentiation. Effective leadership recognizes the scapegoating role for what it represents to the group. Regrettably, many authority figures and leaders collude in scapegoating activity in the mistaken belief that they are getting rid of stupid and difficult people. While those who are assigned the scapegoating role may have some valency for the role (i.e. they may be the challenger or the aggressor of the group), killing them off or banishing them does not deal with the group's inherent anxiety. The group may experience temporary relief; however, its anxiety will manifest itself again, possibly 'dressed in other clothing.' One other matter to note is that the scapegoating role is often assigned by the group to someone who is 'different.'

This may be in age or race or gender, or someone who is too competent, or too independent of the group's dynamics.

Regression: A Consequence of Group Life

Group situations evoke feelings of anxiety, loss of control, or a sense of being overwhelmed. This experience of being part of a group triggers emotions that evoke primitive responses such as the types of defense we developed in early childhood. This behavior on our part is termed regression. Regression refers to a reversion to less mature patterns of feeling or behavior reminiscent of earlier stages of mental life. For example splitting and projective identification are defense mechanisms we developed to cope with frightening ambivalences when we were infants. The more we engage unconsciously in this activity, the more psychologists tell us we are engaged in regressive behavior.

Bion argued that regression in groups is significant and associated with the earliest phases of mental life. As he explains: 'The belief that the group exists, as distinct from an aggregate of individuals, is an essential part of this regression, as are also the characteristics with which the supposed group is endowed by the individual' (Bion, 1961: 142).

A consequence of regression is that the power individuals impute to a group then serves to overwhelm them, placing them in even more anxiety (Smith et al., 1987: 127). Another dynamic of regression is that some people create all kinds of fantasies about what the group can do for them and by doing so diminish their own sense of potency and agency, i.e. they cede their personal power to the group (ibid.: 128). A further dynamic is that the individual member suppresses his or her own self in service of the group. Regression has all kinds of repercussions, especially ethical ones.

Regression, psychologists tell us, and we can experience and observe (!), is an intrinsic characteristic of group life. Regression increases, the more the anxiety the group experiences. In order to exercise leadership effectively one must be cognizant of the regressive tendencies of the group (and the organization at large) and work with those behaviors rather than against them. Working with means understanding and empathizing with the group's defenses yet not giving in to them and allowing the group to swallow itself up or implode through dysfunctional behavior.

THE ETHICAL ORIENTATIONS OF GROUPS

We touched on the issue of ethics and morality in our discussions of obedience and authority in Chapter 5. Here we outline briefly some ethical considerations that require our awareness when we encounter and/or participate in group behavior. We delve into ethics and morality in greater detail in Chapter 8, 'Leadership and Ethics.'

- The group will do whatever it needs to do to survive. This includes physical, emotional and/or psychological survival. Many group members will resort to **survival ethics**. Survival ethics holds that my primary ethical responsibility is to ensure my own survival.

- Because group members (and groups themselves) are always engaged in power struggles around competing interests, power-driven issues override ethical ones.

- As group life is emotionally preoccupied with managing anxiety, fear-based behaviors and defenses predominate. An attention to ethical issues is diminished in a fear-based environment.

- Unhealthy role specialization that results in group stereotyping, and especially scapegoating, results in human distress and as such is unethical behavior.

- Due to the group's regressive tendencies, ethical behavior in times of change and stress is likely to be diminished. Effective leadership will require extra special attention to ethics during these times.

In Chapter 8, we explore the nature of ethics and morality and discuss the role of ethics and morality in times of change.

ORGANIZATIONAL CULTURE AND CHANGE

Organizational culture refers to the basic assumptions and beliefs shared by members of an organization (Schein, 1985: 6). These assumptions and beliefs operate consciously and unconsciously and define an organization's view of itself and its environment. They are learned responses to the organization's challenges for survival, both in the external environment and with respect to struggles for internal integration.

An organization's culture usually evolves from the basic beliefs and practices of its founding leaders. Over time, these beliefs and practices are both reinforced and challenged. Based on the organization's experiences in the environment and shaped by various leaders over time, certain beliefs, assumptions and practices become engrained in the culture and dictate the norms and practices of organization members.

Culture can be formal or informal; can tolerate conflict or cannot; emphasizes the individual or the group; encourages or discourages risk taking; has strong or weak leadership; strongly socializes its members to its culture or does not; is a culture of trust or mistrust.

Organizational culture serves as a containment function for group anxieties and expectations. By establishing norms, customs and the 'way we do it around here' behaviors, organizational members have some kind of certainty and reassurance that everything is somehow under control. Even when they resist certain cultural behaviors, culture provides something to hold onto in times of uncertainty and ambiguity. It also provides a sense of community and, when times are frightening, no one wants to be alone.

An organization's openness and receptivity to new realities is radically influenced by its way of seeing things. General Electric (GE), the culture of which has most certainly been shaped by the charismatic Jack Welch, is known for making change one of its critical features. Change is expected and encouraged – in fact demanded – of all employees and business units. The culture dictates levels of institutional redundancy, making it a highly competitive and aggressive environment in which to work. Having taught strategy to several GE executives, I have had first-hand experience of their huge ambition to get ahead and to be sure they are not the next redundancy. Their anxiety about besting change is quite palpable.

Not all organizations adopt such a radical approach to change; some prefer to slow its arrival and temper its impact. Some cultures quite overtly resist change. State-owned organizations provide good examples of institutionalized resistance to change.

Whatever the culture of the organization, clearly it will influence group dynamics. If business is as usual, the culture will operate toward balancing tensions and containing anxiety. Once new realities arrive, however, the containing function of organizational culture may be radically challenged, thus increasing the organization's anxiety even further.

Leaders play a large role in both forming and challenging cultural norms. To exercise leadership effectively it is vital that leaders take the time to understand not only how the culture of an organization operates but also the role it plays in containing anxiety. Culture tends to institutionalize member defenses. Simply dismissing a culture as being ineffective or outmoded is a hasty strategy that might backfire. This was a sobering lesson for Lawrence Summers, the President of Harvard University, who tried to change the university culture to an economic model. Within two years the faculty revolted and within five years he was fired. Even though many of the Harvard trustees supported his ideas, the culture won!

Dismantling organizational defenses that have been institutionalized requires putting other containment functions in place. This is where innovative and creative leadership comes in, that understands the challenges of adaptive work.

Refer to 'Creating a Holding Environment,' p. 170.

THE ANXIETIES, DEFENSES AND TENSIONS OF CHANGE

We have reviewed a group relations framework for analyzing the conscious and unconscious processes of group life. What the framework brings to our attention is that an organization consists of a huge cauldron of human anxiety ever ready to boil over. The flip side of this anxiety is the organization's huge potential for creativity, innovation and adaptation (learning). An organization, therefore, exists and depends on an optimal level of tension. Tension holds it together; excessive tension rips it apart. The energies that create the tension – anxiety and creativity – are the same energies, just channeled differently.

We are reminded that, according to systems theory, systems strive to attain dynamic equilibrium, which is an optimal balance between order and chaos (Chapter 2). Optimum performance requires an optimum tension. New realities often create disequilibrium, which is where learning occurs. The challenge for leaders lies in allowing for a certain amount of disequilibrium without letting excessive tension detract from the organization's learning potential. This is the containment function we refer to in the next section.

While we have dwelt on what might appear to be the debilitating side of organizational life, it is the positive energy of anxiety that sparks the creative, adventurous and risk-taking spirit. Anxiety is therefore not a bad thing. On the contrary, without a healthy level of anxiety, organizational life is dull, passive and, in the extreme, dead! As John Kotter, of the Harvard Business School points out, effective change processes depend on a sense of urgency in the organization. This urgency is created by mobilizing the energies engaged in anxiety productively. To do this well requires some grasp of the source of these anxieties and the defensive behaviors used to alleviate them. It also requires some sense of the intensity of the anxiety being experienced along with strategies for reducing the levels of intensity. Most importantly, neither anxiety nor individuals' and group member's defenses against anxiety can ever be eradicated. Healthy anxiety is essential for both human and organizational functioning, and defenses are needed for psychological survival. If one wants to exercise leadership successfully, one acknowledges and works with these realities.

Brief Review

The group relations framework helps us understand how once an individual becomes a member of a group, he or she becomes caught up in the anxieties inherent in the work of the organization and the characteristic unconscious defenses against those anxieties. In no time he or she succumbs to a habitual way of seeing the world from the group's perspective (the group mind) and fails to question its overt or covert cultural or moral processes (Obholzer and Roberts, 1994: 8).

At an unconscious level the individual group member develops defenses to help him or her deal with ambivalent feelings about being part of a group. He or she engages in splitting, projective identification and succumbs more or less to some form of role specialization.

The group as a whole is engaged in two simultaneous mental modes: one devoted to the work of the organization and one engaged in avoiding work through all kinds of defense mechanisms. Work group behavior is overt and task-oriented, necessitating cooperation and effort. Basic assumption behavior by contrast is covert and regressive in nature.

The group is also at any point in time caught up with the power struggles within the group while mediating both the group and the individual members' feelings and response strategies to authority (Chapter 5). Attitudes toward authority are influenced by the group's anxiety regarding the changing nature of hierarchy and the increasing trend toward distributed leadership. Distributed leadership exists where exercising leadership is expected at all levels of the organization, thereby increasing individual anxiety about having to perform at higher levels of accountability (Huffington et al., 2004: 68).

At both the conscious and unconscious levels, the management of change is the management of anxiety and of resistance arising from that anxiety (Obholzer and Roberts, 1994). While primitive anxiety in the organization is ever present and all pervasive (a form of existential angst), new realities up the ante! As new realities keep arriving ever faster, bringing with them increasingly radical forms of 'creative destruction,' the organization is challenged to contain its increasing anxieties to levels where it can still be creative, innovative and adaptive. This places a huge strain on the emotional life of the organization and its members and of course on potential leaders.

SUMMARY OF INDIVIDUAL AND GROUP DYNAMICS AND DEFENSES

Individual dynamics	Defense mechanisms
Ego, façade personality	Splitting
Shadow behavior	Suppression, repression
Authority issues	Transference; response strategy
Fear of power and competition	Display of pseudo-innocence
Anxiety of reality	Selective screening
Anxiety of new realities and change	Denial and technical work

Anxiety of failed dependency on organization authority structures.	Passive aggressive behaviors

Group dynamics	**Defense mechanism**
Anxiety re. work, e.g. competence	Basic assumption mentality
Anxiety of being part of a group	Splitting; projective identification and role specialization
Anxiety of group survival	Scapegoating
Anxiety of power struggles and competition between members	Excessive splitting; development of factions and alliances
Anxiety of new realities	Denial and escape into technical work
Anxiety of separation from group	succumbing to group mind

CAPACITY TO ADAPT IS INFLUENCED BY DEFENSES

An individual's mental health and capacity to cope and adapt are determined by the kinds of defenses used. We know the more a person resorts to rather primitive defense processes such as splitting (viewing the world and the people inhabiting it as either all good or all bad), idealization (overestimating others), projection (ascribing to others what one rejects in oneself), and denial, the more problematic his or her adaptive capacity. The adoption of such defenses indicates a tendency to oversimplify attitudinal positions and a need to externalize individual responsibility. (Kets de Vries, 2003: 113)

Group dynamics add even more color to the landscape we have painted so far. While the group is engaged in its various defenses against anxieties it often 'splits' into sub-groups and factions (further explicit evidence of splitting). These sub-alliances serve as strategies that either assist or prevent the group achieving its primary task. Through alliances and factions, group members are helped to contain excessive anxiety by providing overt support and reassurance to one another. These also serve as splitting mechanisms by creating a 'them versus us' dynamic within the larger group. The more factions there are and the greater the intensity of conflict they create in the group, the greater the anxiety in the entire group. The group creates competing factions to enact its basic assumption mentality of fight–flight. If the group cannot get the leader to create an enemy to defend against its will, create its own in its midst. Yet again this behavior is a defense aimed at real work avoidance. Frightening new realities often spark the creation of all manner of factions within the organization. Group 'stuckness,' 'group paralysis,' infighting or other divisive behaviors are appeals for 'attention and help' while at the same time creating work avoidance. Defusing attempts to distract the organization from its real work remains a critical leadership challenge.

Responses to Change

By now we know that change heightens organizational members' anxiety. Different people have different thresholds to the anxiety they can contain before they turn to regressive behaviors. We have all noticed, I am sure, how different people overtly seem to respond to change. There are the sycophants – the proverbial 'Yes – how high shall I jump?' people – and there are the saboteurs, who both consciously and unconsciously do everything they can to sabotage change efforts (Huffington, 1990: 87). Neither of these two types of people exhibit adaptive behavior. There are then those people who fall in between these extremes: some are extremely negative, resist and perpetually challenge the forces of change, while others are more constructive challengers who have the potential for shifting to more adaptive ground. Clearly every organization and every leader wishes all its members would fall into the latter category. Alas, this is a pipe dream. The reality is that there will always be the unthinking grovelers and diehard (literally) resisters. In the world of new realities and change, some will always be lost on the way.

Expanding Group Dynamics to the Organization

Until now our focus has been on group dynamics. How do we take this to the organizational level? Recall the macrocosm–microcosm principle in Chapter 2. This principle holds that the characteristics and force fields that exist in a system (for example, the organization as a whole) are recapitulated in its sub-systems and vice versa. The group dynamics we observe under the microscope at the group level will replicate themselves in some pattern or other at the organizational level.

   At the organizational level we see the larger system made up of sub-systems, notably groups. We can use the images and metaphors and what we have learned about the group and expand these to the organization. For example, groups as systems will behave in similar ways to members within groups. Groups will have anxieties about being part of the larger organization. They will experience the same ambivalences that individual members feel with regard to their groups. Groups will experience anxiety about the organization's work. They will engage in splitting and projective identification (the HR department are the good guys, the accountants are the bad guys), role specialization (the new product development department represent the silent, emotionless nerds), and regression (marketing and sales hate one another and persist in destructive conflicts).

Groups will contribute their shadow to the collective shadow of the organization. Some groups will be the sycophant group and some the saboteurs. Some groups will demonstrate anger, some indifference and others conviviality, just as individual members contribute these behaviors to the group. Whatever we observe at the individual and group level, we can extrapolate one level higher – to the organization as a whole system. If we have sufficient information we can of course do this at the industry level too.

An optimal approach to analyzing organizational dynamics is to shift back and forth between the organization and its groups. By doing this one also gains greater clarity with respect to the critical point of impact of new realities. Remember, systems import both information and emotions from the systems of which they are part. A systems thinking mindset reminds us to look for patterns and interrelationships and to try to understand what we can learn from them. If possible we should refrain from judging or blaming a group or individual in isolation. Systems thinking reminds us that everything must be seen in a systems context. This does not mean of course that irresponsible or unethical people should not be chastised or even fired, as long as we remember that individual activity is rarely (if ever) an isolated event. The individual and the group are always interrelated.

Attention to both the organization and system dynamics should be an ongoing process, a kind of leadership by 'psychically moving around' (as opposed to management by walking around), rather than a sudden, one-off activity when the organization is already in dysfunction. As mentioned in Chapters 1 and 2, to achieve optimal personal and organizational effectiveness, new realities and systems thinking should be a way of life.

CONTAINMENT FUNCTION OF LEADERSHIP

Understanding the true nature of organizational life, including the enormous anxieties it both creates and contains, as well as the increasing pressure to remain relevant and competitive in a radically changing world, raises renewed questions about the nature of leadership. More than ever, effective leaders are going to need more than just emotional intelligence. Given the radical upheaval we are facing and the enormous individual and organizational anxieties being created, leaders are going to have to be in tune with the psychic nature of individual and organizational life. The psyche refers to the soul, spirit and mind. The soul, spirit and mind of the organization are so much more than its physical or emotional functioning. Soul, spirit and mind include the mysteries of human behavior!

THE SOFT STUFF IS THE HARD STUFF!

Sensitivity to soul, spirit and mind only comes with a certain awareness of the pulse of life. Can this awareness be cultivated? Surely. But not in a hurry! A one-year executive MBA course will not do it! Practise in continuous self-reflection, humility, curiosity and a genuine empathy for others provides fertile ground for developing psychic maturity. A 'wise and seeing heart' will have the necessary compassion for the struggles individuals face at work, and the wisdom to know when to back off and contain anxiety and when to push forward to ensure the primary task of the organization is achieved.

New realities never go away. The challenge of organizational (and of course individual) life is how to optimally contain the anxiety of new realities and change, since, well-contained and managed, it can be the prime source of the organization's creativity and learning. Poorly managed it will be the prime source of its demise. A critical task of leadership is thus the containment function. How can leaders provide a holding environment that helps contain members' anxiety so they can most effectively deploy their energies in learning and adapting to change?

Creating a Holding Environment

- Demonstrate empathic acknowledgment of the challenges and losses associated with new realities and the distress this creates.

- Provide time and space for people to express their anxieties and to wrestle with their defenses.

- Pace the work of change; allow for some resistance and anger but do not encourage denial.

- Develop several hypotheses, including competing ones, of what is occurring in the group situation. Think systems! Avoid diagnosing the behavior of individuals and second-guessing their psychological make-up. Explore through conversations with others what the new reality presents to the group as a whole; what its challenge symbolizes; what feelings are emerging through the activity of organizational members; and what service roles are performing on behalf of the group.

- Pay attention to work that is being effectively performed and work that is not getting done. Why is there attention to certain work and not others? What does the work in either case represent to the organization or certain members?

- Recognize that excessive anxiety affects competence. If people are feeling or acting with greater incompetence, investigate the source of their anxiety and try to moderate it.

- Resist getting caught up in basic assumption dependencies by offering creative solutions.

- Encourage learning. Refrain from providing solutions. Rather, generate thoughtful questions. Let others devise the solutions.

- Involve people in ideas. Do not tell them what to do but focus on what needs to be achieved.

- Help people stretch their competencies. Give them room to use their own experience and creativity to find solutions. Minimize criticism of failure or fear of failure.

- Hold people's feet to the fire around the existence of new realities and stay with them in their struggles to adapt. Dropped bombshells followed by absentee leadership is a recipe for disaster.

A last comment on the holding environment: one person does not have to do this work alone. A small group of people who have the trust of organizational members, a sensitivity to group issues, and acknowledged competence in the group's work can provide critical assistance in creating a healthy holding environment. Bear in mind, however: with a group, no matter how small, expect group dynamics!

ORGANIZATIONAL EXERCISE

1   How would you describe the culture of your organization? What institutional defenses against anxiety does it include?
2   What role do you play in your organization/department? How does it serve you and the rest of the group?
3   What member roles stand out in your organization? What hypothesis or interpretation can you make about their existence?
4   Are any departments or people being scapegoated in the organization? If so, what do they represent to the organization/group?
5   What do you see as the greatest anxiety in your organization? How, if at all, is it being contained?

EXECUTIVE SUMMARY

This chapter focuses on the behavioral dynamics within organizations. The many existential anxieties people experience plus the anxiety of being part of an organization affect the organization's creative and adaptive capacities. Effective leaders are aware of the many fears people bring to work and the impact that new realities have on those fears. They realize that human behavior provides important information about what is going on, and paying attention to that information is critical if one wants to effect transformative and meaningful change. Systemic Leaders focus on addressing people's fears and resistance to change through adaptive work.

Key points in the chapter:

- Understanding group dynamics requires systems thinking. Systems thinking focuses on relationships, patterns, values and roles rather than on particular people or events.

- New realities invariably increase the tension within an organization. A critical task of leadership is to keep an optimal tension between creativity and productive anxiety.

- Just as individuals have a shadow, the group exhibits shadow behavior. Being aware of this phenomenon and addressing it appropriately helps address what may appear as dysfunctional behavior.

- Organizational leadership has two essential tasks: the primary task that refers to the organization achieving the goals of its mission, and the secondary task that refers to maintaining the emotional health of the members of the organization.

- The Systemic Leadership approach embraces the group relations approach to understanding organizational dynamics.

- The anxieties that people experience in organizations, plus the added anxieties related to new realities lead to defensive and regressive behaviors. These behaviors need to be understood and managed. The Systemic Leadership approach addresses these behaviors from a systems rather than an individual perspective. This approach alleviates tension and limits blaming and scapegoating.

- Group pressure to conform and support the group's fear for survival negatively impacts the ethical sensibility of group members.

- An organization's culture plays an important role in containing the anxiety of the organization. Effective leaders are sensitive to organizational culture and work with it in the process of change.

- A critical task of leadership is the function of containment. The containment function requires leaders to hold the fears and anxieties of the organization through appreciation and empathy, as well as having strategies for alleviating the distress without detracting from the work of change. Distress-alleviating strategies include humor, allowing for a certain amount of appropriate technical work and working with group fears.

KEY CONCEPTS

Conscious and unconscious processes
Containment
Defenses
Ego, façade personality
Group relations
Irrational behavior
Primary task, secondary task
Projections
Projective identification
Psyche
Psychodynamics
Regression
Repression
Scapegoating
Shadow
Splitting
Suppression, repression
Survival ethics
Tavistock tradition
Work group, basic assumption mentality

CASE STUDY
COMPASS ELECTRICAL

Compass Electrical is a thirty-year-old utility company. It delivers power throughout the county of Kent in England. It buys power from the Grid and then redistributes it through its own power stations, power lines and transformers.

Compass Electrical is structured according to activity. It has a department responsible for line repair and maintenance. It has another department responsible for the maintenance of stations and transformers. A further department is responsible for installing new lines; another one responsible for meters and billing, and another for design. The administrative functions are also structured according to activity: sales, accounting, customer support, and so on.

Over the past years Compass Electrical's performance has been abysmal. In the past year over £1.6m in revenue was not billed due to supposedly faulty meters, or meters not being activated on time. New lines have been installed but not properly connected to existing lines, causing unexpected delays and costs. The repair and maintenance department has union problems and so quality of performance has deteriorated.

The senior management of Compass Electrical has decided that the way the organization is structured is not good for business. They agree to create a new department called Special Projects. This department is supposed to work across departments to assure better interdepartmental performance. Special Projects will be responsible for all new installations and for any significant repair work to existing installations. Special Projects will also carry out *ad hoc* projects for senior management.

You have been appointed the lead engineer as head of Special Projects. You are given no staff. You are it! You are expected to identify the projects that should be managed by your department. You are expected to negotiate resources from within existing departments. You report directly to the Senior Executive Vice-President. He has assured you that if people do not work with you they will have to account to him.

You have been working at Compass Electrical for eighteen months. Most people there are old-timers although there are a few young engineers recently out of graduate school. You are highly experienced and well-educated. Your experience has been gained in a higher tech environment than that of Compass Electrical and you do not find the technical aspects of your job very challenging. You chose to take a position at Compass Electrical as you were promised a fast track to the top. You realize that giving you the Special Projects position is a test of your leadership capabilities.

You have been amazed at Compass Electrical's outdated technology and slow-moving management style. You are not very impressed with the managers you have worked with so far. They do, however, have a lot of experience in dealing with the crises of storms and power outages. It is under extreme pressures that they seem to work best.

Questions:

1 What do you understand to be the culture of Compass Electrical?

2 What group dynamics do you anticipate in response to your new position?

3 How are you going to exercise leadership here?

ORGANIZATIONAL EXERCISE: A FINAL SUMMER!

Dr Lawrence Summers, a former Bill Clinton cabinet member and Secretary of the Treasury, was appointed president of the prestigious Harvard University in 2001. Summers was hired to bring a new vision and discipline to an old and established university. On June 30, 2006, five years later, Summers was forced to quit. In his efforts at creating change and turning Harvard University into a streamlined organization, run more on the lines of a business model, he attracted the ill will and to some extent loathing of many of the senior tenured faculty.

Summers came into office with plans to expand the campus, give new focus to undergraduate education and integrate the university's schools. He saw Harvard's culture as complacent and out of touch with the changing world. He made no attempt to disguise his intention of taking the culture head on. Summers eventually alienated many professors with a personal style that many saw as arrogant and bullying. He was castigated for his poor communication skills and his apparent contempt for those who did not agree with him.

Summer's troubles:

- In the early days of his leadership, he demanded that several tenured professors give an account of the direction of their research and teaching.

- After a group of Harvard faculty signed a petition urging disinvestment from Israel, he warned against the recurring theme of anti-Semitism in their actions.

- At an academic conference on the under-representation of women in the sciences, he speculated about innate differences between men and women and claimed that women might lack an intrinsic aptitude for math and science, which accounted for the differences in test scores between men and women.

- At convocation ceremonies he congratulated Harvard students who served in the ROTC (Reserve Officers' Training Corps), which Harvard had banned since the Vietnam War.

- It was argued that, though Summers did reasonable things, he betrayed Harvard's progressive, liberal ethos.

Summers seemed to be more popular with the students than the faculty. One student claimed he was forced out because he would not bow to the entrenched faculty egos.

Those in favor of Summers's approach said he should keep pushing as it was is good for Harvard to have a strong intellect pushing it. Unfortunately for Summers, his supporters were not strong enough to save him from the 'Ides of March' (March 15), when the faculty voted by a decisive margin a lack of confidence in his leadership. This reflected a wide discontent with a man known for his authoritarian streak and his tendency to call others' questions stupid and to look bored during faculty meetings. He also had a tendency to attack others who disagreed with him.

After a second vote of no confidence by the faculty, Summers was forced to step down.

Questions:

1 What were the new realities facing the Harvard University system when Lawrence Summers was appointed President?

2 Did Summers work with the value tensions being experienced by the system?

3 Describe the distress the system was experiencing and its response.

4 What could Summers have done differently?

FURTHER READING

French, Robert and Russ Vince, eds. *Group Relations, Management, and Organization.* New York: Oxford University Press, 1999.

Huffington, Clare, David Armstrong and William Halton, eds. *Working below the Surface: The Emotional Life of Contemporary Organizations.* London: Karnac, 2004.

Jung, Carl Gustav. *The Undiscovered Self.* Princeton, NJ: Princeton University Press, 1990.

Laszlo, Ervin. *The Systems View of the World.* Cresskill, NJ: Hampton Press, 1996.

Laszlo, Ervin. *Science and the Akashic Field,* Second Edition. Rochester, VT: Inner Traditions, 2007.

Marshak, Robert J. *Covert Processes at Work: Managing the Five Hidden Dimensions of Organizational Change.* San Francisco, CA: Berrett-Koehler, 2006.

Obholzer, Anton and Vega Zagier Roberts, eds. *the unconscious at work.* New York: Brunner-Routledge, 1994.

7 THE SHADOW SIDE OF LEADERSHIP

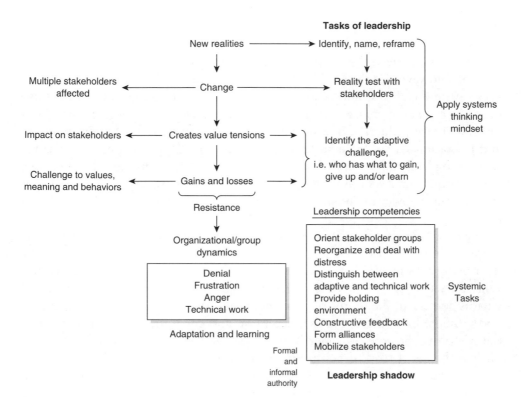

Tasks of leadership

New realities ⟶ Identify, name, reframe ⟩

Multiple stakeholders affected ⟵ Change ⟶ Reality test with stakeholders

Apply systems thinking mindset

Impact on stakeholders ⟵ Creates value tensions ⟶ Identify the adaptive challenge, i.e. who has what to gain, give up and/or learn

Challenge to values, meaning and behaviors ⟵ Gains and losses ⟶

Resistance

Organizational/group dynamics

Denial
Frustration
Anger
Technical work

Adaptation and learning

Formal and informal authority

Leadership competencies

Orient stakeholder groups
Reorganize and deal with distress
Distinguish between adaptive and technical work
Provide holding environment
Constructive feedback
Form alliances
Mobilize stakeholders

Systemic Tasks

Leadership shadow

Figure 7.1

INTRODUCTION

In Chapter 3 we discussed the allure of leadership and our endless fascination with the lives and exploits of leaders. We did not stress at the time the enormous personal challenge of taking on the role of leadership. The role of leadership is an extremely difficult one, especially if one is going to do it well. Difficulties lie not only in the challenge of mobilizing others to face new realities and change, but also in the many temptations that accompany having **power** and influence over others.

Our fascination with and projections on leaders often results in us selecting the wrong people to lead us. We expect superior moral behavior from them and we accord them superhuman powers. We applaud their successes and vilify them when they fail us. We seduce them with our transference, projections and adulation and demean and discard them when we think they have let us down. We lay on them our expectations and our disappointments, our hopes and our fears. How many people truly have the strength, stamina and wisdom to hold this all?

What we frequently fail to acknowledge is that we are as much to blame for their failures as they are. So-called leaders (not a phrase we use much in this text since we do not promote the idea of assigned formal leaders) and so-called followers co-create the successes and the failures of leadership behavior. This does not however let the leader off the hook! Effective leaders who keep their eyes on new realities, and who are intent on holding others to the adaptive process, do not encourage dependency, transference and projections. They understand the seduction of power and they know the extent of their own fears and limitations. They fight to keep a foothold in reality; surround themselves with thoughtful supporters who feel free to challenge them; and do their own work around their shadow side. Effective leaders are ethically good leaders as they use their power to enhance the adaptive capacity of others to deal with real issues.

The shadow side of leadership begins with a false sense of reality. This false sense relates to both personal reality and the reality leaders perceive regarding their own position and that of the organization. Once a false sense of reality prevails, especially where there is a serious disjunction between what is real and what is perceived, the motivation of leaders and the activities they engage in are on the skids! Exploitation, abuse, deception and corruption inevitably result. If the person in the role of leader is an unhealthy narcissist, the results are most likely to be destructive, if not catastrophic.

The **shadow** side of leadership refers not only to misleading others with regard to real issues but also exploiting the use of power for personal gain. Bad or ineffective leaders use people as means to their own ends and often show callousness and lack of caring that defies belief. They use and abuse people at whim; they are dishonest and deceitful; they support cronyism, nepotism and favoritism; and they bully and coerce others into obedience and submission. Sadly, we all know people who exhibit these behaviors.

At this time there is no shortage of fallen heroes. The scandals and corruption, in the financial sector in particular, continues unabated. Intelligent, experienced and well-liked individuals, once given power and opportunity have turned these to their own advantage at a huge cost to society. When are we going to learn that to invest so much trust, to assign so much power and to give so much authority to someone in a so-called leadership position only leads to failure and disappointment? Also, when are leaders going to learn that wallowing in so much trust, having so much power and grasping so much authority can be a fatal moral trap?

LEADERSHIP TRAPS

- **Charisma** does not guarantee determination or perseverance.
- Self-confidence is not ability.
- Enthusiasm does not compensate for competence.
- Good looks do not translate to competence.
- Charm cannot replace perseverance.
- Political connections never count as much as one thinks.
- Emotional intelligence does not equal a 'nice' person.
- Toughness does not equal smartness.

THE SEDUCTION OF LEADERSHIP

As was pointed out in Chapters 5 and 6, the roles of both authority and leadership attract all kinds of transference and projections that are not easy to ward off. These transferences and projections are often highly seductive. Followers frequently set leaders up as heroes and saviors. Under the stresses of managing others, being able to sidestep those kinds of transferences and projections requires enormous self-awareness, self-control, confidence and personal courage. People do not like their transferences and projections to 'miss the mark,' as they see it. Being able to hold one's own in the face of followers' frustrations regarding their failed expectations adds to the complexity of group dynamics.

Another seductive trap for leaders is when followers demonstrate excessive dependency (basic assumption mentality) and encourage the leader to provide solutions and give commands. This behavior readily feeds leaders' egos and love of feeling needed and wanted. Trying to avoid being caught up in this dynamic is not easy either, especially when it is so readily handed on a platter by followers. (Think how Barack Obama feels as 84,000 people wave flags, chant his name and adoringly listen to him outline is presidential plan.) The difficulty of trying to be independent is compounded as followers become angry and act out when their seductive behaviors are ignored or shunned.

Many people long to assume the mantle of leadership as they consider this a step up, a promotion from ordinariness, and an entry card to the club of entitlements. Plato advocated in *The Republic* that people who dearly wanted to become leaders were the very leaders we should *not* have. The reason he gave is that those desiring leadership spend their attention and energies convincing others that they should be leaders instead of focusing those energies on the important issues at hand. Regrettably demagoguery still has most people in its thrall, and we continue to appoint people eager to join the ranks of leaders rather than people who truly help us deal with the new realities that demand change.

Nothing can lead people astray as much as having power. Power is seductive. Because of people's egos and desire to get their own self-interests met they are only too delighted when they find that others will give them power over them. The role of leadership is associated with power. Hundreds of thousands of people rush to be trained as leaders, not only because they want to deal with new realities, or become more adaptive, but also because they want the power associated with being considered a 'leader.' Because people want leaders they are always looking for people who they think fit their leadership profile. Once a suitable person is found, he or she is often catapulted into a position of power, prestige and adulation. Adulation is accompanied by admiration, praise and privilege. It does not take long for many leaders to fall into a place of entitlement…and that is when the problems begin.

THE WARNING SIGNALS OF SHADOW LEADERSHIP

As we have seen often in this text, being a true and effective leader is difficult and immensely challenging. Undoubtedly, taking on a leadership role can provide huge payoffs (and paychecks) in terms of a sense of self-accomplishment and growth in self-esteem, not to mention receiving the accolades and adulation of others. Even more importantly, effective leadership actions genuinely result in greater well-being for others over the longer term. Short-term, quick fix results, so much the measure of the stock markets, do not provide an accurate gage of the true effectiveness of leaders. We discuss this further in Chapters 9 and 10.

Genuine and authentic leaders care more for the benefits they generate for others than for self-aggrandizement. Unfortunately the path of leadership is one filled with all kinds of snares that readily entrap even the most well-intended individual. Good intentions do not guarantee effective leadership. As one very famous person told his disciples, 'You must be wise as serpents and harmless as doves' (Matthew 10: 16). We do not typically think of serpents as wise, but by combining these metaphors, Jesus in his paradigmatic fashion is showing us that wisdom includes a wily element, needed in order to survive the entrapments waiting for the unwary.

In the list below I provide some warning signals that alert us to both our own and others' proclivities for engaging in destructive leadership behaviors. Not all the behaviors people engage in are consciously intended to be destructive. Regrettably, ignorance is no excuse. Self-awareness is the first and primary requirement of anyone wishing to exercise leadership or take on a formal leadership position. This applies to us as much as it does to others! If you have read the chapters so far, this list will come as no surprise.

Warning Signals for Destructive Leadership Behaviors

- Limited or unrealistic self-awareness;
- Lack of attunement to new realities; preference for self-orienting fantasies;
- Fear of change;
- Limited or poor personal adaptive capacity;
- Behaviors driven by limited and unchallenged mental models;
- Lack of critical thinking skills;
- Inability to see the bigger picture; preoccupation with minutiae;
- Poor emotional intelligence;
- Personal authority issues projected onto others;
- Belief that those in authority define reality;
- Belief that those in power are entitled to obedience from others;
- External locus of control; feeling victim to events;
- Poor grasp of how to give and receive feedback and use feedback as an opportunity to learn;
- Inability to hold difficult conversations;
- Leadership style that promotes management by **fear**;
- Tendency to easily get caught up in the transference–counter-transference trap;
- Minimal or no sensitivity to personal shadow issues;
- Poor grasp of group dynamics;
- Tendency to see the world in terms of black and white, or good and evil.

This list is by no means conclusive, nor does it provide insights into why people behave the way they do. We explored some of the causative factors earlier, notably in Chapters 5 and 6. In the rest of this chapter we develop some of these ideas further and highlight how important it is that both 'leaders' and 'followers' grasp the huge number of seductive issues that lead people in leadership roles astray, and the joint responsibility to minimize these dangers.

PERSONAL EXERCISE

- List your expectations of the people you support as 'leaders'.
- How many so-called leaders that you have known have let you down? List the reasons.
- How do you behave toward the people you consider as leaders? List the types of responses you give them.
- List the physical attributes you like in leaders.
- List the personality types you like in leaders.

Question: What can you learn about yourself from this reflection?

THE CHALLENGE OF REALITY

A Glimpse of Reality

We know by now that the major contribution leaders make to organizational life is to help the organization face and embrace new realities. The earlier new realities are detected the greater the opportunity for organizations to turn these to their advantage. Astute leaders are continuously on the lookout for new realities. As we know, identifying new realities takes time, attention and insight. The key issue to bear in mind when we talk about 'new realities' is the word 'realities.' Not fantasy; not hope; not imaginings. Reality!

Reality is a holistic concept. It includes the totality of all things that exist. One cannot 'cherry pick' or 'cut and paste' reality. If one wishes to embrace reality as best one can, one has to be open to all that is true or exists in actuality. We know the impossibility of one person alone perceiving reality in its entirety. At best, several people together can co-conceive some aspects of reality. Leadership is about stimulating this joint apprehension and holding people in the organization to maintaining this as their prime focus. This is really hard work! It is so much easier for leaders to single-handedly decide on a reality they wish to deal with and then focus on those parts they believe they can manage and control. Leaders can appear so masterful and clever when they apparently clean up the problems that are getting in everyone's way. They seem so insightful and decisive when they act so confidently in charting a course ahead at breakneck speed, but are they really confronting reality or just their version of it?

Manipulating or avoiding actual reality is a huge trap for leaders. Clearly they want to be successful, admired, and able to hold on to their power and influence. People reward decisive and seemingly effective problem solvers. They do not give much credence to those who say they need time to clarify the problem and who do not readily have answers. In an attempt to win people's confidence and approval many leaders pounce on problem symptoms rather than root causes and hastily implement technical solutions. These quick fix solutions soon require further 'fixing.' More and more 'fixing' goes on, until the reality of the problem is so far away from the attention of the organization, it takes a dramatic and radical turnaround for it to be found again. By then many leaders have moved on to the next organization, leaving the new incumbent to deal with his or her new reality!

Manipulating Reality

For the reasons stated above, one of the many temptations leaders face is to corrupt reality by manipulating some version of it in their favor. Typical tactics include:

- orienting the organization to a reality of their own making that does not reflect actual reality;

- colluding with the organization to deny the arrival of new realities and pretend business is as usual, i.e. fostering an organizational bunker mentality;

- actively creating a new reality that does not resonate with **reality** in order to shore up political support or popularity;

- not reality testing the perception of new realities with constituents across the organization, thereby upholding the mistaken idea that only one or a few special people have the right to define reality;

- entering into power plays with others as to who gets (or has the power) to define reality;

- deceiving others with regard to the impact of new realities, i.e. pretending it is no big deal and minimizing the adaptation required;

- assuming responsibility for the adaptive work of others by taking on their problems and promising them solutions that are entirely misleading;

- hastily rushing into change initiatives in an attempt to show activity and action without grasping the systemic nature of the problem;

- rushing into technical work before an appropriate amount of the adaptive work has been carried out.

The challenge for leaders is not to succumb to any of these temptations even though they will receive a great deal of support and approval for doing so. Inviting others to participate in leadership and in the reality-testing process can provide critical help in not rushing into a 'quick fix reality.' Consulting with others, especially those who have different points of view, provides important checks and balances in creating a realistic vision for the organization as it moves forward. This leadership approach means of course sharing power, something insecure leaders are afraid to do.

THE ABILITY TO REALITY TEST FACILITATES ADAPTATION

Another factor influencing mental health, adaptation and coping ability is the individual's ability for reality testing. The ability to distinguish inner from outer reality, fact from fantasy, determines the extent to which behavior, judgment, and feelings can be impaired in stressful situations. The capability for reality testing demonstrates how well a person's cognitive processes are integrated or the extent to which that person's thinking processes are limited to pure wish fulfillment. (Kets de Vries, 2003: 113)

The Reality of Leaders

Many metaphors are used for the role of leadership. Leadership is an art; leadership is a dance; leadership is like conducting a symphony – these are some popular examples. The role of leadership indeed includes many of these aspects. Whatever metaphor one prefers, the essential component of any leadership role is that it deals with reality; with *what is*. This *what is* does not only refer to new realities regarding the external environment, competitors, markets, products, government regulations and so on, but also to *what is* regarding what is going on within the leader and within others. In other words, the role of leadership requires working with reality in every sphere and every domain of life. New realities, as we have discussed them, are not limited to the organization's economic environment but extend to every aspect of human interaction within the organization.

Effective and worthwhile leaders, who leave a lasting imprint on the organization by having fostered a healthy environment and established the grounds for a realistic trajectory into the future, are attuned to their own psychic reality. They are self-aware about their world views, their mental models and their perceptual biases. Poor leaders, who are fixated on proving how wonderful they are, who fail to test and refine their world views and mental models, invariably focus on self-aggrandizing technical fixes for any and every organizational problem. One poignant and oft-repeated example is the mega-zillion mergers and acquisitions these erstwhile leaders engage in only to have them fail time after time.

The Reality of the Shadow

From a leader's personal perspective, he or she has to deal firstly and most importantly with his or her *own* reality. He or she needs to be acutely aware of his or her strengths and weaknesses, competencies and propensities for certain types of behaviors, actions and reactions. Most importantly, he or she needs to be aware of the inevitable existence of his or her own shadow side. This shadow side includes unlived hopes and dreams as well as suppressed and repressed angers and disappointments. Shadow issues include those issues deemed not culturally acceptable such as fear, envy and anger. In most organizational cultures people are expected to contain their fears, swallow their envy, and contain their anger. These emotions are treated as if they do not exist. Given this fact it is no surprise that few people know the art of having difficult conversations or dealing with people's fears and anxieties.

People in leadership roles need to be aware of their fears and their angers. They need to know what makes them fearful and their strategies for coping with their fears. They need to face those fears and own them. If they fail to do this the likelihood is that they will either project their fears on to others or take them out on others with mean, irrational, unkind and abusive behaviors. Because leaders have power over other people, their shadow behavior can have devastating and destructive results. Few people challenge leaders, which often means the leader gets away with increasing levels of abuse and escalating levels of aggression. Enron and WorldCom, the two huge organizations involved in massive corporate scandals, were known for the abusive cultures fostered by their leaders.

One further reality that leaders need to get to grips with is that both the individual shadow and the organization's collective shadow can never be totally eliminated or eradicated. A shadow in one form or another will always exist. This does not mean one has to remain victim to the shadow. Two things help deal with shadow issues. The first is to acknowledge that a shadow side always exists and that it is part of the totality of what is. It is the yin and the yang of existence. The second is to try to allow space for unconscious issues to be made conscious. This means leaders should speak to their own and others' fears, ambivalences and angers. Making room for shadow issues to emerge often dissipates their intensity and dilutes their destructive potential. Doing this constructively calls for a great deal of self-assurance and sensitivity. Leaders who do not have self-assurance and sensitivity will either miss or ignore the important information that shadow behavior provides. We explore these leadership requirements further in Chapter 10, 'The Leader in You.'

THE TEMPTATIONS OF LEADERSHIP 1

- Ignoring reality.
- Selectively defining reality.
- Manipulating reality.
- Upholding a reality that is popular rather than true.
- Ignoring his or her own realities.
- Believing that she or he does not have a shadow side.
- Pretending that a personal or collective shadow does not exist.

LEADERS AND NARCISSISM

Recently a growing portion of leadership literature has changed its focus from the glorious side to the shadow and narcissistic side of leadership. Much of the discussion centers on how and why so many people fall for self-absorbed, narcissistic and toxic leaders and support them even in the face of their abusive and clearly self-interested agendas.

One aspect of leadership that has attracted increased attention is that of **narcissism**. Manfred Kets de Vries (and others) points out that narcissists are frequently chosen as leaders because they have the ability to act out the fantasies of their followers. As Kets de Vries writes, 'Their sense of drama, their ability to manipulate others, their knack of establishing quick, superficial relationships serve them well in organizational life' (2003: 23).

Leaders who exhibit excessive narcissistic tendencies tend to be destructive people. Absorbed with their own image, and seeking to create everything as mirrors of themselves, these individuals pay minimal attention to true reality, preferring to identify and create their own. Their insatiable need is for greatness, fame and power. Their main concern is preservation of their own position and importance. They tend to be contemptuous of the needs of others, especially emotional ones. They behave with self-righteous arrogance and inattention. Filled with hubris, they are unable to exchange ideas, especially those that contradict their own. They avoid self-development and self-questioning and have a limited capacity for self-analysis. Their charismatic, yet domineering and abusive behavior fosters submissiveness and passive dependency. Contrary to how they may seem outwardly, narcissists have no sense of self and feel empty inside. To compensate for this state they turn every issue or event into something special about them. Unfortunately the safeguards and checks and balances in organizations frequently fail to pick up the danger signals of the narcissistic personality (Kets de Vries, 2003). We do not have to look far to see many organizations headed by narcissistic personalities.

Jean Lipman-Blumen, in *The Allure of Toxic Leaders: Why We Follow Destructive Bosses and Corrupt Politicians – and How We Can Survive Them*, discusses how bad leaders deliberately exploit our basic human needs for safety, simplicity and certainty. She argues that toxic leaders are plentiful. She describes them as having the effect of poison (2005: 17). They demonstrate lack of integrity; have an insatiable ambition; feed enormous egos; and exude arrogance. Toxic leaders tend to have a poor internal moral code, are greedy, reckless and cowardly, and often show incompetence in the face of problems.

Unfortunately for us, Lipman-Blumen explains, they know how to prey on our psychological needs. They know we have a need for reassuring authority figures to fill our parents' shoes; a need for security and certainty; a need to feel special or chosen; and a need for membership in a human community. They understand our fear of ostracism, isolation and social death and sense our fear of personal powerlessness to challenge them. Toxic leaders play on our fears and paint illusions that feed our needs. Because we have angst and fear life, death and everyday change, we want superhuman and divine leaders who alleviate these fears and provide us with solutions (ibid.: 87). Toxic leaders promise us this elixir, which we cling to desperately as we endure their abusive self-centered behavior. Lipman-Blumen's description of toxic leaders certainly fits the profile of the narcissistic leader.

The Roots of Narcissism

Since **narcissism** reflects a psychological type of behavior we can turn to the psychologists for guidance on understanding this phenomenon. Unsurprisingly, we find the roots of narcissistic behavior in early life. We also learn that we all have some degree of narcissistic tendencies essential for survival. Without it we would not value ourselves any more than anyone else. According to Sigmund Freud narcissistic tendencies are fostered in early infancy when we find ourselves at the center of a loving world, where we are loved and protected. We feel safe from harm and cocooned from the harsh realities of the world. Life is filled with self-contentment and unchallenged repose. This is our imagined experience of paradise.

As we grow older we soon find out that the world is not a loving place and that we are most certainly not at the center of it. We find we are never quite loved enough, we cannot be totally protected, and we come to realize our mortality. Paradise lost! Freud suggests that our psychological escape from this sobering reality is to create or find an **ego ideal**.

The Freudian term 'ego ideal' represents an imagined image of ourselves if we could get rid of all the things that cause us anxiety – our feelings of being unloved and vulnerable and our anxiety about our mortality. In order to defend ourselves against these depressing feelings we attribute our anxiety to a person or a place or a group and direct aggression at that 'bad stuff.' In this way we endeavor to create an image for ourselves of a 'good world' devoid of the bad stuff. We identify the bad stuff in the world by projecting our anger, rage, jealousy, greed, lust, shame, laziness and aggression on the 'other': typically those different to us. In other words we create an 'axis of evil'; and if we could get rid of it, this would give us the good world we desire. People or things that are different are often used as our repository for things that are bad and that we don't want to admit about ourselves. The lazy Irish, the Italian Mafia, the racist South Africans and so on…Since we prefer something in our own image, we tend to identify difference with something bad or to be feared. The creation of the ego ideal is along the lines of the splitting phenomenon we discussed in Chapter 6.

The good world, reminiscent of early childhood when we are loved and pampered, provides us with the possibility of returning to a state of narcissism. In this good world we can do whatever we want to do, the world has us as its reason for being, everyone loves us, and we are free from all anxiety. It is our anxiety that drives us to pursue the ego ideal, which involves rejecting who we really are and how we really feel.

Narcissism and the Organization

Howard Schwartz in his book *Narcissistic Process and Corporate Decay* (1990) develops Freud's ideas on narcissism by illustrating several ways in which the ego ideal may be formed. One way is to create a perfect object such as an organization to function as the ego ideal.

As explained above, the creation of the ego ideal serves as an attempt to return to narcissism. In the case of an organization, the individual's projected idea of the 'perfect organization' unites everyone in a universal 'oneness.' According to the individual this is what the good organization is supposed to do and would do except for the influence of the 'bad stuff' in the world. The devoted employee for whom the perfect organization is the ego ideal is committed to bringing about his or her idea of what the perfect organization should be. He or she assumes that others in the organization share the same interests and obligations to create this idea. This assumed sharing eliminates conflict and along with it all social anxiety. Where the organization represents the ego ideal it mirrors back the participant's love for the perfect image of him or herself. This reminds us of the tale of Narcissus, who falls in love with his own image in a pond, hence the idea of a return to narcissism.

As Schultz explains, individuals who define themselves in terms of the ideal organization put themselves into an interesting relationship with others who have done the same; that is, a relationship of idealized love and a relationship of mutual responsibility where each one upholds the organizational ideal for the others. In this situation the organization's injunctions represent the ethical standard and individuals' relationships with one another are sanctioned by their mutual need to maintain their projected ideal. Conflict, challenge and difference are thus suppressed. The consequence of these processes is that the individual rejects his or her spontaneous self and what he or she stands for in order to alleviate anxiety. In reality that anxiety can never be totally alleviated and so he or she keeps on striving and further denying his or her true self. This self-denial leads to increasing disavowal of the individual's own personal moral agency, resulting in an organization where members feel self-alienated and refuse to see their personal responsibility for their actions. Moral decay soon sets in.

Organizational totalitarianism is obvious in many companies that encourage employee adoration and devotion. Remember Enron, Arthur Andersen and other similar institutions where employees had a grandiose idea about the company and their part in its magnificence – the image they see of themselves. Enron employees saw themselves as 'The smartest guys in the room!' Look at the organizations that promote the wearing of T-shirts, baseball caps and other adornment intended to remind the loyal employee of his or her unquestioning commitment to the organization ideal. Once the idea of the organization takes such a hold of employees' minds, independent thought and responsibility is ceded to those in power who are considered to embody this beautiful image. Loss of objectivity, balance and a foothold on reality is the inevitable sad result.

Narcissism and Organizational Totalitarianism

In his book Schwartz explains where this whole dynamic (creation of the organization as an ego ideal) becomes a real problem. According to him the projection of the **organizational ideal** degenerates into a form of totalitarianism due to the effect of institutionalized power. Organizations have power over participating individuals. This power is entrenched in various layers of bureaucratic hierarchy. The more status one has in the hierarchy, the greater the perceived progress in the return to narcissism. The higher up an individual is on the ladder, the more his or her actions are deemed to represent the organization's actions. Progress in the hierarchy is not only progress in the attainment of the projected ego ideal for the individual but is also considered progress for others as well. For the individual, acquiescing to the perfection of those in power becomes a moral obligation collectively enforced by others who have done so and with whom the individual defines him or herself in community. In turn, the powerful feel self-righteous, believing they are of service to the community – which in a bizarre sense they are!

Here we can understand the danger of narcissistic leaders who both create and reinforce a culture where the organization serves as the ego ideal. Narcissistic personalities care less than other people about what others think of them. They answer mainly to their own internal needs (Maccoby, 2007: 87). According to Freud, narcissists have not internalized any parental models. They tend to lack a superego that provides them with a moral code. Whilst productive narcissists are independent thinkers who want to project their vision on to the world and are able to inspire followers with their passionate conviction, unproductive narcissists tend to be arrogant, grandiose, rarely listen to others, paranoid, exceedingly competitive, ambitious and highly aggressive. The latter are the ones to fear.

The danger of narcissistic leaders is well-documented. Typically these leaders see themselves as the definer of reality, which is biased towards personal self-enhancement (Maccoby, 2007: 25). Subordinates are made to see the world as one that edifies the leader, and in turn deny their own tendencies for self-enhancement. Because both peers and those in authority are caught up in this dynamic, there is extreme pressure from all sides to conform, resulting in personal isolation and self-alienation. Because the perfect ideal is not experienced (it is not possible), excessive splitting occurs along with all kinds of scapegoating. The narcissistic leader enthusiastically initiates and endorses these tactics to keep others distracted from the realization that they are not dealing with reality for the benefit of the organization. The culture in organizations led by narcissistic leaders is usually one of paranoia and suspicion. Everything and everyone is caught up in taking sides. Those on the side of the leader are supported – at least temporarily – while others are denigrated, humiliated and moved out. The leader's self-confidence in her or his dysfunctional regime is interpreted by supporters as competence, while challengers become cynical and disaffected. Many organizations caught up in the multitude of corruption and financial scandals are headed by narcissistic leaders who bully subordinates into silence and submission.

PROFILE OF A DESTRUCTIVE NARCISSIST

- A pathological preoccupation with the self.
- Inclined to nurture grand schemes and harbor illusions that circumstances and enemies block their success.
- Tendency toward grandiosity and distrust.
- Driven to gain power and glory.
- Often charismatic.
- Surround themselves with sychophants.
- Dominate.
- Highly sensitive to criticism.
- Cannot tolerate dissent.
- Crave empathy from others but not empathic themselves.
- Have an intense desire to compete.
- Not interested in personal reflection or discipline.
- Take risks and push through on difficult decisions without personal qualms.

(Maccoby, 2000 : 53–61)

FEAR AND POWER – THE DEADLY MIX

The Pervasiveness of Fear

New realities invariably challenge our fears. Will we survive? What will we gain? What will we lose? Can we adapt? New realities challenge organizational fears in the same way. As we saw in Chapter 6, organizations are fear-filled places. They are the containers of organizational members' tension between creativity and anxiety. New realities heighten this tension.

Fear and anxiety are intrinsic parts of life, with fear of mortality being a big factor and a huge part of organizational life. Fear is energy that can be productively channeled into creative and compassionate behaviors or destructively channeled into fear-based and cruel and abusive behaviors. Fear well channeled can lead the organization to new heights, new creations and new insights; badly channeled it can tear the organization apart and destroy the lives of its employees and other stakeholders.

Because people in positions of authority (formal and informal) have power over others, the manner in which they handle their own fears and those of the organization has a significant impact on organizational well-being. Leading people through the processes of change requires extra sensitivity to the 'fear factor,' both personal and organizational. People who have power and who do not respect and attend to their own fears take out their fear on people in the organization. As a result, decisions become fear-based and relationships are based on managing their fears.

Fear is at the base of most destructive and unethical behaviors. Fear leads to greedy, corrupt, abusive, deceitful, intemperate, callous and inconsistent behavior. The source of hubris is fear, not confidence. Bullies are deeply fearful. Domineering, arrogant, strident, rigid and evil people are fearful. Narcissists fear how empty they feel inside. Fearful people in positions of power are dangerous because they use their power dangerously. During times of heightened change they become even more dangerous as they feel less in control and even more exposed.

Leadership Fears

Every person harbors some level of fear or anxiety, even if it is only fear about death. In reality no one is totally fearless. That is a good thing! Fear has a constructive role to play. It keeps people's egos in check, prevents people from doing hopelessly brash and stupid things, and encourages thoughtfulness and care. Fear also teaches people compassion as they reach out to others who are experiencing things they fear. Fear is uniting in that people can come together around their fears and share them. Destructive leaders might use this sharing of fears for negative purposes so as to set up enemies, but constructive leaders can use this sharing to bring out the positive elements of the human spirit.

It is the shadow side of fear that has destructive elements. From a leadership perspective, consider the many fears leaders might experience:

- fear of failure;
- fear of losing popularity;
- fear of losing power;
- fear of being upstaged;
- fear of not having the answers;
- fear of being blamed;
- fear of being overtaken;
- fear of being outwitted;
- fear of being alone;
- fear of being betrayed;
- fear of being second best;

So, besides existential fear, the role of leadership brings along with it many added fears. Leaders often set themselves up to be perfect, indestructible, talented and self-sufficient. Maintaining this image for themselves as much as for others takes a great deal of energy and invites a further fear of whether this image management is sustainable or not. They question: will they be found out as less perfect, brave or smart than they have everyone believe? What a let-down to everyone and, of course, themselves!

Unmanaged excessive fear invariably creates a destructive force field. When people are consumed with fear they lose their sense of self. Fear erodes confidence, challenges a person's sense of self-worth, and makes people self-protective and defensive. Fear is the root cause of many irrational, hasty, thoughtless and unkind behaviors. Fear is also the root of greed and corruption. The shadow side of leadership is keeping the many potential fears in check so they do not lead to unethical and destructive behaviors.

Exploiting the Fears of Others

In Chapter 6 we saw that the human energy contained within the organization exists in tension between creativity on the one hand and excessive or debilitating anxiety on the other. Leaders and authority figures together help keep this creativity/anxiety tension at a level of productive equilibrium. New realities challenge that equilibrium, invariably increasing levels of anxiety. Effective leaders help contain that anxiety. Ineffective or destructive leaders ignore or exploit that anxiety and promote a fear-based culture.

The neurotic response to fear

In *The Neurotic Organization*, Manfred Kets de Vries and Danny Miller (1984) provide us with descriptions of neurotic leaders who suffer from excessive anxiety and who act out their anxiety in the life of the organization. They explain how organizations are influenced by the fantasies of their top executives mixed in with their beliefs and aspirations. They show how the mental or intrapsychic processes of executives' minds play themselves out in the behavior of the organization, especially under the pressure of change. They claim the mindset of organizational executives provides the source of dysfunctional resistance to change and adaptation (Kets de Vries and Miller, 1984: xi).

The Neurotic Organization focuses on five types of organizational problem syndrome influenced by five neurotic styles of top managers. These five styles are identified as paranoid, compulsive, dramatic, depressive and schizoid. Each of these styles generates a variety of different problems that affect the strategy, structure, decision making, culture and adaptive capacity of the organization. These problems all become magnified when the organization is experiencing radical change (ibid.: 22).

The five styles are following:

1 *Paranoid*: Leaders are suspicious, distrustful, hypersensitive, coldly rational and unemotional. Reality is distorted due to preoccupation with confirmation of suspicions.

2 *Compulsive*: Leaders are obsessed with perfectionism and have a preoccupation with trivial details. Relationships are seen in terms of dominance and submission. Leaders have an inward orientation, are indecisive and fear making mistakes, placing excessive reliance on rules and regulations. They also have difficulties in seeing the big picture.

3 *Dramatic*: Leaders practise incessant drawing of attention to themselves; have a narcissistic preoccupation; alternate between idealization and devaluation of others; are highly exploitive. They tend to be superficial and overreact to minor events and are inclined to be abusive.

4 *Depressive*: Leaders live out feelings of guilt, inadequacy and worthlessness; feeling at the mercy of events (low internal locus of control). They are overly pessimistic; have difficulties in concentration and performance; and show inhibition of action.

5 *Schizoid*: Leaders are detached, withdrawn; show lack of excitement or enthusiasm; are indifferent to praise or criticism; and appear cold and unemotional. Emotional isolation causes frustration of the dependency needs of others, who experience a leadership vacuum.

Leaders and executive managers who suffer from excessive anxiety that is not contained do a great deal of damage to the healthy emotional life of the organization. It does not take long before their neurosis and their destructive behaviors become part of the organizational culture.

A fear-based culture

Fear, especially excessive fear, makes people regress to feeling like powerless children. A child fears those in power and authority. A child fears getting caught; fears punishment; fears not being loved; fears being left out or left behind; and fears not feeling good about him or herself. When adults live out of fear, all these 'child fears' reassert themselves. This fear overwhelms their moral sensibilities. It overrules their moral voice and intimidates their natural moral courage. Fear causes people to forget who they are and what they really stand for. It traps them in the rationalizing corridors of their minds, where they see no light and only the darkness, which they feel compelled to escape.

Where fear has such a primitive and pervasive hold of the psyche, all actions and behaviors reflect fear. Decisions are made from fear-laden alternatives. Problems are solved with fear-based solutions. People are managed with fear-based tactics. The world is seen and responded to through the spectacles of fear.

Fear-based actions and behaviors are always power-seeking. Power-seeking behavior stems from a desperate desire for control. People imagine that when they have control they can manage or get rid of the fear and all the things that make them fearful. Alas, of course this is an illusion.

The fear–power dynamic makes everyone a victim. Those in power are victim to the power plays required to hold on to their power. Those not in power, but anxious to participate in the power hierarchy, are victim to the power plays required to get power. Those without power or not aspiring to have power become victim to those who have or aspire to have power.

A culture of fear where power dynamics reign supreme destroys ethical sensitivity and moral courage. Fear dulls sensitivity. Fear discourages risk taking, discourages imaginative thinking, limits the capacity to observe and learn, and depresses the human spirit. A culture of fear does not promote creativity, learning or adaptation. A culture of fear supports resistance to change. Leaders who promote a culture of fear destroy the healthy spirit of the organization and resort to power for abusive purposes.

SYMPTOMS OF A FEAR-BASED CULTURE

- People are afraid to speak up.
- People always agree with the person in authority.
- People do not trust others in the organization, especially those in authority.
- The system has many bullies who demonstrate aggressive behavior.
- People are full of excuses and blame others.
- Scapegoating occurs frequently.
- There are huge power differentials between those in authority and others.
- Senior executives engage in secretive decision making.
- There are adverse repercussions for speaking up.
- The messenger of bad news gets shot.

The Catch-22 of Positional Power

We discussed authority and **power** in Chapter 5. There we outlined two broad forms of power: positional power that is ascribed to a position and personal power that is internal to a person regardless of his or her formal or informal position. We also highlighted that positional power, since it is ascribed to a position, is transient. It is not personally owned and can be taken away at any time. The catch-22 is that the very condition of having positional power creates the fear of losing it. The more power one has, the more can be lost. The knowledge that positional power can be taken away heightens people's desire for more power in the hope that they will eventually attain a position where they are invulnerable, i.e. their power can never be taken away. Alas, a position of total invulnerability does not exist. If nothing else takes away one's power then death (and maybe taxes) will!

People in leadership roles who are attached to their power, and who fear losing it, are dangerous! Power should be used in the service of something. That something is enhancing individual, group or organizational adaptive capacity. Power simply used to satisfy people's egos and serve their self-interest is important energy squandered irresponsibly.

THE TEMPTATIONS OF LEADERSHIP 2

- Denying personal fears.
- Surrounding oneself with sycophants.
- Surrounding oneself with like-minded people.
- Avoiding or silencing challengers.
- Claiming to have no time to think or reflect.
- Taking the popular course of action.
- Initiating or participating in scapegoating.
- Getting caught in the fear–power dynamic.
- Getting rid of dissenting voices.

JOINT RESPONSIBILITY FOR THE SHADOW OF LEADERSHIP

The Systemic Leadership approach takes the perspective that nothing occurs as a single event or isolated set of activities. No one person is a sole actor or has the ability to control events. Everyone and everything is in relationship to everything else. Linear cause and effect does not exist. Rather, many activities occur at once, and every one event affects everything else.

With a systems mindset we can see that someone who takes on a leadership role is not able single-handedly to maneuver or manipulate others in the group or organization. As much as the leader is playing his or her role, members of the organization are playing theirs.

In Chapters 2 and 6, we pointed out that systems select people to take on certain roles, leadership being one of them. The strengths and weaknesses of the leader are thus a reflection of the group, not vice versa. Strong systems or organizations appoint strong leaders. Dysfunctional systems reflect dysfunctional leaders. If we realize this dynamic, we see there is no point in blaming the leader entirely for her or his failures. Members of the system contribute both consciously and unconsciously to their leader's effectiveness. The system uses the leader as much as the leader may wish to use the system. Unfortunately leaders are often scapegoated by the system in an attempt to eradicate the system's failures. So many books, courses and seminars focus on 'fixing the leader' or grooming the right leader for the job, without taking cognizance of the fact that the system will select the leaders it wants or needs to fulfill certain functions or roles.

The systems approach to leadership just described does not exonerate the person in the role of leader if he or she engages in destructive behavior or supports dysfunctional system behavior. Effective leaders are those who grasp systems theory and who are therefore attuned to group dynamics. They realize the power of the system and make constructive interventions to get the system to face the new realities they are inevitably avoiding. Effective leaders realize they cannot take this task on alone. They seek out strategic partners who help them work with the system dynamic. In this way leadership is not an isolated activity but becomes part of the organic efforts of the system. We discuss the requirements of effective leadership more fully in Chapter 10, 'The Leader in You.'

THE SHADOW SIDE OF MORALITY

In Chapter 8 we discuss leadership and ethics in greater detail. An important matter we delve into is the difference between ethics and morality and why that difference matters. We discuss morality and its emphasis on conformity to customs, norms and rules. Customs, norms and rules are only as good and as effective as the people who made them. The shadow side of leadership includes readily hiding behind rules as a way of doing business. Elaborate codes of conduct in no way guarantee ethical behavior. On the contrary, they can deliberately detract from the creation of an ethical culture and the ethical responsibilities of leadership.

EXECUTIVE SUMMARY

This chapter focuses on the shadow side of leadership and the need for leaders to be aware of the seduction and moral trap of assuming a leadership role. An important aspect of the discussion is that followers create a moral minefield for leaders that is challenging to navigate. Self-awareness, courage and self-confidence are critical requirements for anyone eager both to assume the role of leadership and to avoid these traps.

Key points of this chapter:

- The role of leadership is seductive. People like to admire leaders; project all kinds of fantasies on to them and cede their power to them. This understandably feeds leaders' egos.

- The prime task of leadership is to remain grounded in and focused on reality. Reality can be harsh and uninviting. Pointing out reality does not guarantee popularity with others. In fact, the opposite can result.

- Leaders need to recognize that the shadow side of people's behavior always exists. Working with the shadow rather than denying its existence is essential in order to deal with what is real.

- Narcissistic leaders tend to do a great deal of harm to organizations and the people who work in them. Unfortunately many narcissistic people are charismatic and thus attractive as leaders. Organizations need to be more attentive and wary about being seduced by narcissists.

- The role of leadership invites many added fears and challenges. Leaders fear failure in its many guises. This fear alone can cause them to act irrationally, irresponsibly and unethically.

- Fear and power are a deadly mix! People who are fear-filled and who have power use that power in abusive ways. Leaders who are fear-filled are abusive. Abusive leaders prey on the fears of others and perpetuate a culture of fear. Sadly, many organizations suffer at the hands of abusive leaders and executives.

- Power invariably corrupts to some degree. Organizations need to ensure they have the necessary checks and balances to keep destructive uses of power limited.

- Leaders are mirror images of the people they lead. Corrupt or destructive leaders are called into service by corrupt and destructive systems. Leaders and followers create the corruption–destruction dynamic together. Both parties are responsible for the result.

- A thoughtful and responsible leader is someone who is ethical and who does not hide behind moral codes and rules.

KEY CONCEPTS

Charisma
Ego ideal
Fear

Narcissism
Organization ideal
Power
Reality
Shadow leadership

CASE STUDY
A FINAL SUMMER

1 Based on the information provided in Chapter 6, p. 175, and any further research you might engage in, how would you describe Lawrence Summers as a leader?

2 In what way do you think he was acting out of his dark side – if at all? What shadow behaviors did he reflect?

3 What new reality tensions was he not personally adapting to?

4 Was he solely responsible for his leadership demise? What could the organization and its members have done differently? In what way did the system collude with both his appointment and his downfall?

FURTHER READING

Horney, Karen MD. *Neurosis and Human Growth: The Struggle Towards Self-realization*. New York: W.W. Norton, 1991.

Johnson, Craig E. *Meeting the Ethical Challenges of Leadership*, Second Edition. Thousand Oaks, CA: Sage Publications, 2005.

Kellerman, Barbara. *Bad Leadership*. Boston, MA: Harvard Business School Press, 2004.

Kets de Vries, Manfred F.R. *Leaders, Fools and Imposters*. New York: iUniverse, 2003.

Kets de Vries, Manfred F.R. and Danny Miller. *The Neurotic Organization*. San Francisco, CA: Jossey-Bass, 1984.

Lipman-Blumen, Jean. *The Allure of Toxic Leaders: Why We Follow Destructive Bosses and Corrupt Politicians – and How We Can Survive Them*. Oxford: Oxford University Press, 2005.

Maccoby, Michael. *The Leaders We Need: And What Makes Us Follow*. Boston, MA: Harvard Business School Press, 2007.

Nahavandi, Afsaneh. *The Art and Science of Leadership*, Fifth Edition. Upper Saddle River, NJ: Prentice Hall, 2006.

Ryan, Kathleen D. and Daniel K. Oestreich. *Driving Fear out of the Workplace*. San Francisco, CA: Jossey-Bass, 1998.

Schwartz, Howard S. *Narcissistic Process and Corporate Decay*. New York: New York University Press, 1990.

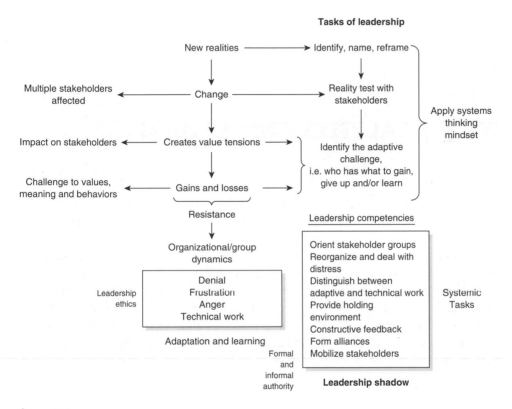

Tasks of leadership

New realities ⟶ Identify, name, reframe

Multiple stakeholders affected ⟵ Change ⟶ Reality test with stakeholders

Impact on stakeholders ⟵ Creates value tensions ⟶

Identify the adaptive challenge, i.e. who has what to gain, give up and/or learn

Challenge to values, meaning and behaviors ⟵ Gains and losses ⟶

Apply systems thinking mindset

Resistance

Organizational/group dynamics

Leadership ethics

Denial
Frustration
Anger
Technical work

Leadership competencies

Orient stakeholder groups
Reorganize and deal with distress
Distinguish between adaptive and technical work
Provide holding environment
Constructive feedback
Form alliances
Mobilize stakeholders

Systemic Tasks

Adaptation and learning

Formal and informal authority

Leadership shadow

Figure 8.1

INTRODUCTION

This chapter focuses on how Systemic Leadership, which is primarily and fundamentally concerned with new realities, is concerned with the **truth**. Wrestling with the truth; trying to frame it; grasp it; respond to it and embrace it are essentially ethical endeavors.

Here we point out that leadership and **ethics** are intertwined. Effective leadership is intrinsically ethical leadership. Effective leadership cannot exist where people act unethically since ethics relate to living a life that faces reality honestly and openly and always strives to be more attuned to the truth.

In this chapter we explore what ethics and **morality** mean and the importance of engaging in the **ethical quest**. We again illustrate how effective leadership includes the ethical quest and accentuates the importance of living a life that exceeds a moral one. We point out how the coercive nature of groups and the pressure to conform to group norms, whether they are in the ethical interests of the group or not, often force group members to collude in unethical behavior or in collusive silence. We highlight the corruptive temptations that exist in organizations and the situations that tend to lead to corruptive behavior. Effective leaders are sensitive to the ethical and moral challenges that organizations face and realize that attuning people's energies to new realities creates a healthy ethical climate.

NEW REALITIES AND ETHICS

Throughout this text I have argued that the most important task of leaders is to keep their eye on new realities and to hold up these new realities to others. I have explained new realities as being trends in the environment that literally reflect *new realities*, i.e. changing circumstances that reflect a new actuality.

New realities can be big events like floods and hurricanes, a change in ruling political parties, stock market crashes or epidemics. They can also be relatively small and less significant events, such as a broken tooth, a puncture, or a lost item of clothing. Big or small; rough or gentle; loud or soft – new realities keep arriving. New realities are 'in the making' all the time. No sooner have they arrived and we find ourselves in the midst of dealing with them, than the next new realities arrive and we have to deal with them. New realities are like waves on the seashore – ceaseless and unrelenting. Further, they always imply some kind of change. Whether we embrace that change or not is another matter. New realities bring the perpetual change we discussed in Chapter 2.

New Realities Affect Everyone

New realities have a ripple effect. Our responses to new realities create new realities for others. Ultimately everyone and everything is affected, hence the systemic nature of new realities. For example, if you are suddenly appointed manager of a new manufacturing plant or distribution center in Bangladesh, that is a new reality for you and for the people in Bangladesh. You respond by traveling more often to Asia. This in turn presents a new reality to your family. Your family responds in various ways and this in turn affects other people. The people in Bangladesh respond to the new reality they are facing by possibly hiring more people. This creates a new reality for them, their families and their community and so on.

New Realities Bring Different Value Tensions

The same new reality has different impacts on different people. If the new reality is soaring energy prices, some people will experience a negative impact, while the energy organizations and their employees will likely experience a positive impact. The responses people have to new realities depends on the gains and losses (value tensions discussed in Chapters 1 and 4) they experience. Their responses to their value tensions in turn create new realities for others who in turn experience different gains and losses. One new reality, therefore, has a multiplicity of effects on the various stakeholders in a system.

New Realities are neither Good nor Bad

New realities in themselves are neither good nor bad. How we experience them or respond to them is what makes them either 'bad' and negative experiences, or 'good' and positive experiences. In and of themselves, new realities simply occur. They are devoid of intrinsic 'goodness' or 'badness'. You might wonder how that is possible. For example, a devastating flood or epidemic we would consider a bad new reality, but that is from our human perspective. From a cosmic perspective, floods, hurricanes or whatever are part of the yin and yang of existence. We can never see the bigger picture. We are limited in our vision to our lives and what directly affects us. What may seem adverse to us may in the larger scheme of things or in the longer term have many positive consequences. If we experience a new reality as having an adverse affect on our lives we call it 'bad.' If there is a positive effect we call it 'good.' Bad and good are thus relative to our perspective.

Reality is the Truth

The most important activity of leadership is to be attuned to new realities. By definition, reality does not go away. We can pretend it has never arrived or that it is inconsequential or has nothing to do with us. That is our choice. Reality however remains. It cannot be wished or ignored away. Reality is actuality. It is the truth. What is true is what is real. When we talk about telling the truth we mean we are telling what really happened or what is real. Leadership is about wrestling with reality, which is the truth.

If we talk about ethical principles such as honesty, truthfulness, integrity or transparency we are referring to ethical ideals that focus on what is real: on reality. If I choose to live an honest life, for example, it means I choose to deal with reality openly, straightforwardly and without deceit. It means I deal with what is real in my life without trying to manipulate it, pretend something else is true, or avoid whatever is unpleasant. I confront reality as openly and directly as I can. I seek the advice of other wise and mature people to help me reality test the reality I believe I am living. Being aligned with reality is critically important to me.

Here is where we can see how leadership and ethics are directly related. If we agree that leadership is first and foremost about facing reality and helping others do that too, we can see that leadership is intrinsically an ethical endeavor. What can be more ethical than dealing with reality directly and honestly and without contrivance, dissemblance or deceit?

Leadership is an Intrinsically Ethical Endeavor

Our discussion points to the fact that leadership which focuses on embracing new realities is intrinsically an ethical endeavor. Leaders who mobilize others to respond to the truth are clearly engaged in ethics. (We explore the meaning of ethics in detail below.) Truly effective leaders are ethical leaders. Effective leaders hold people's attention and focus on what is real and therefore true. Under the Systemic Leadership definition, one cannot be an effective leader and at the same time be an unethical one.

Effective leaders try to establish a coherent truth, live by it, and encourage others to do the same. Effective leaders are engaged in the ethical quest (see p. 208). Many leadership theories do not tie leadership and ethics together. Under those theories people are often considered effective leaders because they have achieved some goal or have influenced their followers in a particular way. Whether they were ethical or not in achieving their goals is sometimes considered an aside.

Measuring effective leadership from the Systemic Leadership perspective is much more difficult than in the case of other leadership theories. It is not just the achievement of goals or the motivation of followers that matter in Systemic Leadership, but how these goals have been achieved and whether or not the achievements advance people's adaptive capacities to cope with ever-changing new realities. In other words, are people getting better at coping with truths no matter how challenging or seemingly aversive? If the answer to this question is 'yes,' this signals the measure of effective leadership. Adaptive capacities take time to evolve. They are not easily defined or measured. Effective leadership, therefore, needs time to prove its worth. This time is likely to extend many years rather than a few. Most leaders today only hold their leadership positions for two to five years before they move on. This short time frame does not provide an appropriate window for measuring leadership effectiveness.

> ## TRUE LEADERSHIP CARES FOR THE GOOD OF THE LED
>
> Plato's view is that true leadership is concerned with the good of the led, not the good of the leader him or herself. He states:
>
> > every kind of rule, in so far as it rules, doesn't seek anything other than what is best for the things it rules and cares for, and this is true both of public and private kinds of rule. (Plato, *The Republic* 345d–e)

The effective exercise of leadership takes time and patience. As we discuss below, ethical behavior, because it relates to the way we live our lives, is a delicate matter that requires sensitivity, thought and guidance. It is not easy to be an ethical person because life's challenges that come with new realities are endless. The ethical path is thus a journey; a quest – we never really arrive. We can only hope we grow in wisdom. Systemic Leadership helps find the path, holds our focus, and encourages the quest.

Before we delve deeper into the ethical quest, let us clarify our understanding of what ethics and morality really mean.

UNTANGLING ETHICS AND MORALITY

Many people, incorrectly in my view, use the terms **ethics** and **morality** interchangeably. One explanation for using these terms synonymously might be that both terms – 'ethics' (Greek, *ethos*) and 'moral' (Latin, *mores*) – derive from the word for 'custom.' Both ethics and morality do in some way relate to 'custom' or 'customary' behavior. How these terms relate to these concepts, however, is very different. This difference is important, as we shall see. Briefly, the distinction between ethics and morality reveals the tension between ethics as principles by which we intend or desire to live, and morals being how we actually live.

Ethics

Let us look at the term ethics. Ethics is a more complex term than morality. Conceptually, ethics both guides and analyzes moral choices. To understand the concept completely requires looking carefully at the different elements subsumed in the term. Ethics refers to all of the things that lead up to what people do, and how they behave.

Ethics is primarily concerned with how we should live. What kinds of attitudes, motivations and behaviors should we exhibit that will result in a 'good,' beneficial or worthwhile life? In asking these questions an important consideration is that we live our lives among others and that our welfare and theirs is inextricably intertwined.

Many theorists offer different definitions of ethics. The one I use here is as follows:

> Ethics is concerned with the principles of right conduct and the systematic endeavor to understand moral concepts and to justify moral principles. Ethics analyzes concepts such as right, wrong, permissible, ought, good and evil in their moral contexts. Ethics seeks to establish principles of right behavior that may serve as action guides for individuals and groups. It investigates which values and virtues are paramount to the worthwhile life or society. (White, 1993: 1–5)

Using this definition of ethics, let us explore what it means.

First, ethics is a cognitive discipline that includes a wide array of ethical principles intended to guide moral choices. Examples of ethical principles include 'you should do your duty,' 'every person should be treated justly,' or 'the ends justify the means.' There are many ethical principles available to us. These have developed over the last 2,500 years or so. New ethical principles evolve in every age in response to the moral dilemmas of the times. Ethics, as a discipline, therefore, is continuously evolving. Contrary to say 200 years ago, we now have business ethics, bioethics and environmental ethics. These 'new ethics' propose new principles aimed at prescribing how we should respond to business, biological and environmental moral dilemmas.

As there are several ethical principles from which we might choose, the second element of ethics is concerned with how we justify our choice of a particular principle. For example on what basis would we justify choosing 'do your duty' as a moral guide as opposed to say 'care for the relationship'? How do we justify the fact that sometimes we care about our duty, sometimes we put relationships first, and sometimes the anticipated consequences drive our decisions? Why do we not use one ethical principle to drive all our moral choices? How can we, or do we, justify these different approaches or different prioritizations of ethical principles?

The third element of ethics is the **moral reasoning** behind our choice of ethical principle. Moral reasoning includes the factors we took into account in selecting our guiding principle. It includes those factors we excluded and our reasons for the exclusion. It includes how we prioritized our concerns. Moral reasoning asks in what way this particular moral dilemma was different from, or the same as, other moral dilemmas. How did we decide what was 'good' or 'right' or 'fair' or 'bad' in this circumstance? How does the thinking here compare with universal (where they exist) ideas about 'good, bad, right, wrong and reasonable'?

A fourth element of ethics is the reflection on why things are the way they are and how value conflicts (concerning honesty, loyalty, compassion) should be understood and mediated. Reflection includes asking questions as to whether known and used ethical principles are relevant or irrelevant to the times in which people are living. Do the principles require alteration or revision? The issue of slavery provides a good example. The idea that people should be treated equally goes back in Western cultures at least 2,500 years. The problem with this principle was that it only applied to 'equal' people: i.e. only equal people were to be treated equally. In other words those not considered 'equal' – women, children and slaves – did not fall within the ambit of this principle. It has taken thousands of years for ethics to catch up with the idea that all people by virtue of their humanity are equal and, therefore, all people without exception should be treated equally. The task of ethics is to continuously reflect on the validity and appropriateness of the principles available, challenge them and propose new ones. Typically societies have looked to their prophets, philosophers, theologians and social critics to perform this ethical function.

Morality

Morality refers to the norms, customs and mores approved by a particular group, society or nation as values and standards perceived to be good and right for that group, society or nation (McCollough, 1991: 7). The moral norms of a group are usually established by those in power (those in power make the rules), or those in the majority. Like it or not, for someone to be accepted by the group (usually) requires conforming to the group's accepted norms.

Morality refers essentially to people's behavior: what it is they actually do. A person's behavior is deemed either moral or immoral depending upon whether it does or does not coincide with moral norms. An example of a moral norm is monogamy. Anyone who chooses to have more than one spouse in a monogamous culture would be considered immoral by the rest of the group or society.

A group can establish its own norms. For example, one could have a Sunday afternoon reading group that bars anyone who attends from swearing. If someone showed up and insisted on swearing, according to our definition he or she would be behaving immorally.

Let us take a more serious example. For several hundred years prior to the civil war in the United States, owning slaves was considered a completely moral endeavor. Once objections arose and social activists began to highlight the injustices of slavery, those challenging existing norms, known as abolitionists, were considered immoral. Once the civil war ended, new norms became the rule, the abolitionists prevailed, and slavery was no longer an acceptable norm. Now slavery is considered highly immoral.

Moral customs and norms are established by people to facilitate the coexistence of a group, society or nation with the intention of enhancing their optimal coexistence. Moral customs also serve as a form of disciplinary control over group members. Moral norms and customs act together with laws to keep people's self-interested behavior in check.

Moral customs and norms are influenced by the prevailing ethical thinking espoused by philosophers, theologians, ethicists and social critics. New customs and norms evolve as times change and people's social consciousness changes. For example one hundred years ago, in many Western societies, women were not allowed to vote. This has changed significantly. At this time, women not only vote, but run and are elected as presidents and prime ministers.

SUMMARY

- Morality is about choices of behavior, given group or societal norms.
- Ethics is about prescribing broad principles that guide behavior; analyzing the choice of principle(s) that people make; looking at the justifications put forward for the choice; evaluating the process of moral reasoning that went into the choice; and reflecting on how effective or appropriate given ethical principles are in light of the times.
- Moral reasoning is the intellectual effort that goes into choosing a guiding ethical principle appropriate for the context and circumstance.

Ethics and morality are clearly different concepts. Ethics is complex, continually questioning and analyzing, and forever evolving. We also note that ethics is about principles, while morality is about rules and codes of conduct intended to guide us in the messy real world of choices. Ethics is the discipline, while morality is the subject under study. Ethics is therefore the critical analysis of morality. Ethics searches for the foundational principles that transcend the relative historical particularities of the situations that moral choices deal with. Ethics is an intellectual engagement at a higher level of abstraction than morality. Morality by contrast is about actual behavior. Human behavior, as we know, is not only intellectual, but emotional, affective and embodied.

By comparing the meaning of the terms ethics and morality in detail it is obvious they cannot really be used interchangeably. These distinctions also bring home to us the tension between the two concepts. Theory and practice test and challenge one another. Good theory seeks to mirror real-world practice.

PERSONAL EXERCISE

- Are you an ethical person? If so, how do you support your answer?
- Are you a moral person? If so, why do you choose to be moral?
- Which ethical principles most guide your behavior?

- When you last faced a moral dilemma, which ethical principle or moral rule guided your choice of action? In hindsight, would you have done anything differently?
- Think of a person you know who exercises leadership. Does he or she demonstrate clear ethical principles in his or her choices?
- When did you last behave immorally? Why?

Now let us see how we use the terms ethics and morality in our discussions. If one claims that someone is unethical, one is stating that this person lacks self-awareness, is unreflective and appears not to have any principled framework that guides his or her actions. For example, CEOs who lie, steal and cheat are unethical. No self-aware, reflective and principled person would behave in this fashion. Further, no validating principle can be found that could rationally justify this kind of behavior in someone appointed to a position of stewardship over those very assets that he or she is lying, stealing and cheating about. So when we are talking about ethics we are referring to the cognitive, intellectual facility to rationalize and justify the standards of behavior by which we hope to, or in actuality do, live.

On the other hand, if one claims that someone has been immoral, one means that person has acted counter to the current folklore, customs, norms and community expectations considered moral behavior. In the case cited above, our lying, stealing and cheating CEO acted immorally since our society does not condone this behavior. When we talk about morality we are talking about actual behavior within a particular time and context. So in our example we have an unethical CEO who has behaved immorally.

Moral Relativism

Moral relativism is another frequently misunderstood concept. In sum, moral relativism refers to the belief that no objective, absolute ethical principles exist that should be applied regardless of place, situation or circumstance.

Let us return to the women as equal to men example. Here we see the issue of 'moral relativism' at work. Should each culture or society be entitled to have its own social norms that decide people's morality, or are there some meta-ethical principles that should override and guide all local norms regardless of situation or context? In this example, is it acceptable that in some cultures women may be horribly oppressed whereas in others they are treated equally with men? Should the ethical principle that all people are equal, regardless of gender, color, race or creed, apply across societies regardless of local moralities? This is the moral relativism question.

The issue of moral relativism and universal norms presents some very pressing questions for organizations that operate globally. They must continually ask themselves whether or not the moral codes of the home country should apply in other countries. For example, should women be treated equally in a country where moral custom insists that women are inferior and most certainly should not be promoted over men? This type of question is a difficult one since it challenges deeply held values and entrenched norms. From a leadership perspective new realities reflect a growing tide of emancipation of women. Exercising leadership would require pacing the adaptation around this new reality, assessing value tensions within various stakeholder groups, and holding people's feet to the fire regarding the inevitability of the growing emancipation of women. So-called 'fundamentalists' reject new realities that challenge traditional values and norms. Working with this resistance provides significant leadership challenges.

A BRAVE HEART

Paraphrasing Pericles' funeral oration, the secret of happiness is freedom and the secret of freedom is a brave heart.

THE ETHICAL QUEST

Now we have discussed ethics and morality, let us consider their relevance to us, especially with leadership and change in mind.

The Ethical Question

A few thousand years ago, arising with our self-awareness that we are more complex and intelligent than animals, we began asking ourselves how we should live. Our growing self-awareness of our capacity for rational choices brought with it a growing responsibility for consciously shaping our lives. Socrates, a Greek philosopher, set the ethical agenda with his immortal statement, 'The unexamined life is not worth living' (Plato, *Apology* 38a) Since that time we have challenged ourselves with questions such as these.

- How should we live?
- What sort of choices result in well-being?
- How should we treat one another?
- What is justice?
- What does a good society look like?
- What kinds of institutions does a good society need?
- What types of leaders do we need to bring out the best in us?

We tend to refer to these types of question as **the ethical question**. The ethical question has been with us a long time and continues to challenge us to this day. The ages come and go, our historical context changes and we continue to ask 'the question.' At its heart, the ethical question is a living question. There is no one absolute answer for all time. The question lives with us. As our circumstances change, we live the question. Some principles may seem immutable – for example, the idea of equality or justice – yet how we live these principles changes. As human beings, living in society, we cannot avoid living the ethical question. We may choose not to openly or publicly articulate our thoughts, concerns or ideas about ethical issues, but we have no choice in living those questions. They are the fabric of a conscious life.

Ethics, as we have discussed, concerns who we are, the kinds of choice we make and how we engage with the world. It refers to how we live our lives; what we value; how we set our priorities; how we make our choices; what tradeoffs we are prepared to tolerate; how we handle our relationships; how we care for others, and how we take care of ourselves. Being aware or 'being awake' as to how we live our lives is our ethical responsibility.

Ethics is a 'scary' topic. As the lived question, it challenges us. The ethical question can act as an awkward mirror, reflecting back to us our motivations, our intentions, and our responses to life's choices. Ethics is a subject that places us under scrutiny. With ethics we are the ones under the microscope, and the laboratory of life is not as well-sealed and controlled as we would like it to be.

Ethics calls us to account. It asks us to reflect on whether or not (a) we have chosen good ethical principles that guide our choices and (b) how well our moral behavior reflects those principles.

Our ethics tell us apart. Our ethics define how we live in the world; who we consort with; who we vote for; how we bring up our children; to whom we give allegiance; how we spend our money. The topic of ethics is pervasive as it has to do with the principles behind the choices we make, and everything in life concerns choices. There is no choice-free day, hour or moment. We are making choices as long as we breathe, are conscious and live engaged in the world. Living the ethics question consciously needs to be one of our premier ethical principles.

Self-awareness and Reflection

From a leadership and change management perspective, the ethical quest concerns being ever present to the challenge of the truth – i.e. wrestling with reality. From a practical perspective this requires several active tasks. First and foremost, ethics are about self-awareness and self-reflection. Self-awareness and constructive self-reflection require humility and openness to one's personal limitations and failings.

Effective leaders make time for self-awareness and reflection. They acknowledge the seductive aspects that accompany the power imputed to them as leaders. They realize that people look to them to provide answers and to alleviate personal responsibility for problems. They understand how others willingly place them on a pedestal and look to the leader to provide ethical guidelines and moral agency. As discussed, many people prefer having someone else tell them what to do, especially a charismatic leader. All of these projections and expectations act as deathly moral traps for leaders. Failing to give the work back to others and assuming they have solutions to other people's adaptive problems is simply hubris and deceit.

Power and Fear

Effective leaders are also aware of the potential to abuse the power vested in them. They understand the **moral power** of authority (remember the Milgram experiments in Chapter 5) and do not exploit it to their advantage. They understand the lure of feeling and acting as entitled people outside the normal limitations and moral requirements that others must contend with. They also appreciate that their real and true power lies in personal rather than positional power and they do not use their position to dominate or prevail. Mostly they submit to the need for temperance and balance in their lives.

Effective leaders are in touch with their fear. They acknowledge it, confront it, work with it, and refrain from using fear-based tactics to conceal the fears they face. This means effective leaders have courage. They are prepared to make difficult decisions. They do not deny or avoid unpleasant new realities. Through communication and collaboration they invite others to participate in confronting the truth. They accept and acknowledge the fact that they do not have all the answers. They encourage others to help define suitable solutions.

An Ethical Life Exceeds a Moral Life

Effective leaders understand the importance of being ethical. They realize that being a moral person is only part of the challenge. Conforming to rules and norms takes one only so far. An ethical person lives a principled life. An ethical person thinks about the rules and norms, and challenges them when they are not appropriate. An effective leader is not a slave to norms and rules and does not encourage others to be so. An effective leader realizes that an ethical life goes well beyond a moral one.

Effective leaders understand the nature of their responsibilities. They live up to their stewardship obligations; they strive to be competent and acknowledge the limitations of their competency; they defer to others who have wisdom and insights in areas where they feel they are lacking; and they know when to demonstrate empathy and compassion.

The Systemic Leadership approach we have been studying is an intrinsically ethical approach to leadership. Systemic Leadership embraces the transformational approach to leadership and goes one step further in that its fundamental and prime task is holding up new realities. Systemic Leaders knowingly and sometimes unknowingly are actively engaged in the ethical quest.

THE ETHICAL QUEST

- Self-awareness and reflection.
- Humility and acceptance.
- Give the work back to others.
- Take responsibility for power.
- Focus on personal power.
- Face one's fears.
- Act with personal courage.
- Face unpleasant new realities.
- Be unconstrained by group norms.
- Know one's limitations.
- Strive to live a principled life.

THE MORAL POWER OF GROUPS

In Chapter 6 we discussed the ethical orientations of groups. We noted that groups are preoccupied with the need for survival. This often results in a survival ethic that encourages group members to act in any manner they think will ensure the group's survival. A survival ethic is a minimalistic ethic in the sense that it is totally self-centered and self-referential. A survival ethic shows little concern for taking the moral high road or caring for the welfare of others.

We have also discussed how power issues within groups dominate and have seen that ethical issues are frequently subordinated to the competing interests within the group. Due to the anxieties inherent in groups, often exacerbated by the tensions that come with new realities and change, fear-based behaviors, scapegoating and regressive tendencies do not tend to bring out the best ethical or moral behaviors of group members.

Many philosophers and sociologists have written about the ethical orientations and moral behavior of groups. To illustrate some of the thinking on this topic I have selected two well-known twentieth-century figures who argue vehemently against the possibility of groups rising above their own self-interests.

The first is Protestant theologian Reinhold Niebuhr. Niebuhr wrote in great detail about the coercive power of groups and its impact on group morality. In *Moral Man and Immoral Society* (1960), he claimed that, in professional life, personal values are mediated by other forces inside the organizational structure that may alter the role played by personal values in decision making.

According to Niebuhr, individuals are endowed by nature with qualities of sympathy and consideration. These prompt them to a sense of justice, which education can refine to a point, and which can enable them to be objective even when their own interests are involved. On the other hand, Niebuhr argued that in 'every human group there is less reason to guide and check impulses, less capacity for self-transcendence, less ability to comprehend the needs of others, and more unrestrained egoism than the individuals who compose the group reveal in their personal relations' (Niebuhr 1960: xi–xii). He explained that the inferior morality of groups as opposed to individuals arises from the collective egoism of the group. He referred to humans' collective behavior that can never be brought under the dominion of reason and conscience, and the dominating force of collective power that invariably exploits the weak. According to Niebuhr, relations between groups are always predominantly political rather than ethical, and will be determined by the proportion of power that each group possesses. All social cooperation on a larger scale than small intimate social groups requires a measure of coercion, resulting in the dominant group being able to impose its will (Niebuhr, 1960: xxiii).

Niebuhr's argument seems compelling when reviewing the moral performance of economic institutions. In our day, economic rather than political and military power has become the significant coercive force of society. While as individuals people may believe they ought to have harmonious relations and establish justice with one another, as groups they are intent on taking for themselves whatever power they can command. The pressure of society on individuals drives their morals, rather than individuals' own moral barometers.

Increasing the size of the group increases the difficulties of achieving group self-consciousness. The larger the group, Niebuhr claimed, the less inclined to ethical behavior and the more people are held in the sway of the coercive pressures within the group. According to him, 'Conflict, a seemingly unavoidable prerequisite for group solidarity, and the preoccupation of gaining or surrendering power turns a group of moral individuals into an unruly mob' (Niebuhr, 1960: 48).

Carl Jung also had something to say about the moral power of groups. He argued that:

> Every man is, in a certain sense, unconsciously a worse man when he is in society than when acting alone.... Any large company of wholly admirable persons has the morality and intelligence of an unwieldy, stupid, and violent animal. The bigger the organization, the more unavoidable is its immorality and blind stupidity.... Society, by automatically stressing all the collective qualities in its individual representatives, puts a premium on mediocrity, on everything that settles down to vegetate in an easy, irresponsible way. Individuality will inevitably be driven to the wall. (Jung, 1959: 240)

The idea that groups diminish the moral agency of individuals is an alarming one. Does this mean that nations are less moral than small groups of individuals, or than individuals themselves? Depending on our perspective on history we may agree with Niebuhr and Jung.

The interplay of group dynamics and the collective group's shadow discussed in Chapter 6 plays a significant role in the ethics of groups. This fact is borne out by research carried out into the corporate culture of organizations embroiled in corporate scandals such as Enron, Arthur Andersen and WorldCom. The climate in these organizations is described as one of intimidation and fear. Here anyone who dared challenge superiors or deviated from group norms would earn immediate reprimand or group alienation. Often they would lose their job and struggle to find another one. As a result of group pressure impinging on people's sense of moral freedom, well-intentioned people are readily caught up in a collusion of silence.

Howard Schwartz, whom we met in Chapter 7, writes in *Narcissistic Process and Corporate Decay* that the organization's processes appear to define moral value for its employees and the organization seems to exist in a moral world of its own (Schwartz, 1990: 3). If we consider the incredible spate of corporate scandals and the behavior of some of the executives, we cannot but agree that group pressure to conform effectively silences many. When people fail to challenge the system or fear whistle-blowing they have good reason – group pressure is intense and the price of challenging group norms is very, very high.

Effective leaders understand the moral pressure groups place on their members. They recognize how inhibiting it is for a member to challenge group norms, especially when the group is in fear. Working with these anxieties and these pressures takes a great deal of courage and perseverance. As stressed in other chapters, it is extremely difficult and dangerous for anyone to take this on alone. Effective leaders collaborate with group members to help break moral strangleholds and to continue to push forward in making progress in embracing new realities.

PERSONAL EXERCISE

- Have you ever made a decision based on what the group expected of you rather than what you would have preferred to do? If yes – why? If never, what ethical principle justified your breaking out of group norms?
- Do you ever encourage a group you participate in to challenge its norms?
- Have you ever supported anyone else who has challenged group norms?
- When do you think group norms serve a constructive purpose?

CORRUPTION

Unfortunately **corruption** plays a hugely significant role in organizational life. It would seem the financial services sector engages in a disproportionate amount of corruption compared with other parts of the economy. The current financial scandals that surround the sub-prime mortgage crisis exceed anyone's reasonable expectations. The scale of the dishonesty, deceit and incompetence of organizations in the financial services sector defies belief. How this has come about and why this sector appears riddled with corruption lies beyond the remit of this text.

Corruption is usually, but not always, due to collusion or collective action. Here individuals or groups attain some benefit at the cost of the organization. This benefit is achieved through dishonesty, deceit, downright theft or manipulation. Corruption, in one way or another, results in organizational resources being diverted to the illegitimate use of an individual or group. Research shows that certain factors within the organization heighten the motivation and opportunities for corruption. These include:

- narcissistic leadership;
- weak leaders surrounded by sycophants;
- an excessively competitive organizational culture;
- a culture resistant to new realities and the changes required;
- a culture that promotes elitism and entitlement;
- organizational systems that lack transparency;
- reward systems that emphasize achievement of results at any cost;
- excessive bureaucratic controls;
- a culture of non-accountability;
- a fear-based culture. (*Academy of Management Review*, 33(3), July 2008 and Annabel Beerel, 'How the Culture of Fear Influences Unethical Leadership': research project, 2007)

The temptation of corruption lurks somewhere in every organization. Effective leaders are aware of this phenomenon. They realize the best way to reduce the probability of corruption occurring is to keep the organization's eye and energies focused on new realities.

EXECUTIVE SUMMARY

This chapter explores the ethical and moral aspects of leadership. It highlights the critical link between leadership and ethics and the need for an ethical rather than a moral organizational culture.

Key points include the following:

- New realities refer to the search for the truth.

- Systemic Leadership that focuses on new realities is concerned with the truth and hence is an ethical endeavor.

- There is an important difference between ethics and morality. Ethics refers to living a principled life while morality refers to conforming to the norms of a group or society.

- Effective leadership focuses on developing an ethical rather than a moral organizational culture.

- Effective leadership means engaging in the ethical quest.

- The moral power of groups inhibits group members from acting as autonomous moral agents. Effective leaders are aware of this pressure.

- Corruption flourishes in certain climates. Effective leaders focus on new realities in order to build a healthy and adaptive ethical climate.

KEY CONCEPTS

Corruption
Ethics
Ethical quest
Ethical question
Morality
Moral power
Moral reasoning
Moral relativism
Truth

CASE STUDY
SECRETS

Cantaloupe Insurance is looking for a new senior customer services director. This is a very important position in the company. The previous director, Jack Wheeler, left after a difficult six months. Jack never really fitted into the organization. Despite many interviews, two personality tests and good references, Jack did not perform as anticipated. People speculated why this was so. Some said he was too arrogant. Others claimed the fact that he was friendly with Cantaloupe CEO's brother gave him an inside track. Yet others insisted it should have been an internal appointment and that bringing in an outsider would not work as too many internal people deserved a shot at the job.

Sheryl Dander, Vice-President of Human Resources, was in a bind. In general she believed in supporting internal promotions as much as possible. However, in this instance she was convinced that someone new and experienced in customer services, and who could bring a new perspective, was what was needed. Sheryl discussed this with the CEO, who agreed. Sheryl had also recently received a résumé from a colleague she had worked with at a previous job, who was a highly experienced customer services manager and who she believed would fit the position perfectly.

Sheryl and her assistant, Eric, crafted a new job description for the vacant position. They publicized it in the company newsletter and distributed it internally among the staff. Sheryl and Eric discussed the probability that at least three existing employees of Cantalope would apply. The new job posting created quite a stir in the customer services department. Members of the department speculated as to the possibility of an internal hire actually taking place. Frank Williams, Martha Seabald and Ernest Black considered themselves eligible for the position, and each one duly applied. Due to the competitiveness between them nobody divulged their actions.

Sheryl and her nominating committee screened the myriad applications they had received and settled on inviting seven people in for interviews. The seven included Frank, Martha and Ernest, Sheryl's previous colleague Therese, and two other outside applicants. During the six weeks of receiving applications and selecting interviewees there was much consternation in the customer services department. People were agitated and distracted. Work quality deteriorated. People snooped around trying to find out who had been short-listed for an interview. Frank, Martha and Ernest were barely talking with one another. Rumors spread about who was going to be the next customer services director. Morale in the department deteriorated. Everyone was in suspense, waiting for the announcement.

Sheryl meets you for a drink after work. She is tired and frustrated. She tells you what is going on. She explains how this hire has created dynamics that seem way out of proportion.

Questions:

1 What are the new realities facing Cantaloupe Insurance and Sheryl?

2 What are the moral pressures Sheryl is facing? Describe how these are operating in the system.

3 What is the ethical challenge here?

4 What advice would you give Sheryl?

ORGANIZATIONAL EXERCISE: PARMALAT – WHERE CHEESE DOES NOT MEAN 'SMILE'

The unraveling of Italy's eighth-largest industrial empire, the food giant Parmalat, caused reverberations around the world. Parmalat was the flagship producer of some of the most popular dairy products, cookies and beverages and controlled 50 percent of the Italian market in milk and milk derivative products. Headquartered in the Italian city of Parma, it was launched as a family business as a small cheese and sausage shop and grew into an international food and beverage concern. In 2004 Parmalat was the largest bankruptcy in European history, representing 1.5 percent of Italian GNP.

Parmalat's downhill trend began in 1997 when it decided to become a global player and started a campaign of international acquisitions financed largely through debt. The acquisitions, instead of bringing in profits, brought significant losses. Losing money on its productive businesses, the company shifted more and more to the high-flying world of derivatives and speculative enterprises.

Parmalat's founder and CEO, Calisto Tanzi, engaged the firm in several exotic enterprises, such as a tourism agency and the purchase of a soccer club. Huge sums were poured into these enterprises, which incurred losses from the beginning. While accumulating losses and using the debt of banks, Parmalat started to build a network of offshore mailbox companies to conceal its losses. Bonds were issued against the fake assets of these mailbox companies, supported by fraudulent balance sheets. According to Parmalat the banks were not only in cahoots with the scheme they developed but also suggested it.

The Parmalat crisis broke in December 2003 when the company defaulted on a €150 million bond. Within days Parmalat's true illiquidity was uncovered and the company went into bankruptcy. Thousands of people lost their jobs, many suppliers were never paid, and investors lost several billion dollars. Although the Tanzi family had siphoned off millions of dollars to serve their own interests, right until the end Calisto Tanzi insisted he was not fully informed of what had gone wrong.

Questions:

1 What were the new realities Parmalat was avoiding? (Think of the time in history when they decided to go global.)

2 Based on the limited information provided, what corporate indicators do you see that supported corrupt activities?

3 Why did it take four years before Parmalat's unethical behavior was uncovered?

FURTHER READING

Denise, Theodore C., Nicholas P. White, and Sheldon P. Peterfreund. *Great Traditions in Ethics*. Florence, KY: Wadsworth, 2008.

Howard, Ronald A. and Clinton. D. Korver. *Ethics (For the Real World)*. Boston, MA: Harvard Business School Press, 2008.

Johnson, Craig E. *Meeting the Ethical Challenges of Leadership*, Second Edition. Thousand Oaks, CA: Sage Publications, 2005.

Johnson, Craig E. *Ethics in the Workplace*. Thousand Oaks, CA: Sage Publications, 2007.

MacKinnon, Barbara. *Ethics: Theory and Contemporary Issues*, Sixth Edition. Florence, KY: Wadsworth, 2009.

Price, Terry L. *Understanding Ethical Failures in Leadership*. New York: Cambridge University Press, 2006.

9 SYSTEMIC LEADERSHIP AND STRATEGY

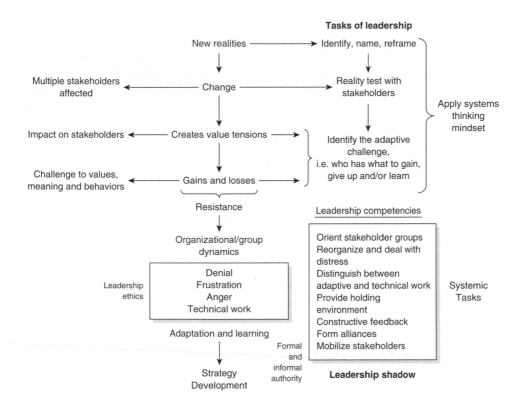

Tasks of leadership

Figure 9.1

INTRODUCTION

In this chapter we discuss some of the leadership and change management aspects that influence the organization's **strategy development.** We do not develop the strategic process in full (we leave that to many other detailed strategy texts), nor do we outline the strategic planning process. We focus instead on how effective leadership that keeps the organization attuned to new realities provides the necessary direction for the organization's strategy development.

Developing the organization's strategy and executing it is the primary task of senior management. An organization's **strategy** is essentially its plan for remaining relevant. The adaptive work we discussed in earlier chapters provides enormous insights into the strategies that are required. Strategy therefore addresses new realities and sets out the organization's response by way of innovation, product and market strategies and resource allocation plans. Detailed strategic plans also include the organization's goals for mobilizing resources to face the challenges of the new realities.

Any organizational strategy includes the organization's plans for transformation and learning and how these are put to effective use for future survival. Effective leadership ensures that transformation and learning are continuous, so strategy development is an ongoing process. Effective organizational leadership recognizes that strategic strength lies in strengthening network relationships, leveraging network ties and that using network innovation to the full is a far stronger and more enduring strategy than trying to be a market leader all alone. Scenario planning provides a very helpful method for developing strategic plans that resonate with uncertain and ambiguous new realities. Strong scenarios can form the basis of flexible and creative strategic plans.

NEW REALITIES AND REMAINING RELEVANT

In Chapter 1 we discussed how the primary goal of organizations is to remain relevant. To remain relevant requires the ability to read new realities and to respond to them appropriately. Once organizations lose their **relevance** they are destined to failure. Sometimes radical repositioning may bring the organization back into the zone of relevance, but that takes a great deal of energy, determination and good fortune. Steve Jobs managed to bring Apple back to relevance in the late 1990s, saving it in the nick of time before the world of PCs closed all competitive opportunities. Many organizations are not fortunate enough to get a second chance.

By now we know that new realities are the forces that herald change. Facing new realities, embracing them and using them to help the organization learn and transform remains the critical challenge of leadership. If an organization fails to remain relevant it loses 'power' and can no longer survive. Embracing new realities and remaining relevant go hand in hand.

We have also seen that change is constant and pervasive. We live, communicate and compete in a virtual world where time and space have been collapsed into a virtual here and now. The communications and information technology revolutions have accelerated the pace of arrival of new realities. These new realities continue to challenge existing paradigms and common assumptions and expectations. For example, phones became cell phones. Cell phones have now become clocks, radios, computers, cameras and TVs. What next? Maybe cell phones will become language translators and sonic guides for the blind – if they are not already doing that!

Remaining relevant depends on adaptation, which means creativity, transformation and learning. Remaining relevant requires more than running faster; it requires seeing the world with new eyes; it requires a new mindset, a different consciousness and a new openness to change. Remaining relevant necessitates abandoning existing habits and practices and developing new ones. Remaining relevant is only possible if one is continually asking new and different questions in light of the constant unfolding of new realities. These new realities hail from the environment, or the larger system of which one is part.

In Chapters 1 and 2 we examined how important it is for the organization to identify and name the new realities that affect its system. I also pointed out that the organization needs to trace the source of new realities outside of its own system. New realities, always systemic in nature, affect an entire system, which includes its many sub-systems. If the organization simply focuses on the impact on any particular sub-system, it fails to grasp the totality of the new realities' impact. A limited understanding of the impact of new realities dilutes the potency of any strategic response.

ADAPT OR DIE: ADAPTATION AND THE LEARNING ORGANIZATION

Strategy Development Emerges from Adaptive Work

As new realities arrive, in order to stay alive and relevant, organizations must continually engage in change. Real change, rather than a fix or simple adjustment, is adaptive and transformative. Adaptive change includes embracing the emotional aspects associated with that change. The emotional aspect refers to the value tensions discussed earlier. Just as people confronted with change experience value tensions, so does the system as a whole. In the same way that value tensions challenge people's sense of self and self-esteem, they challenge the organization's sense of self. When an organization is coping with new realities, it too must look at what it stands for, the values being challenged, and the new attitudes and behaviors required to respond to new market needs.

As we know, exercising leadership means dealing with both the individual and the group dynamics that result from the emotional challenges of change. Strategy development emerges from the adaptive work encouraged by leaders and undertaken by members of the organization, both individually and collectively. Continuously developing new strategies to deal with new realities requires both adaptive and technical work. Technical work relates to all the plans and execution details required to create or revise products and services, to refine market positioning, develop new systems, and expand supply chain and delivery alternatives.

Adaptation Results from Learning

True adaptation requires transformation. It means not just acting differently but also being different. Transformation is always accompanied by learning. Learning means knowing differently. The learning process affects the way a person constructs and reconstructs meaning (Beerel, 1998). Learning is not the addition of new information. It is not the training in new skills. Learning means seeing things differently by developing new insights and new mindsets. The more one encourages one's innate proclivity to learn, the better a learner one becomes. Through learning we recreate ourselves. Through learning we extend our capacity to create. Learning enhances one's adaptive capacity. It opens up new vistas of consciousness that allow for new insights and new experiences.

New Realities Provide Learning Opportunities

Adaptation results from taking advantage of learning opportunities. The incentive to learn is always there as part of the DNA of living systems. New realities provide a continuous stream of learning opportunities. Effective leaders shine the torch on those opportunities and encourage others to avail of them.

Learning opportunities are often challenging. Especially as we get older, we are reluctant to learn new things, which require us to change. Challenging long-held assumptions and deeply engrained prejudices and biases, and forming new habits is not only uncomfortable work but also hard work. Effective leaders stimulate the learning process even when they are met with resistance. They find ways to demonstrate that learning is both essential and beneficial. Most of all, they help make learning exciting and personally rewarding. They recognize that superior performance depends on superior learning. Effective leaders place a high emphasis on being designers, teachers and stewards. They know a **learning organization** is an adaptive enterprise. A learning organization is an organization that is continually expanding its capacity to create its future (Senge, 1990). Only a learning organization will survive in the longer term. Strategy development should be a continuous learning process. Organizations need to build learning into their strategies by encouraging innovation and creativity and focusing on the effectiveness of feedback loops (as discussed in Chapter 2).

Many organizations experience all kinds of learning blocks or learning disabilities. Of course, the first is the inability to face and embrace new realities. Once an organization shies away from keeping new realities foremost all the time, all kinds of other internal aspects will collude to keep it from doing the hard work.

Excessive fear in the organizational system will also detract from people's ability to learn and be creative. Of course, fear makes people regress, which often leads to a downward spiral where they become incompetent and uncommunicative. Below is a list of some of the contributors to learning ineffectiveness.

Blocks to learning organizations.

- Denial or complacent response to new realities.

- Inattention or minimal attention to the stresses and anxieties around change.

- Organizational failure to engage in adaptive work.

- Excessive fear and anxiety in the organization's systems.

- A reward system that focuses on performance rather than creativity.

- Overemphasis on execution.

- A punitive system for risk takers.

- Mental models that emphasize entrenched methods of problem solving.

- A culture that does not encourage fun at work.

PERSONAL EXERCISE

- List the three personal lessons you have learned in this past year.
- List the three professional or work-related lessons you have learned in this past year.
- List one transformative lesson you have experienced in this past year. What made it transformative? What did you gain and what did you give up? In what way has this lesson changed who you are, how you see things, and how you behave?
- How can you relate this transformative lesson to a new reality you experienced?
- What can you learn about yourself from these reflections?
- As a manager, parent and/or friend, what positive advice could you give others based on this reflection?
- How could you build these lessons into your experiences at work?

DISTRIBUTED MARKET LEADERSHIP

Just as one leader cannot keep abreast of all new realities and critical change signals in the market, neither can one organization hope to exercise leadership alone. Just as decision making is becoming more broadly distributed throughout the organization, so must strategic strength and intelligence be distributed throughout the organization's immediate system. Both customers and suppliers are critical stakeholders and sources of innovation and strategic resources. Clearly an organization needs customers to survive. Excessive focus on the customer and changing customer needs is a critical activity required to ensure continued organizational relevance. Continuously adjusting the organization's business model to ensure financial sustainability is another strategic aspect of running a business. Keeping customers or getting new ones, along with a sustainable business model, is dependent on relative product excellence, value for money, and strategic distribution channels.

Globalization has brought along with it **'the disassembly' line** (Meredith 2008). In order to drive down costs and increase quality, companies are rushing to break down their products into sub-assemblies that are transported on **supply chains** across the world. Traditional **assembly lines** have become totally fragmented. Even a cheap toy may be assembled from pieces made in a dozen different factories strewn across China, India, Taiwan, or all three. The disassembly line is the backbone of globalization. The ability to fragment the assembly line and stretch it across the world has dramatically changed the roles of companies and their workers. Companies move their work to wherever they find cheap labor, efficient transport systems and a good infrastructure. The disassembly line has enabled companies to become extremely efficient as they view their factory as a global network of producers each doing what they do fastest, cheapest and most effectively. Using this global network provides enormous opportunities to tap the strengths of countries and cultures and to stimulate network innovation (see p. 225). Organizational strategy needs to be viewed as maximizing the synergy of the network. (Remember systems thinking in Chapter 2.) Network relationships and **network innovation** will provide the key to success. Enabling each participant in the network to exercise leadership will reinforce network strength. Individual organizations no longer count nearly as much as the innovative and responsive strength of the network. Strategic collaboration is the name of the strategy game. Successful strategies for the future require the organization to think systems, networks and **distributed leadership**.

THE DISASSEMBLY LINE

A clothing company like Marks & Spencer might order 100,000 copies of a shirt. First, it might buy yarn from a Korean producer, then ship the yarn to Taiwan to be dyed and woven into cloth. Buttons might be ordered from a specialized Japanese company with a factory in China, and the buttons plus the freshly woven cloth will be shipped to Thailand to be cut and sewn into a shirt. Because fashions change quickly, and the company wants the shirts on its shelves as soon as possible, the cloth and buttons might be sent to five different Thai factories so that each could rush to finish and ship 20,000 shirts, completing the 100,000-piece order faster than if one factory produced the entire lot. Five weeks after they are ordered, identical shirts can be found on store shelves halfway around the world. (Meredith, 2008: 100)

NETWORK INNOVATION

Network innovation is a strategic approach to developing new products quickly and efficiently while using the intelligence and innovative strengths across the organization's network. Apple, known as an integrator of technologies, is a master at this approach to innovation. It is known for stitching together ideas from its network and then packaging them in an elegant and user-friendly fashion. Apple's focus is on the needs of the user and simplicity and ease of use. For example, the iPod was dreamt up by one of its many consultants. Apple quickly adapted the idea and turned it into yet another winning product. (*The Economist*, June 9, 2007)

THE STRATEGY PROCESS

The Strategy Game

The key feature of the strategy game is change (Stacey, 1996). An organization develops its strategies on the basis of its understanding of the nature of change (new realities) and the new context created. The prime goal of the strategic process is to ensure the organization's continued relevance in the marketplace and to its stakeholders combined with a business model that ensures financial sustainability. The strategy process includes the identification of early warning signals for new realities along with the creation of a corporate culture that encourages and rewards learning. For organizations to be strategically adept, they need to learn faster than their competitors. They also need to anticipate strategic growth opportunities and prepare against strategic growth threats (Charan, 2007). This is only possible if the organization is literally 'obsessed' with keeping its eye on new realities. Recall that new realities are evident in the here and now; they are not the subject of fancy futuristic forecasting. Everything in the strategy 'game' is about anticipating and reading the change signals brought about by new realities. Surviving the strategy game requires being adaptive and innovative. Adaptation and innovation are totally dependent on the organization's ability to learn. Strategy is therefore about adaptive transformation and learning.

STRATEGY: A DEFINITION

A strategy is the pattern or plan that integrates an organization's major goals, policies and action sequences into a cohesive whole. A well-formulated strategy helps marshal and allocate an organization's resources into a unique and viable posture based on its relative internal competencies and shortcomings, anticipated changes in the environment and contingent moves by intelligent opponents. (Mintzberg and Quinn, 1991: 5)

Leadership and Strategy

We have seen that leadership is about facilitating the process of change. Organizations are under continuous pressure to change. New realities keep arriving and organizations need to have effective screening mechanisms for detecting those new realities that are immediately and directly pertinent to their remaining relevant to their stakeholders. Exercising leadership is about getting the organization to respond to new realities relevant to their fate. This explains why leadership is such an essential role in any group or organization. This is why people automatically look to someone to exercise leadership and to tell them 'what to do.' People recognize that their fate often depends on the role of effective leaders. If things were not changing and everything was as usual, there would be no need for leaders. Effective leadership, by orienting the organization to new realities, is instrumental in helping the organization devise strategies needed to remain relevant.

As we have explored, contrary to what people want, exercising leadership is *not* about telling others what to do. Effective leaders realize that people have to do their own learning; others cannot do it for them. Effective leaders assist in helping the organization frame new realities correctly so that the organization's response is strategically effective. Effective leadership and strategy development go hand in hand.

Good Strategy and Bad Strategy

Change is essential; however, there is good change and bad change. Changing for the sake of changing is not strategically helpful, and 'bad' change is downright destructive in that it squanders important creative energy and the scarce resources needed to stay vital, exciting and relevant. Good and bad changes are directly related to good and bad strategies.

Good change responds directly to new realities. Bad change takes the organization and its strategic efforts further away from the realities it needs to respond to. Strategy setting is part of the reality testing referred to in earlier chapters. As members of the organization, guided by those exercising leadership, look at new realities, frame and reframe them and discuss their relevance to the organization, initial strategy formulation emerges. Good change efforts result in enhanced adaptive capacities that improve the organization's ability to change in the future.

Strategy Setting Needs to Reflect Reality

Setting organizational strategy in the twenty-first century needs an approach that differs from that of the past. Creating rock solid business plans that define the future and then charting a course through a set of predictions is no longer effective and no longer reflects reality as we currently understand it. Recall the findings of the new sciences outlined in Chapter 2. There we discussed how everything, everywhere is in continuous motion moving toward an infinite number of possibilities. Reality is reflected in networks of relationships that represent values and roles in a system. Systems are part of an infinite number of other systems. Systems import and export new realities. Nothing is stable, and no one event can be isolated from any other. Observing or studying any system or part thereof influences the activity of the system. No objective view or understanding of reality is possible. Reality is co-created by all participants. Developing an effective strategy requires reflecting this understanding and appreciation of reality in our strategy-setting processes. How does one do this?

Clearly strategy development must reflect reality. Reality, as we know it, comprises multiple networks of relationships engaged in continuous and simultaneous interaction. Linear cause and effect cannot be identified. Everything is in motion, and everything is possible. New relationships create new options. Power distribution across the network is continually changing. Capturing this complexity, motion and uncertainty is not possible in linear and quantitative planning methods. Even with the use of many variables and multiple regression techniques, it would not be possible to simulate reality using a linear model, contrary to what economists or mathematical theorists might say. One method that has proved more effective than others in simulating reality is scenario planning. Scenario planning, as described below, explicitly embraces ambiguity and uncertainty. It also allows for many possibilities without insisting that a plan end with one final exact or even approximate solution. Scenario planning focuses on inviting multiple questions that the organization 'lives,' rather than creating a defined course that confines the organization's responses.

The Power of Scenario Planning

Many claim that **scenario planning** is a tool that overcomes the weaknesses of many other planning methods in that it more closely approximates reality (Beerel, 1998; Van Der Heijden, 1996). Reality, as we experience it, is a series of multiple stories occurring at the same time. People live their lives in narrative form. Life, anywhere and everywhere, is a continuous unfolding story. Scenario planning looks at the future through the lens of stories about how the world might be tomorrow, given the new realities of today. The purpose of the stories is to help us recognize the complexity and nuances of the many participants and the changing environment to which we need to adapt.

Scenarios help us order our perceptions about alternative future environments and allow us to play out the various decisions we would make under different circumstances. Scenarios are written like a script for a film or a play. They have themes and plots that have been carefully selected to highlight significant elements in the world environment which challenge the future of the organization (see below). Well-written scenarios adopt systems thinking in developing their plot or theme. By considering a number of different scenarios, the organization can think through the consequences of a range of decisions. It can review how and what might change those decisions when the scenario theme or plot is changed.

Working with and through scenarios is like rehearsing the future, where, like the actor on the stage, different lines can be used depending on which play is being run. The reader of the scenario has the benefit of observing all the events and players from a distance, and can explore the issues, options and challenges from a vantage point that the actors in the story do not have.

SCENARIO PLANNING IS ORGANIZATIONAL LEARNING

Scenario planning distinguishes itself from other more traditional approaches to strategic planning through its explicit approach towards ambiguity and uncertainty in the strategic question. The most fundamental aspect of introducing uncertainty in the strategic equation is that it turns planning for the future from a one-off episodic activity into an ongoing learning proposition. In a situation of uncertainty, planning becomes learning, which never stops. (Van Der Heijden 1996: 5)

Scenarios: The Art of Strategic Conversation, Kees Van Der Heijden. 1996. Copyright John Wiley & Sons Limited. Reproduced with permission.

Developing scenarios

Developing scenarios that interweave the realities of the external and internal organizational systems while addressing their opportunities, limitations and constraints, is both an art and a science. Scenarios are stories that describe a possible future, with the organization, or departments in the organization, as the protagonist(s). They are crafted so as to address the critical new realities and the adaptive challenges the organization is, or should be, facing. Key driving forces, for example political, environmental or demographic issues, should stand out so that scenario readers can identify causal influences on changing trends in the environment.

Scenario stories describe issues, events and players from various perspectives. Just as in a good story, the plot unfolds on the basis of past events and predetermined and unexpected things that may occur in the future. A concatenation of events can present an opportunity or threat to which players or actors may or may not be able to respond. A key feature incorporated in a well-written scenario, just as in a good book, is a number of plots and a number of different events that occur at the same time.

A well-written scenario incorporates the systemic issues of all the interlinking systems and pays attention to the explicit and implicit relationships that network the systems together. The scenario should inject novelty and creativity. Totally unlikely events or ideas should be included. The scenario should exude energy and motion, should have interesting real-life plots filled with the profiles of real people and events, and should be plausible yet stretch the boundaries of people's imaginations. Scenarios need to be grounded in the real world, reflecting genuine possibilities.

Benefits of scenario planning

Some benefits of scenario planning include the following:

- It is performed in the narrative and builds on the power of storytelling.

- It invites imagination, curiosity and play, which stimulates creative thinking.

- It allows for the reframing of the same issue from various perspectives.

- It is useful when the future environment is difficult to predict and there are many variables.

- It does not fixate on exact answers, which is the tendency of quantitative planning approaches.

- It provides the opportunity of looking at multiple perspectives, which can be held in tension without forcing a decision in favor of only one. This frees up people's psyches to see creative and constructive alternatives to a single path or solution.

- It can highlight the nuances of an environment by making things evident without reducing the many facts to just data or evidence.

- It provides the opportunity of combining analysis and synthesis.

- Scenario planning enables and encourages the inductive thinking discussed in Chapter 1. Inductive thinking allows for the development of new heuristics to challenge new and different problems.

- Through the use of analogies, scenario planning provides a vehicle for turning up the heat on new realities without being overly confrontational.

- It enables one to move backwards and forwards between tomorrow's possibilities and today's potential and constraints.

- It enables one to move from the present to the future without the usual discontinuous leaps that are intrinsic in other planning methods.

At this time, in this precarious uncertain environment, scenario planning brings many positive aspects, which explain its use as a core strategic planning technique.

Turning scenarios into strategic plans

There are several ways in which an organization can use its scenario-planning processes to create formal plans. Some organizations use scenarios simply as a backdrop to the more conventional strategic-planning processes, using some of the scenario discussions as a basis for creating strategic planning assumptions. Attention to alternative scenarios facilitates flexible thinking if plans later require alteration.

Other organizations convert the market and product implications of chosen scenarios into numbers, using the most 'likely' scenario as the basis for the numerical plan. In this case, ongoing discussions and attention to alternative scenarios provide input to addendums to the formal plan, thereby facilitating later adjustments.

Less frequently, organizations rely on a number of chosen scenarios as the basis for their formal planning effort. Here they develop forecasts and strategic goals based on each scenario resulting in several plans. The drawback of this approach is that management is not quite sure which plan to adhere to and to be measured against. They may either keep switching plans or may delay decision making as they wait to see which plan is most likely to unfold.

Using scenario planning as the backdrop to the formal plan and/or selecting a main scenario and planning around that one appears to be the most effective method (Beerel, 1998).

IBM IN INDIA

Who would have ever thought, IBM, the true blue of the U.S. computer industry would find its center of gravity in India? IBM has sold its personal computer business to a Chinese multinational, Lenovo. It has also switched its core business from manufacturing to services. Over 40,000 servers outside India are being managed from Bangalore. With 53,000 employees, India is at the core of IBM's strategy. The domestic Indian market is one of the fastest growing markets for IBM where it plans to invest a further $6 billion having already invested $2 billion. Its recent annual investors' day usually held in New York was held in Bangalore. (*The Economist,* April 7 2007)

NEW REALITIES

At the time of writing this book, the world faces many new realities. Some are not really new but only recently acknowledged as such, for example the environmental issue and global warming. The most pressing new reality at present is the worldwide financial crisis brought about by excess liquidity in global financial markets caused by inflated asset prices. The main assets inflated have been home prices. The trigger that sent the global markets spiraling downward is the sub-prime mortgage market that first unraveled in the United States.

The sub-prime mortgage débâcle was inevitable. Due to overcapacity in the financial markets and the fight for market share to stay alive, banks lent money to people to buy homes they could not afford. Mortgage funds were readily available to everyone without careful checks on their capacity to repay. Excessive demand for houses drove prices up. This led banks to believe their security in high-risk homes was safe. In order to compensate themselves for high-risk lending, the banks created kick-in clauses, which, after a certain time, sent mortgage interest rates on high-risk mortgage borrowers, sky high. The risk of defaulting on loans became a self-fulfilling prophecy. High-risk mortgage borrowers by definition could not afford high interest rates. Once these kicked in they began defaulting. Within no time, the housing market collapsed. Due to globalization and the interconnectedness of banks worldwide, this malaise spread quickly across the world, to other countries that had been engaging in similar lending tactics to US banks.

The results of the financial meltdown will bring ripples of new realities for some time to come. No corner of the globe is likely to escape. Both individuals and organizations will have to take radical action. Adaptive capacities will be tested to the extreme. Worldwide consumer demand will plummet, due to the existence of less liquidity in all markets. This will cause the demise of many organizations, layoffs, bankruptcies and organizational mergers. Only strong networks will survive. Relationships will count more than ever. I predict that relationship-oriented organizations that have strategically developed goodwill and strategic leverage on their networks have the greatest potential for survival. Individual strength is insufficient. Only resilient networks will survive. They too will face reconfiguration and the need to adapt and learn.

Some Other New and not so New Realities

Demographics

Growth in world population to 9.2 billion by 2050.

Population of developed world living longer.

Elderly population growing dramatically.

Worldwide mass migration – radically redistributing populations.

Energy

Huge demand for energy in developing countries.

Innovation opportunities in new energy resources.

Environment

Global warming and climate change on the increase.

Impact of the above will affect health, diseases, ecology, food production.

Socio-cultural

Globalization resurfaces old tensions as religious and ethnic loyalties resurge.

Technology

Innovation accelerates and will impact all sectors.

Biotechnology

Unexpected results from stem cell research.

New diseases will call for new solutions.

Geopolitical

Oil and water needs perpetuate and create new tensions.

EXECUTIVE SUMMARY

This chapter focuses on leadership as setting the appropriate direction for developing an organization's strategy. That direction is facing new realities. Key points made in the chapter include the following:

- The goal of strategy development is keeping the organization relevant.

- Remaining relevant requires adaptation, transformation and learning.

- The source of new realities is always outside the existing system. Tracing this source is critical when developing the organization's strategies.

- The adaptive work of the organization provides critical insights into strategies needed for future survival.

- New realities always provide opportunities for learning. Effective leadership helps build these learning opportunities into the organization's future plans.

- Globalization increases the need to utilize worldwide networks for strategic effectiveness.

- Encouraging collaboration and innovation across networks will create greater leverage opportunities than trying to devise a strategy or innovate entirely alone.

- Scenario planning is a powerful tool for developing strategic plans in a world of continuous change and uncertainty and where many players are acting at once.

- At this time the world is facing many 'new' realities. One critical new reality is the financial fallout across the globe that will challenge many organizations' adaptive capacities.

KEY CONCEPTS

Assembly lines
Disassembly lines

Distributed leadership
Learning organization
Network innovation
Relevance
Scenario planning
Strategy
Strategy development
Supply chains

CASE STUDY
SUSAN AND FAMILY FRIENDLY LAUNDRIES

Susan Schneider has just been appointed the President of Family Friendly Laundries (FFL). FFL has been in business for over ninety years. It started out as one of the first independent laundry services in the suburbs of south Boston that would also provide sewing services and a hotline cleaning advice service.

Over the ninety years FFL has become a very successful chain of seventeen outlets throughout the greater Boston area. Part of the organization's success has been its reluctance to franchise its operation, preferring to own the outlets and have direct control over the cleaning services provided. Business has boomed due to the deep understanding the founders and subsequent managers have of the cleaning business. A key part of the organization's strategy has been to make it a point to buy the latest equipment and to seek special advice from technical experts in order to care for clothing in an exemplary manner. Customer friendliness and service have also always been great aspects of the business. The only challenge the organization has had over the years has been to hold staff once they achieved a managerial position. The turnover of managers has thus always been a problem. Some said that the President was too patriarchal and others said that the culture at FFL was such that business managers would never get to share in the power – the family would always run the show.

Prior to Susan's appointment, her grandfather, who started the business, was President for fifty years, followed by her father who was President for forty years. Susan has worked in the business for the past fifteen years and is well known by all the staff. Much to her father's chagrin, Susan started to promote management courses in the organization in order to encourage people to want to become managers and to see a long-term future with the organization. She has had small successes but management turnover remains high. Good managers continue to leave and go to competitor organizations.

Susan has been President for three months. She has decided to develop a formal strategic plan, something her father or grandfather never did. She knows the business needs to grow to survive. In the past, this has not been that difficult. Now the business climate is moving into recession and she realizes she needs to have a strategic plan and some thought-through strategic options. Keeping senior staff is one of her main concerns.

Susan asks you to be her consultant and to give her some advice on how she should go about developing her strategic plan.

Questions:

1   How should Susan go about developing her strategic plan?

2   What new realities should she build into her planning process?

3   What adaptive work needs to be carried out prior to the development of her future strategy?

4   What organizational learning is required?

ORGANIZATIONAL EXERCISE: TATA GROUP

The Tata Group was founded in Bombay, India, by Jamsetji Tata in 1868. Jamsetji was a nationalist and dreamed of self-sufficiency for his country. In 1886, he started Swadeshi Mills to promote the purchase of Indian textiles instead of imported British clothing. Gandhi, with his spinning wheel, became the Swadeshi movement's most famous advocate. In 1902, Mr Tata opened the Taj Mahal, the first Indian-owned luxury hotel, after being denied entry to a British hotel where he wanted to entertain clients.

Among other ambitions, Mr Tata set out to make India self-sufficient in steel production. His son was able to realize his dream by founding India's first steel company, Tata Iron and Steel, in 1907. His son's successor, J.R.D. Tata, supplied the steel needed for India's post-independence five-year plans. J.R.D. Tata was a pilot and founded India's first airline, which became Air India.

In the 1990s, as India slowly opened its country to foreign trade, efficient foreign firms entered the market and local Indian businesses were unable to compete. By 2006 foreign companies had overtaken Indian brands of many household consumables. The challenges facing the century-old Tata group again paralleled those facing the nation.

When Ratan Tata took the reins during the 1991 economic crisis, many of the then conglomerate's complacent companies were unable to compete outside India or even against foreign companies selling inside India. In order to survive, Ratan Tata restructured; sold factories; jettisoned more than half of its employees; and partnered with foreign brands to return to profitability. Tata Steel was one of the toughest cases to turn around. By 2007 Tata Steel became one of the world's most efficient steel producers.

Ratan Tata is the visionary behind the development of India's first self-developed passenger car, the Nano. The Nano is a $2,500 automobile designed to make automobiles more affordable to Indians. Ratan Tata hopes to keep families off scooters and motorbikes in the crazed Indian traffic where many place their lives in daily jeopardy.

Today Tata Group is the largest private company in India. It has interests in steel, automobiles, information technology, communication, power, tea and hotels. The Tata Group has operations in more than eighty-five countries. It comprises ninety-eight companies, twenty-seven of which are publicly listed. The charitable trust of Tata holds 65.8 percent of the ownership of the Tata Group. The Tata Group is a leading buyer of foreign businesses. These include:

Britain's Tetley Teas

The Pierre Hotel in New York

Daewoo Commercial Vehicle Company

Tyco Global Network

Millennium Steel Thailand

Eight O'Clock Coffee

Ritz Carlton Boston

Campton Place Hotel, San Francisco

General Chemical Industrial Products

Jaguar Cars and Land Rover

China Enterprise Communications

Neotel, South Africa

The Tata Group has helped establish and finance numerous quality research, educational and cultural institutes in India. It is a leading and highly respected philanthropic corporate entity and in 2007 was awarded the Carnegie Medal for Philanthropy.

Questions:

1 How would you describe the Tata Group's strategy?

2 Does this strategy respond to new realities? What evidence do you have to support your response?

3 Given the new realities at this time, where is the Tata Group's Achilles' heel?

(You may have to do a little research on India to answer these questions in any depth.)

FURTHER READING

Charan, Ram. *Know-How*. New York: Crown Business, 2007.

Freedman, Mike. *The Art and Discipline of Strategic Leadership*. New York: McGraw-Hill, 2003.

Handscombe, Richard S. and Philip A. Norman. *Strategic Leadership: Managing the Missing Links*, Second Edition. New York: McGraw-Hill, 1993.

Mintzberg, Henry and James Brian Quinns. *The Strategy Process: Concepts, Contexts and Cases*, Second Edition. New York: Prentice Hall, 1991.

Stacey, Ralph D. *Strategic Management and Organizational Dynamics*, Second Edition. London: Financial Times/Prentice Hall, 1996.

Van Der Heijden, Kees. *Scenarios: The Art of Strategic Conversation*. New York: John Wiley, 1996.

10 THE LEADER IN YOU

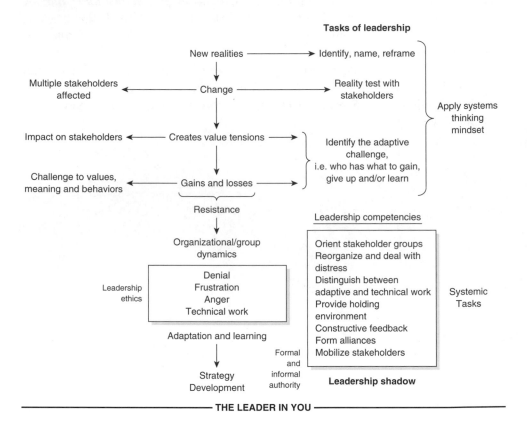

Figure 10.1

INTRODUCTION

This book has explored the implications of leadership and change management in depth and stressed the Systemic Leadership approach. The Systemic Leadership approach places a great deal of emphasis on the emotional health of the organization and how it influences the organization's ability to respond to new realities.

Systemic Leadership is task-oriented in that leadership is measured by the types of task carried out rather than the skills or traits of the leaders. Systemic Leadership is measured by the extent to which 'leaders' increase the organization's long term-**adaptive capacity**, rather than their achievement of short-term goals or financial results.

Systemic Leadership takes a transformational approach. The emphasis is on creating greater adaptive capacities of the organization and its members, thereby improving their ability to respond to change. While Systemic Leadership does not focus on the skills and traits of leaders, certain dispositions and strengths help in making Systemic Leaders more effective.

One thing Systemic Leaders pay attention to is the power of the system and the group. They are sensitive to the anxieties inherent in organizations and the **group dynamics** that change creates. They understand that excessive anxiety impairs the organization's creative and learning abilities. An important aspect of Systemic Leadership is not to try to lead alone and become the subject of emotional or psychological assassination, but to find strategic partners in the leadership and change process.

CRITICALITY OF NEW REALITIES

There is nothing more important, compelling or urgent than the existence of changing realities and wrestling with what that implies for the healthy survival of a system or organization.

REVIEW OF THE SYSTEMIC LEADERSHIP APPROACH

This book stresses that the Systemic Leadership approach is the most effective approach at this time of tumultuous change and uncertainty. The Systemic Leadership approach claims that leadership concerns facilitating change and that the most important task of leadership is to help the organization identify new realities and respond to them appropriately.

Four major assumptions underpin the concept of **Systemic Leadership**:

- Leadership is defined by the tasks performed rather than the skills or traits of particular individuals.

- Leadership is not something that only those in positions of formal or informal authority are able or expected to do. Therefore, in Systemic Leadership, we refer to *exercising leadership* rather than referring to 'the leader' or 'the leadership.'

- Anyone can conceivably exercise leadership from anywhere in the organizational hierarchy. Function, discipline or level in the hierarchy should not inhibit the opportunity to exercise leadership.

- The role of leader is distinct from that of authority. Not all people in positions of authority automatically exercise leadership (see Chapter 4, p. 90).

Systemic Leadership also takes a transformational approach to leadership. This means that leadership is understood to take care of others, motivate them and, in the best sense of the term, encourage and help them to be all they can be. Systemic Leadership is primarily concerned with enhancing both the organization as a whole, and its members' adaptive capacities.

Systemic Leadership focuses on the tasks carried out rather than on the skills and traits of the person doing them. This does not mean talents, propensities, skills and traits are unimportant. Rather, the Systemic Leadership approach takes the view that no one person has all the talents, skills and/or traits required. Organizational leadership is most effective and enduring when it is distributed; when the organizational culture allows for and encourages all of its members to exercise leadership when they can. Systemic Leadership holds that everyone can rise to the occasion. Everyone has some of the many talents and skills required to keep the organization adaptive, creative and flexible in times of rapid change.

There are several tasks and activities that fall under the heading of Systemic Leadership. Activities include integrating the primary and the secondary tasks of organizational management. The primary task is achieving the organization's mission through strategy development and execution. The secondary task is taking care of the emotional life of the organization, i.e. providing a containment function for the anxiety within the organizational system. Change, especially rapid and highly uncertain change, increases organizational anxiety. Systemic Leaders are aware of this and actively work to contain that anxiety while continuing to keep the organization attuned to the new realities it is facing.

THE OVERALL TASKS OF SYSTEMIC LEADERSHIP

1 Identify new realities.
2 Identify and name the adaptive challenge.
3 Orient stakeholder groups to deal with value tensions.
4 Identify who has what to gain and what to give up or lose.
5 Recognize signals of distress.
6 Distinguish between the group/organization's adaptive and technical work.

7 Provide a holding environment or container for distress.
8 Make constructive interventions to keep people on track.
9 Get on the balcony to gain new perspectives.
10 Give the work back.
11 Form alliances across group factions and constituencies.
12 Mobilize resources.

PERSONAL EXERCISE

- When did you last deny a new reality?
- What were the consequences of your denial?
- What did you learn about yourself when you realized you were in denial?
- Who did you discuss this with? If no one, why was this?
- What did you learn from your discussion or lack of discussion?

OPTIMAL SKILLS AND CAPABILITIES REQUIRED OF SYSTEMIC LEADERS

In Chapter 3 we discussed some of the optimal skills and capabilities that contribute to effective Systemic Leadership. We recognize that no one person can possibly have all of these skills. Here is a review of the capabilities and skills we listed:

1   To identify new realities:

- openness, attentiveness and curiosity about a changing global environment;

- strength in systemic thinking;

- an ability to see patterns and relationships;

- good inductive reasoning capabilities.

2   To identify the adaptive challenge (value tensions):

- intellectual and emotional alertness;

- strong cognitive abilities – the ability to entertain competing mindsets at once;

- emotional intelligence.

3   To work with the challenges of change:
   •   self-awareness around one's own feelings of change;
   •   the ability to empathize without faltering on what is required;
   •   critical thinking skills to understand what is really going on and to follow through with rigor;
   •   strong conflict management skills.

4   To deal with organizational anxiety and distress:
   •   high levels of cognitive development;
   •   emotional maturity;
   •   endurance.

5   To focus others to co-create a vision for the future:
   •   confidence and patience;
   •   lack of hubris – willing to co-create the future without having to demand all the accolades.

6   To act ethically:
   •   courage;
   •   a brave heart;
   •   and more courage.

Essential Skills of the Systemic Leader

There are a few skills, however, that are essential for the potential Systemic Leader. These are the following

1   Self-awareness regarding one's own strengths and weaknesses; self-awareness regarding one's emotions and how they impact one's behavior; and self-awareness regarding one's shadow side, one's issues with authority, one's desire to be respected and admired, and one's fears and how one handles them.

   Self-awareness is a sign of maturity. It provides an indicator that one is self-reflective, and that one is able to look at oneself critically. Self-awareness shows an interest in and a concern about the kind of person one is and how one engages in the world. Self-awareness is a critical component of cognitive and emotional intelligence. Without it one is likely to be less adept in dealing with complex and stressful situations. Unreflective people are less thoughtful and aware of other's states of mind or feelings. Dealing with the stresses of change and developing one's adaptive capacity certainly requires a focus on **self-reflection and awareness** as an ongoing endeavor.

2   General **mindfulness** and awareness refers to the ability to be attentive to the present and to be observant. Unobservant people will find it difficult to exercise effective leadership.

Mindfulness, i.e. being present and being attuned to what is happening in the present, is the hallmark of good leadership. New realities are revealed in what is going on in the present. Only by seeing the present with curious and attentive eyes can one recognize many of the new realities that seem hidden in plain sight. Mindfulness implies a certain amount of patience, thoughtfulness and openness to seeing new and different things.

General mindfulness and awareness also implies an avid interest in learning; in observing new and different situations and seeing what they mean. An interest in learning is important for the tasks of leadership as adaptation and responding to change always requires some element of learning. Without an avid interest in learning, this effort will be seen as a burden rather than as something that is life giving and essential to thriving in the future.

3   The ability to see the big picture is important for Systemic Leadership. Systems thinking helps one understand new realities and their impact. To exercise leadership requires being able to take this larger perspective and not get bogged down in minutiae. This is not always easy to do as sometimes the details and smaller issues distract us and trip us up. Helping the organization face new realities, however, requires an ability to move back and forth between the big picture and the detail. Being able to see the big picture requires confidence and imagination.

4   **Courage** is an essential ingredient of any type or form of leadership. Courage is required to stand up to the challenges of others, to be able to hold steady when one fails their projections and expectations, and when one is blamed for the discomfort of having to adapt to new realities.

Courage is required to stand up to the personal temptations and seductions of power and the glory that is often attributed to those in power. Courage is required to be able to face one's own fears and not to project them on others. It takes courage to give people the work back; to make them do their own learning when they would prefer someone else to tell them what to do. It takes courage to admit one does not have all the answers even when others pretend one does.

Only courageous people can be ethical. Only courageous people can withstand the seduction of power that comes with leadership. Only courageous people can face the truth when it is unpleasant and try to make others do the same regardless of the personal cost. Only courageous people can challenge unfair norms, biased precedents, and the coercive power of groups or systems. True courage is the heart of Systemic Leadership.

PERSONAL EXERCISE

1   Do you see yourself as a reflective and self-aware person? If you asked three other people you know, would they agree with your answer?
2   Are you someone who is mindful and observant? If you asked three other people you know, would they agree with your answer?
3   Are you able to see the big picture? Are you able to hold both the big picture and details at the same time? List two circumstances where you have demonstrated this capacity.
4   Do you see yourself as a courageous person? If you asked three other people you know, would they agree with your answer? Can you provide examples of where you were courageous?

THE IRON RULE

The iron rule is never ever do for people what they can do for themselves. It is the opposite of learned helplessness. The iron rule respects people's dignity. Teach people confidence in their own competence.

EXERCISING LEADERSHIP IN RESPONSE TO GROUP BEHAVIOR

Throughout this text we have stressed that leadership is about facilitating the process of change. We know change is challenging and that for all kinds of reasons people resist change. If nothing else, change always challenges our values and behaviors and requires us to revisit our priorities. Change also challenges our self-esteem and our sense of self. If new realities are considered unpalatable, our resistance to change can bring out our anger and fear in unpleasant ways. Leaders have to deal with our anger and fear if we are to adapt and embrace the new reality. This is tough stuff.

When groups face challenging new realities, their responses can be brutal; sadly, in some cases, murderous. Group sentiment and power can be hugely destructive.

Working with group resistance requires understanding and compassion and at the same time strength and resilience. Courage is required to engage in difficult conversations and to withstand pressure from the group to avoid unpleasant new realities and to be distracted into technical work.

Systemic Leaders understand that leading change is as much an emotional as a rational process. It involves confusion, uncertainty, ambiguity, paradox, irrationality, intuition and imagination. In fact, exercising leadership calls on all of a person's innate potential, hence the need for self-awareness and reflection so as to know where that potential does (or does not) lie.

Group (system) pressure is truly one of the most complicated and difficult things for leaders (or anyone in a system) to deal with and they must withstand its coercive nature. Effective leaders need to be able to distinguish themselves from their role, so they are not emotionally devastated by the anger they may attract. They need to recognize they may be the lightning rod or target for difficult situations and that this can lead to their being scapegoated or disempowered. They need to know how to pace the adaptive work; how to turn up the heat yet not generate too much anxiety. Most importantly, they need to know how to create strategic alliances so that they do not have to drive all the adaptive work alone. They need to leverage others' strengths in the system and to know when to take a step back or retreat without colluding with denial or escapism into non-reality. Finding strength and courage in the face of group issues around change is one of the hardest tasks of leadership, especially if one stays true to holding the system to facing new realities.

STAYING ALIVE

An important consideration in exercising leadership is **staying alive**. There is no point in being the insightful, perspicacious and courageous leader if the result is 'assassination' or 'suicide.' Unfortunately too many good leaders fall under the axe of group angst and anger. In no time they are scapegoated or done away with so that the group does not have to do its adaptive work. Putting off the adaptive work is destructive because, as we know, new realities do not disappear. However, leaders need to know how to stay alive. This means alive not only in the physical but also in the emotional and psychological senses. I have mentioned the importance of not trying to exercise leadership alone. That makes one too easily the target of other's fears. There are other strategies that help potential leaders stay healthy and alive. These include the following:

- If you are in a position of formal authority, monitor the length of your tenure and limit it.
- Share power.
- Challenge your own hype.
- Stay real.

- Build strategic alliances that support your weaknesses.
- Partner with people who typically disagree with you and have other viewpoints.
- Stay fit and healthy.
- Develop a personal support system.
- Be reflective.
- Focus on how to represent an issue and not become it.
- Find assistance in mobilizing the real stakeholders, not the proxies.
- Try to find a balanced life with opportunities for stress relief.
- Once you have lost your sense of humor, quit and get out of the system for a while at least.
- Find opportunities to retreat and reflect.

THE LEADER IN YOU

All of us have the potential to exercise leadership. All of us do exercise leadership from time to time although it may not be recognized as such. So much of our culture focuses on people in positions of formal authority uttering pronouncements or defining reality for others. That is not exercising leadership as we define it in this text.

Along the way this book has invited you at various points to check in and to check how well you respond to new realities. You have been asked to consider what your tendencies might be and where you have strengths and limitations in dealing with the gains and losses around change. There is no question you have the potential to be a Systemic Leader: everyone has! Hopefully this book has inspired you to exercise leadership more consciously and to realize the transformative power of facing and embracing new realities.

Given the turbulent and challenging world we live in, having a strong adaptive capacity is critical. Being able to withstand misfortune, disappointing new realities and turmoil in what used to be a 'normal life' is essential, not only to survive but also to find a meaningful life.

Exercising leadership begins with personal leadership; with the way in which one lives one's own life and faces one's own new realities – not that these are ever isolated as they are always systemic in nature. Simply being more aware and more reflective strengthens one's capacity and resolve to acknowledge that reality is reality and dealing with it sooner rather than later is always the best choice. Helping others to do the same is a great gift, and a true sign of leadership and courage.

ORDINARY PEOPLE CAN RISE TO EXTRAORDINARY THINGS

Ordinary people can rise to extraordinary things. Simply give them as much freedom as possible. Give them and encourage them to take every opportunity. Take responsibility for their mistakes and reduce their fear of the consequences of failure. Leadership is to facilitate the optimum responses of others. Status, class or caste will not guarantee anything. People learn best through experience. Let their experiences train and educate them. (Professor P.V. Ramana, Chairman and trustee ITM Group of Institutions, Mumbai, India)

EXECUTIVE SUMMARY

This chapter brings together some of the personal requirements for exercising Systemic Leadership. It highlights the following:

- Systemic Leadership facilitates the change management process by understanding and managing the organization's anxieties.

- Systemic Leadership is concerned with the tasks that surround identifying new realities and embracing them.

- While Systemic Leadership does not focus on the skills and talents of leaders, certain dispositions and propensities underpin the Systemic Leadership approach.

- One of the biggest challenges facing Systemic Leadership is the group dynamic associated with the resistance to change. Knowing how to read and understand groups is an important component of Systemic Leadership.

- An important goal of leadership is staying alive.

- Everyone has the potential to be a leader. Organizations would be a great deal better off if they encouraged this potential in each and every member.

KEY CONCEPTS

Adaptive capacities
Courage
Group dynamics

Leadership skills and talents
Mindfulness
Self-reflection and self-awareness
Staying alive
Systemic Leadership

CASE STUDY
SUSANNA JOHNSON

'I fought for your appointment and I hired you because I believed that you are one of the best. So, make that ——— profit forecast whatever it takes!' CEO Don Peruchi stood up and stormed out of the room, leaving Susanna speechless in the wake of his fury. This storm had been brewing for weeks in anticipation of publication of Palermo Inc.'s quarterly financial results. Falling sales, increased costs, and excessive bonuses to favored employees explained some of the poor results for the period. In truth, Palermo Inc.'s way of doing business needed massive rethinking right from the identification of its markets, to pricing, delivery channels, systems and financing.

Susanna Johnson had joined the organization six months previously. She had expected a challenge, but had underestimated the corrosion present in every nook and cranny of the multinational corporate hierarchy. Her exposure to the pervasive corruption within the organization was yet to come.

At first Don Peruchi had seemed competent and thoughtful, not to mention amiable. His charm and persuasiveness had initially impressed her. As the months had passed, however, she had begun to see the real person behind the façade. She had attributed his apparent personality change to his fear regarding the organization's poor performance. Over time, she came to realize that everything was personal for him. When things in the organization went badly and she tried to discuss the problems, he had interpreted her discussions as a personal attack. He seemed to believe that poor organizational performance reflected directly on him as a person and, thus, poor results made him a personal failure. From this stance he could not possibly countenance reporting poor results to the board or shareholders, regardless of the reality.

Palermo Inc. had, financially speaking, 'squeaked' through the first quarter, but the last three months had seen a dramatic decline in sales and a significant increase in fixed costs, to the extent that fixed costs were growing at twice the rate of sales. The euro was also losing value against other trading partner currencies. Susanna had detected this trend from the outset, but had faced fierce resistance from the executive management team whenever she had raised this issue at the weekly management meetings.

Susanna worked late into the night, as she did every night. A qualified CPA with over twenty-five years of business experience, she knew all the accounting 'tricks' in the book. Accelerating charges, changing rates of depreciation, revising valuation of inventories, capitalizing expenses, holding back invoices and not accruing payables, treating expenses as payments in advance – you name it, she had seen it all. Her MBA qualification and training had increased her ambition to get to the top of the corporate ladder and given her greater confidence to be creative and to push the envelope when required.

Palermo Inc. had recently invested an enormous amount in computer hardware, software and systems training. Training costs alone had amounted to over half a million dollars. Susanna had reviewed the software and training payments over and over again, wondering how much could reasonably and honestly be placed on the balance sheet as an asset and then be depreciated over time rather than be written off as an expense. Half a million dollars less in expenses would radically alter the bottom line. Driving home in the early hours of the morning, she pondered whether she could make any 'honest' adjustments to expenses and thus drastically reduce or eliminate if possible the expected quarterly loss.

The next morning, at the regular weekly executive management meeting, CEO Don Peruchi reported that, after his discussion with the CFO the previous day, he was pleased to confirm that the organization's performance for the quarter was on track. Susanna sat at the conference table dumbfounded. He'd done it again! He'd just publicly committed her to collude with him in a lie. She could only challenge him with an outright public counter-challenge that he was lying. She took a deep breath and remained silent, determined to have it out with him later. This, of course, was a fatal mistake.

The members of the management team turned to Susanna in both confusion and admiration. They all knew that the organization's performance for the past three months had been abysmal, so how could it be possible that they would meet forecast profits? On the other hand, Susanna had an excellent reputation as a competent CFO and maybe she could perform miracles – thank heavens for that. They were now off the hook. Smiles all around; the meeting ended early.

After the meeting the CEO asked Susanna to come to his office. He asked her how things were going and how close she was to producing the 'right' figures. Still angry from the meeting but deciding not to say anything, she claimed that she was working on it and that she needed more time. She mentioned briefly that one possibility lay in changing the method of accounting for the investment in computer software and especially the related training, with the possibility of thereby radically reducing expenses. She insisted that, before she finalized any details in this regard, she would need to consult with the organization's auditors. They agreed to meet at the end of the day.

A few hours later a distressed Jack Daniels, Vice-President of Information Systems phoned Susanna. He claimed that he had just met with the CEO, who wanted a schedule drawn up immediately that set out the details of the investment in computer hardware and software plus training over the past six months. The VP was also asked to write a report arguing that certain items of software, but more especially the amounts spent on training, should be considered as balance sheet investments and not expenses. The VP wanted Susanna to tell him what was going on. He expressed surprise at having been approached by the CEO without having been briefed by Susanna first, as hitherto they had had a very good working relationship. He mentioned his fear that somehow he was being excluded from conversations that would influence his power detrimentally and thus negatively affect his ability to get things done. Susanna tried to assure him that she was the one under the gun, and not him, and that his position was safe.

Later that afternoon, Susanna received a phone call from the organization's auditors. Giovanni Malto, the senior audit partner responsible for the Palermo account, indicated that he had just had a long conversation with the CEO. The Palermo account was a significant source of income to the auditing firm and they usually responded to Don Peruchi's requests with immediate attention. Malto stated that he was 'very open' to capitalizing training expenses associated with new systems and assured Susanna that he planned on being cooperative. He suggested that she fax him the sheet of software and training costs prepared by the VP of Information Systems and he would 'see what he could do.' It was 5 p.m. by the time Susanna hung up the phone. As she tossed her once again uneaten lunch into the waste bin, Don Peruchi walked into her office.

Questions:

1   What were the new realities Palermo Inc. was facing?

2   What where Susanna Johnson leadership challenges?

3   Where had Susanna Johnson slipped up?

4   What should she do?

FURTHER READING

Argyris, Chris. *On Organizational Learning*. New York: Wiley-Blackwell, 1999.

Aurelius, Marcus. *Meditations*, trans. M. Staniforth. New York: Viking Penguin, 1964.

Charan, Ram. *Know-How*. New York: Crown Business, 2007.

Dreher, Diane. *The Tao of Inner Peace*. New York: Penguin Group, 2000.

Heifetz, Ronald A. *Leadership without Easy Answers*. Cambridge, MA: Belknap Press of Harvard University Press, 1994.

BIBLIOGRAPHY

A Jossey-Bass Reader (2003) *Business Leadership*. San Francisco, CA: Jossey-Bass.

Ackoff, Russell, L. (1999) *Recreating the Corporation: A Design of Organizations for the 21st Century*. New York: Oxford University Press.

April, Kurt, Robert Macdonald and Sylvia Vriesendorp (2000) *Rethinking Leadership*. Cape Town, South Africa: University of Cape Town Press.

Arbinger Institute (2002) *Leadership and Self-Deception*. San Francisco, CA: Berrett-Koehler.

Argyris, Chris (1990) *Overcoming Organizational Defenses*. New York: Prentice Hall.

Argyris, Chris (1991) "Teaching Smart People How to Learn", *Harvard Business Review*, May–June.

Argyris, Chris (1999) *On Organizational Learning*. New York: Wiley-Blackwell.

Aurelius, Marcus (1964) *Meditations*, trans. M. Staniforth. New York: Viking Penguin.

Avery, Gayle C. (2005) *Understanding Leadership*. Thousand Oaks, CA: Sage Publications.

Badaracco, Joseph L. Jr. (2006) *Questions of Character: Illuminating the Heart of Leadership through Literature*. Boston, MA: Harvard Business School Press.

Balasubramanian, S. (2007) *The Art of Business Leadership: Indian Experiences*. New York: Response.

Banks, Robert and Kimberly Powell, eds (2000) *Faith in Leadership*. San Francisco, CA: Jossey-Bass.

Barabasi, Albert-Laszlo (2003) *Linked*. New York: Penguin.

Barker, Joel Arthur (1992) *Paradigms: The Business of Discovering the Future*. New York: HarperBusiness.

Bass, Bernard M. and Ronald E. Riggio (2006) *Transformational Leadership*, Second Edition. Hillsdale, NJ: Lawrence Erlbaum Associates.

Beach, Lee Roy (2006) *Leadership and the Art of Change: A Practical Guide to Organizational Transformation*. Thousand Oaks, CA: Sage Publications.

Beerel, Annabel (1993) *Expert Systems in Business: Real World Applications*. Chichester, UK: Ellis Horwood.

Beerel, Annabel (1998) *Leadership Through Strategic Planning*. London: International Thomson Business Press.

Bennis, Warren (1989) *On Becoming a Leader*. New York: Addison-Wesley.

Bennis, Warren, ed. (1992) *Harvard Business Review: Leaders on Leadership*. Boston, MA: Harvard Business Review Books.

Bennis, Warren, Jagdish Parikh and Ronnie Lessem (1994) *Beyond Leadership*. Cambridge, MA: Basil Blackwell.

Bion, W.R. (2000) *Experiences in Groups*. New York: Routledge.

Bocchi, Gianluca and Mauro Ceruti (2002) *The Narrative Universe*. Cresskill, NJ: Hampton Press.

Bohm, David (1992) *Thought as a System*. New York: Routledge.

Bolman, Lee G. and Terrence E. Deal (2003) *Reframing Organizations*, Third Edition. San Francisco, CA: Jossey-Bass.

Bordas, Juana (2007) *Salsa, Soul, and Spirit: Leadership for a Multicultural Age*. San Francisco, CA: Berrett-Koehler.

Bowman, Cliff (1990) *The Essence of Strategic Management*. New York: Prentice Hall.

Brown, Marvin (2005) *Corporate Integrity: Rethinking Organizational Ethics and Leadership*. Cambridge, UK: Cambridge University Press.

Burns, James MacGregor (1978) *Leadership*. New York: Harper.

Cameron, Kim S., Robert E. Quinn, Jeff DeGraff and Anjan V. Thakor (2006) *Competing Values Leadership*. Northampton, MA: Edward Elgar.

Capra, Fritjof (1991) *The Tao of Physics*. Boston, MA: Shambala.

Capra, Fritjof (2004) *The Hidden Connections: A Science for Sustainable Living*. New York: First Anchor Books.

Carson, Rachel (2002) *Silent Spring*. New York: Houghton Mifflin.

Cavalieri, Steven and Sharon Seivert (2005) *Knowledge Leadership: The Art and Science of the Knowledge-Based Organization*. Amsterdam: Elsevier.

Celente, Gerald (1997) *Trends 2000*. New York: Warner Books.

Charan, Ram (2007) *Know-How*. New York: Crown Business.

Chen, Min (1995) *Asian Management Systems*. London: International Thomson Business Press.

Ciulla, Joanne B. (2003) *The Ethics of Leadership*. Florence, KY: Thomson Wadsworth.

Clark, Andy (2001) *Mindware*. New York: Oxford University Press.

Clark, Timothy R. (2008) *Epic Change: How to Lead Change in the Global Age*. San Francisco, CA: Jossey-Bass.

Clawson, James G. (2009) *Level Three Leadership*. Upper Saddle River, NJ: Pearson Prentice Hall.

Cloke, Kenneth and Joan Goldsmith (2002) *The End of Management*. San Francisco, CA: Jossey-Bass.

Cohen, Allan R. and David L. Bradford (1989) *Influence without Authority*. New York: John Wiley.

Collins, Jim (2001) *Good to Great*. New York: HarperCollins.

Colman, Arthur (1995) *Up from Scapegoating*. Wilmette, IL: Chiron Publications.

Conger, Jay A. (1992) *Learning to Lead: The Art of Transforming Managers into Leaders*. San Francisco, CA: Jossey-Bass.

Conner, Daryl R. (1998) *Leading at the Edge of Chaos: How to Create the Nimble Organization*. New York: John Wiley.

Cooper, Robert K. and Ayman Sawaf (1996) *Emotional Intelligence in Leadership and Organizations*. New York: Penguin Books.

Covey, Stephen R. (1992) *The Seven Habits of Highly Effective People*. London: Simon & Schuster.

Crocker, Chester A., Fen Osler Hampson and Pamela R. Aall, eds (1996) *Managing Global Chaos: Sources of and Responses to International Conflict*. Washington, DC: United States Institute of Peace Press.

Daft, Richard L. (2005) *The Leadership Experience*. Florence, KY: Thomson South-Western.

Davidson, James Dale and William Rees Mogg (1991) *The Great Reckoning: How the World Will Change in the Depression of the 1990s*. London: Sidgwick & Jackson.

De Caluwe, Leon and Hans Vermaak (2003) *Learning to Change: A Guide for Organizational Change Agents*. Thousand Oaks, CA: Sage Publications.

De Bettignies, Henri-Claude, ed. (1997) *The Changing Business Environment in the Asia-Pacific Region*. London: International Thomson Business Press.

Demers, Christiane (2007) *Organizational Change Theories*. Thousand Oaks, CA: Sage Publications.

Denhardt, Robert B. and Janet V. Denhardt (2006) *The Dance of Leadership: The Art of Leading in Business, Government and Society*. Armonk, NY: M.E. Sharpe.

Denise, Theodore C., Nicholas P. White and Sheldon P. Peterfreund (2008) *Great Traditions in Ethics*. Florence, KY: Wadsworth.

De Pree, Max (1989) *Leadership is an Art*. New York: Dell.

De Pree, Max (1992) *Leadership Jazz*. New York: Dell.

Diamond, Jared (2005) *Collapse: How Societies Choose to Fail or Succeed*. New York: Penguin Books.

Dicken, Peter (1992) *Global Shift: The Internationalization of Economic Activity*. New York: Guilford Press.

Dreher, Diane (2000) *The Tao of Inner Peace*. New York: Penguin Group.

Drucker, Peter F. (1989) *The New Realities*. New York: HarperBusiness.

Drucker, Peter F. (1992) *Managing for the Future*. Oxford: Butterworth-Heinemann.

Drucker, Peter F. (1993) *Post-Capitalist Society*. New York: HarperBusiness.

Drucker, Peter F. (1999) *Management Challenges for the 21st Century*. New York: HarperBusiness.

Eccles, Robert G. Nitin Nohria and James D. Berkley (1992) *Beyond the Hype: Rediscovering the Essence of Management*. Boston, MA: Harvard Business School Press.

Egan, Daniel and Levon A. Chorbajian (2005) *Power: A Critical Reader*. Upper Saddle River, NJ: Pearson Prentice-Hall.

Fairhurst, Gail T. (2007) *Discursive Leadership*. Thousand Oaks, CA: Sage Publications.

Farkas, Charles M. and Philippe De Backer (1996) *Maximum Leadership*. New York: Henry Holt.

Finser, Torin M. (2003) *In Search of Ethical Leadership*. Great Barrington, MA: Steiner Books.

Fisher, Colin and Alan Lovell (2006) *Business Ethics and Values*, Second Edition. Upper Saddle River, NJ: Prentice Hall.

Fisher, Roger and Alan Sharp (1998) *Getting It Done: How to Lead When You Are Not in Charge*. New York: HarperBusiness.

Freedman, Mike (2003) *The Art and Discipline of Strategic Leadership*. New York: McGraw-Hill.

French, Robert and Russ Vince, eds (1999) *Group Relations, Management, and Organization*. New York: Oxford University Press.

French, Wendell L., Cecil H. Bell and Robert A. Zawacki (2005) *Organization Development and Transformation: Managing Effective Change*, Sixth Edition. Boston, MA: McGraw-Hill Irwin.

Fullan, Michael (2001) *Leading in a Culture of Change*. San Francisco, CA: Jossey-Bass.

Gardner, John W. (1990) *On Leadership*. New York: Free Press.

Gillette, J. and M. McCollom (1990) *Groups in Context*. Boston, MA: Addison-Wesley.

Girard, René (1986) *The Scapegoat*. Baltimore, MD: Johns Hopkins University Press.

Gladwell, Malcolm (2002) *The Tipping Point: How Little Things Can Make a Big Difference*. New York: Back Bay Books.

Gladwell, Malcolm (2005) *Blink*. New York: Little, Brown.

Gleick, James (1990) *Chaos*. New York: Cardinal.

Goleman, Daniel (1995) *Emotional Intelligence: Why It Can Matter More Than IQ*. New York: Bantam Books.

Goleman, Daniel, Richard Boyatzis, Annie McKee (2002) *Primal Leadership: Realizing the Power of Emotional Intelligence*. Boston, MA: Harvard Business School Press.

Gould, Laurence J., Lionel F. Stapley and Mark Stein (2004) *Experiential Learning in Organizations*. London: Karnac.

Haas, Howard G. with Bob Tamarkin (1992) *The Leaders Within*. New York: HarperBusiness.

Haines, Stephen G. (1998) *The Managers' Pocket Guide to Systems Thinking & Learning*. Amherst, MA: HRD Press.

Hamel, Gary (2002) *Leading the Revolution*. Cambridge, MA: Harvard Business School Press. p.115.

Handscombe, Richard S. and Philip A. Norman (1993) *Strategic Leadership: Managing the Missing Links*, Second Edition. New York: McGraw-Hill.

Handy, Charles (1989) *The Age of Unreason*. London: Business Books.

Hankin, Harriet (2005) *The New Workforce: Five Sweeping Trends That will Shape Your Company's Future*. New York: AMACOM Books.

Harrison, Jeffrey S. and Caron H. St John (2002) *Foundations in Strategic Management*, Second Edition. South-Western: Thomson Florence, NY.

Hartman, Mary S. (1999) *Talking Leadership: Conversations with Powerful Women*. New Brunswick: NJ: Rutgers University Press.

Hartman, Laura and Joseph DesJardins (2006) *Business Ethics: Decision-making for Personal Integrity & Social Responsibility*. New York: McGraw-Hill Irwin.

Harvard Business Review on Leadership. Boston, MA: Harvard Business School Press, 2008.

Hawkins, David. R. (2002) *Power vs. Force: The Hidden Determinants of Human Behavior*. Carlsbad, CA: Hay House.

Heider, John (1985) *The Tao of Leadership*. London: Humanics.

Heifetz, Ronald A. (1994) *Leadership without Easy Answers*. Cambridge, MA: Belknap Press of Harvard University Press.

Heifetz, Ronald A. and Donald L. Laurie (1997) "The Work of Leadership," *Harvard Business Review*, January-February.

Heifetz, Ronald A. and Marty Linsky (2002) *Leadership on the Line*. Boston, MA: Harvard Business School Press.

Hess, Edward D. and Kim S. Cameron (2006) *Leading with Values*. Cambridge, UK: Cambridge University Press.

Hirschhorn, Larry (1997) *Reworking Authority: Leading and Following in the Post-Modern Organization*. Cambridge, MA: MIT Press.

Hollander, Edwin P. (2009) *Inclusive Leadership: The Essential Leader–Follower Relationship*. New York: Routledge.

Holman, Peggy, Tom Devane and Steven Cady (2007) *The Change Handbook*, Second Edition. San Francisco, CA: Berrett-Koehler.

Horney, Karen, MD (1991) *Neurosis and Human Growth: The Struggle toward Self-Realization*. New York: W.W. Norton.

Howard, Ronald A. and Clinton. D. Korver. (2008) *Ethics (For the Real World)*. Boston, MA: Harvard Business School Press.

Howell, Jon P. and Dan Costley (2006) *Understanding Behaviors for Effective Leadership*, Second Edition. Upper Saddle River, NJ: Pearson Prentice Hall.

Huffington, Clare, David Armstrong and William Halton, ed. (2004) *Working below the Surface: The Emotional Life of Contemporary Organizations*. London: Karnac.

James, Jennifer (1996) *Thinking in the Future Tense*. New York: Simon & Schuster.

Jick, Todd D. and Maury A. Peiperl (2003) *Managing Change: Cases and Concepts*. New York: McGraw-Hill.

Johnson, Craig E. (2005) *Meeting the Ethical Challenges of Leadership*, Second Edition. Thousand Oaks, CA: Sage Publications.

Johnson, Craig E. (2007) *Ethics in the Workplace*. Thousand Oaks, CA: Sage Publications.

Jung, Carl Gustav (1959) *The Archetypes and the Collective Unconscious*. New York: Princeton University Press.

Jung, Carl Gustav (1990) *The Undiscovered Self*. Princeton, NJ: Princeton University Press.

Jung, Carl Gustav (2001) *Modern Man in Search of a Soul*. New York: Routledge.

Kao, John (1996) *Jamming*. New York: HarperBusiness.

Kegan, Robert (1994) *In Over our Heads: The Mental Demands of Modern Life*. Cambridge, MA: Harvard University Press.

Kellerman, Barbara (2004) *Bad Leadership*. Boston, MA: Harvard Business School Press.

Kellerman, Barbara (2008) *Followership*. Boston, MA: Harvard Business School Press.

Kennedy, Paul (1993) *Preparing for the Twenty-First Century*. New York: Random House.

Kets de Vries, Manfred F.R. and Danny Miller (1984) *The Neurotic Organization*. San Francisco, CA: Jossey-Bass.

Kets de Vries, Manfred F.R. (2003) *Leaders, Fools and Imposters*. New York: Universe.

Khanna, Tarun (2007) *Billions of Entrepreneurs*. Boston, MA: Harvard Business School Press.

Klein, Melanie (1952) *The Origins of Transference*. New York: Free Press.

Knapp, John C., ed. (2007) *For the Common Good: The Ethics of Leadership in the 21st Century*. Westport, CT: Praeger.

Koestler, Arthur (1967) *The Ghost in the Machine*. London: Penguin.

Korten, David C. (2006) *The Great Turning: From Empire to Earth Community*. Sterling, VA: Kumarian Press and Berrett-Koehler.

Kotter, John. P. (1995) "Why Transformation Efforts Fail", *Harvard Business Review*, March–April.

Kotter, John P. (1996) *Leading Change*. Boston, MA: Harvard Business School Press.

Kotter, John P. (1999) *John P. Kotter on What Leaders Really Do*. Boston, MA: Harvard Business School Press.

Kouzes, James M. and Barry Z. Posner (1995) *The Leadership Challenge*. San Francisco, CA: Jossey-Bass.

Kouzes James M. and Barry Z. Posner (2006) *A Leader's Legacy*. San Francisco, CA: Jossey-Bass.

Kuhn, Thomas S. (1970) *The Structure of Scientific Revolutions*, Second Edition. Chicago, IL: University of Chicago Press.

Lakoff, George and Mark Johnson, (1980) *Metaphors We Live By*. Chicago, IL: University of Chicago Press.

Landes, David S. (1999) *The Wealth and Poverty of Nations*. New York: W.W. Norton.

Laszlo, Ervin (1996) *The Systems View of the World*. Cresskill, NJ: Hampton Press.

Laszlo, Ervin (2006) *Science and the Reenchantment of the Cosmos*. Rochester, VT: Inner Traditions.

Laszlo, Ervin (2007) *Science and the Akashic Field*, Second Edition. Rochester, VT: Inner Traditions.

Levinson, Harry (1968) *The Exceptional Executive: A Psychological Conception*. New York: New American Library.

Lewis, Richard D. (1996) *When Cultures Collide*. London: Nicholas Brealey Publishing.

Lipgar, Robert M. and Malcolm Pines, eds (2003) *Building on Bion: Roots, Origins and Context of Bion's Contributions to Theory and Practice*. London: Jessica Kingsley.

Lipman-Blumen, Jean (1996) *The Connective Edge: Leading in an Interdependent World*. San Francisco, CA: Jossey-Bass.

Lipman-Blumen, Jean (2005) *The Allure of Toxic Leaders: Why We Follow Destructive Bosses and Corrupt Politicians – and How We Can Survive Them*. Oxford, UK: Oxford University Press.

Locke, Edwin A. and Associates (1991) *The Essence of Leadership: The Four Keys to Leading Successfully*. New York: Lexington Books.

Lukes, Steven, ed. (1986) *Power*. New York: New York University Press.

Maak, Thomas and Nicola M. Pless, eds (2006) *Responsible Leadership*. New York: Routledge.

Maccoby, Michael (2000) "Narcissistic Leaders", *Harvard Business Review*, January–February.

Maccoby, Michael (2007) *The Leaders We Need: And What Makes Us Follow*. Boston, MA: Harvard Business School Press.

McCollough, Thomas E. (1991) *The Moral Imagination and the Public Life*. Chatham, NJ: Chatham House.

MacKinnon, Barbara (2009) *Ethics: Theory and Contemporary Issues*, Sixth Edition. Florence, KY: Wadsworth.

March, James G. and Thierry Weil (2005) *On Leadership*. Malden, MA: Blackwell.

Marshak, Robert J. (2006) *Covert Processes at Work: Managing the Five Hidden Dimensions of Organizational Change*. San Francisco, CA: Berrett-Koehler.

May, Rollo (1972) *Power and Innocence: A Search for the Sources of Violence*. New York: Dell.

Mayfield, Marlys (2007) *Thinking for Yourself*. New York: Thomson.

Maynard, Herman Bryant Jr. and Susan E. Mehrtens (1993) *The Fourth Wave: Business in the 21st Century*. San Francisco, CA: Berrett-Koehler.

Meredith, Robyn (2008) *The Elephant and the Dragon*. New York: W.W. Norton.

Messick, David M. and Roderick M. Kramer (2005) *The Psychology of Leadership: New Perspectives and Research*. Hillsdale, NJ: Lawrence Erlbaum Associates.

Milgram, Stanley (2004) *Obedience to Authority*. London: Pinter & Martin Classics.

Mintzberg, Henry and James Brian Quinn (1991) *The Strategy Process: Concepts, Contexts and Cases*, Second Edition. New York: Prentice Hall.

Moss Kanter Rosabeth (1997) *Men and Women of the Corporation*. New York: Basic Books.

Mumford, Michael D. (2006) *Pathways to Outstanding Leadership: A Comparative Analysis of Charismatic, Ideological, and Pragmatic Leaders*. Hillsdale, NJ: Lawrence Erlbaum Associates.

Murphy, Susan Elaine and Ronald E. Riggio, eds (2003) *The Future of Leadership*. Hillsdale, NJ: Lawrence Erlbaum Associates.

Nahavandi, Afsaneh (2006) *The Art and Science of Leadership*, Fifth Edition. Upper Saddle River, NJ: Pearson Prentice Hall.

Neumann, Erich (1990) *Depth Psychology and a New Ethic*. Boston, MA: Shambala.

Niebuhr, Reinhold (1960) *Moral Man and Immoral Society*. New York: Touchstone.

Northouse, Peter (2005) *Leadership: Theory and Practice*. London: Sage Publications.

Obholzer, Anton and Vega Zagier Roberts, eds (1994) *The Unconscious at Work*. New York: Brunner-Routledge.

O'Hagberg, Janet (2003) *Real Power: Stages of Personal Power in Organizations*, Third Edition. Salem, WI: Sheffield.

Olson, Edwin E. and Glenda H. Eoyang (2001) *Facilitating Organizational Change*. San Francisco, CA: Jossey-Bass.

Oshry, Barry (2007) *Seeing Systems: Unlocking the Systems of Organizational Life*. San Francisco, CA: Berrett-Koehler.

O'Toole, James (1995) *Leading Change: Overcoming the Ideology of Comfort and the Tyranny of Custom*. San Francisco, CA: Jossey-Bass.

Palmer, Parker J. (1998) *The Courage to Teach*. San Francisco, CA: Jossey-Bass.

Parenti, Michael (1978) *Power and the Powerless*. New York: St Martin's Press.

Parks, Sharon Daloz (2005) *Leadership Can Be Taught*. Boston, MA: Harvard Business School Press.

Peters, Thomas J. and Robert H. Waterman Jr (1982) *In Search of Excellence*. New York: Harper & Row.

Pfeffer, Jeffrey (1994) *Managing with Power: Politics and Influence in Organizations*. Boston, MA: Harvard Business School Press.

Pierce, Jon L. and John W. Newstrom (2006) *Leaders & the Leadership Process*, Fourth Edition. New York: McGraw-Hill Irwin.

Porter, Michael E. (1990) *The Competitive Advantage of Nations*. London: Macmillan.

Prahalad, C.K. (2006) *The Fortune at the Bottom of the Pyramid*. Philadelphia, PA: Wharton School Publishing.

Price, Terry L. (2006) *Understanding Ethical Failures in Leadership*. New York: Cambridge University Press.

Puccio, Gerard J., Mary C. Murdock and Marie Mance (2007) *Creative Leadership: Skills that Drive Change*. Thousand Oaks, CA: Sage Publications.

Quinn, Robert E. (1996) *Deep Change: Discovering the Leader Within*. San Francisco, CA: Jossey-Bass.

Ray, Michael and Alan Rinzler, eds (1993) *The New Paradigm in Business*. New York: Putnam Books.

Ricoeur, Paul (1967) *The Symbolism of Evil*. Boston, MA: Beacon Press.

Riggio, Ronald E., Ira Chaleff and Jean Lipman-Blumen, eds (2008) *The Art of Followership*. San Francisco, CA: Jossey-Bass.

Roberts, Wess, PhD (1987) *Leadership Secrets of Attila the Hun*. New York: Warner Books.

Rokeach, Milton (1979) *Understanding Human Values*. New York: Free Press.

Rosenberg, Marc J. (2001) *e-Learning: Strategies for Delivering Knowledge in the Digital Age*. New York: McGraw-Hill.

Ryan, Kathleen D. and Daniel K. Oestreich (1998) *Driving Fear out of the Workplace*. San Francisco, CA: Jossey-Bass.

Schaller, Lyle E. (1993) *Strategies for Change*. Nashville, TN: Abingdon Press.

Schein, Edgar H. (1985) *Organizational Culture & Leadership*. San Francisco, CA: Jossey-Bass.

Schwartz, Howard S. (1990) *Narcissistic Process and Corporate Decay*. New York: New York University Press.

Senge, Peter (1990) *The Fifth Discipline*. London: Century Business.

Senge, Peter, Bryan Smith, Nina Krushwitz, Joe Laur and Schley Sara, (2008) *The Necessary Revolution*. New York: Doubleday.

Shapiro, Edward R. and A. Wesley Carr (1991) *Lost in Familiar Places*. New Haven, CT: Yale University Press.

Shaw, William, H. (2008) *Business Ethics*. Sixth Edition. Belmont, CA: Wadsworth.

Smith, Kenwyn K. and David N. Berg (1987) *Paradoxes of Group Life*. San Francisco, CA: Jossey-Bass.

Shriberg, Arthur, David L. Shriberg and Richa Kumari (2005) *Practicing Leadership: Principles and Applications*, Third Edition. San Francisco, CA: John Wiley.

Smythe, John (2007) *The CEO: Chief Engagement Officer*. Aldershot, UK: Gower.

Stacey, Ralph D. (1996) *Strategic Management and Organizational Dynamics*, Second Edition. London: Financial Times Prentice Hall.

Sterman, John D. (1996) *Business Dynamics: Systems Thinking and Modeling for a Complex World*. Boston, MA: McGraw-Hill Irwin.

Tainter, Joseph (1988) *The Collapse of Complex Societies*. Cambridge, UK: Cambridge University Press.

Thompson, Leigh L. (2004) *Making the Team: A Guide for Managers*. Upper Saddle River, NJ: Pearson Prentice Hall.

Tichy, Noel M. and Warren Bennis (2007) *Judgment: How Winning Leaders Make Great Calls*. New York: Penguin Group.

Torbert, Bill and Associates (2004) *Action Inquiry*. San Francisco, CA: Berrett-Koehler.

Turquet, P. (1974) "Leadership: The Individual and the Group", in G. Gibbard, ed., *Analysis of Groups*. San Francisco, CA: Jossey-Bass.

Van Der Heijden, Kees (1996) *Scenarios: The Art of Strategic Conversation*. New York: John Wiley.

Von Bertalanffy, Ludwig (1969) *General System Theory*. New York: George Braziller.

Waldrop, M. Mitchell (1992) *Complexity: The Emerging Science at the Edge of Chaos*. New York: Touchstone.

Weber, Max (1964) *The Theory of Social and Economic Organization*. New York: Free Press.

Weick, Karl E. and Kathleen M. Sutcliffe (2001) *Managing the Unexpected*. San Francisco, CA: Jossey-Bass.

Wheatley, Margaret J. (1994) *Leadership and the New Science*. San Francisco, CA: Berrett-Koehler.

Wheatley, Margaret J. and Myron Kellner-Rogers (1999) *A Simpler Way*. San Francisco, CA: Berrett-Koehler.

White, Randall P., Philip Hodgson and Stuart Crainer (1996) *The Future of Leadership*. London: Pitman.

White, Thomas 1. (1993) *White Business Ethics*. New York: Macmillan. pp. 1–5.

Wilber, Ken (1998) *The Essential Ken Wilbur: An Introductory Reader*. Boston, MA: Shambala.

William, Dean (2005) *Real Leadership*. San Francisco, CA: Berrett-Koehler.

Youngblood, Mark D. (1997) *Life at the Edge of Chaos*. Dallas, TX: Perceval.

Yunus, Muhammad (1997) *Banker to the Poor*. New York: Public Affairs.

Yunus, Muhammad (2007) *Creating a World without Poverty*. New York: Public Affairs.

Zohar, Danah (1997) *ReWiring the Corporate Brain*. San Francisco, CA: Berrett-Koehler.

INDEX

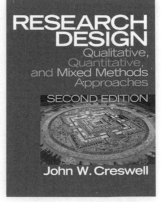

The Qualitative Research Kit

Edited by Uwe Flick

Supporting researchers for more than forty years

Research methods have always been at the core of SAGE's publishing. Sara Miller McCune founded SAGE in 1965 and soon after, she published SAGE's first methods book, *Public Policy Evaluation*. A few years later, she launched the Quantitative Applications in the Social Sciences series – affectionately known as the 'little green books'.

Always at the forefront of developing and supporting new approaches in methods, SAGE published early groundbreaking texts and journals in the fields of qualitative methods and evaluation.

Today, more than forty years and two million little green books later, SAGE continues to push the boundaries with a growing list of more than 1,200 research methods books, journals, and reference works across the social, behavioural, and health sciences.

From qualitative, quantitative and mixed methods to evaluation, SAGE is the essential resource for academics and practitioners looking for the latest in methods by leading scholars.

www.sagepublications.com